HODDER GCSE (9–1) HISTORY FOR Pearson Edexcel

MIGRANTS IN BRITAIN
c.800–present
NOTTING HILL
c.1948–c.1970

Abdul Mohamud • Robin Whitburn
(Justice to History)

In order to ensure that this resource offers high-quality support for the associated Pearson qualification, it has been through a review process by the awarding body. This process confirms that this resource fully covers the teaching and learning content of the specification or part of a specification at which it is aimed. It also confirms that it demonstrates an appropriate balance between the development of subject skills, knowledge and understanding, in addition to preparation for assessment.

Endorsement does not cover any guidance on assessment activities or processes (e.g. practice questions or advice on how to answer assessment questions), included in the resource nor does it prescribe any particular approach to the teaching or delivery of a related course.

While the publishers have made every attempt to ensure that advice on the qualification and its assessment is accurate, the official specification and associated assessment guidance materials are the only authoritative source of information and should always be referred to for definitive guidance.

Pearson examiners have not contributed to any sections in this resource relevant to examination papers for which they have responsibility.

Examiners will not use endorsed resources as a source of material for any assessment set by Pearson. Endorsement of a resource does not mean that the resource is required to achieve this Pearson qualification, nor does it mean that it is the only suitable material available to support the qualification, and any resource lists produced by the awarding body shall include this and other appropriate resources.

The Publishers would like to thank the following for permission to reproduce copyright material.

Acknowledgements

P.56 © Nick C. and Andrew F. from Springbank Community HighSchool. fawcettworkshop@hotmail.com; **p.89** © Crown Copyright; **p.91** © 2021 The Migration Observatory; **p.92** & **117** © 2021 Guardian News & Media Limited; **p.128** © International Times Archive. The publisher would like to thank Abigail Branford, doctoral researcher in history education at University of Oxford, for her review of the content. This book is part of the Hodder GCSE (9-1) History for Edexcel Paper 1 Thematic and Paper 2 British Depth Studies series of textbooks established by Dale Banham and Ian Dawson.

Every effort has been made to trace all copyright holders, but if any have been inadvertently overlooked, the Publishers will be pleased to make the necessary arrangements at the first opportunity. Although every effort has been made to ensure that website addresses are correct at time of going to press, Hodder Education cannot be held responsible for the content of any website mentioned in this book. It is sometimes possible to find a relocated web page by typing in the address of the home page for a website in the URL window of your browser.

Hachette UK's policy is to use papers that are natural, renewable and recyclable products and made from wood grown in well-managed forests and other controlled sources. The logging and manufacturing processes are expected to conform to the environmental regulations of the country of origin.

Orders: please contact Hachette UK Distribution, Hely Hutchinson Centre, Milton Road, Didcot, Oxfordshire, OX11 7HH. Telephone: +44 (0)1235 827827. Email education@hachette.co.uk Lines are open from 9 a.m. to 5 p.m., Monday to Friday. You can also order through our website: www.hoddereducation.co.uk

The authorised representative in the EEA is Hachette Ireland, 8 Castlecourt Centre, Dublin 15, D15 XTP3, Ireland (email: info@hbgi.ie)

ISBN: 978 1 3983 4055 8

© Abdul Mohamud and Robin Whitburn 2022

First published in 2022 by
Hodder Education,
An Hachette UK Company
Carmelite House
50 Victoria Embankment
London EC4Y 0DZ
www.hoddereducation.co.uk

Impression number   10 9 8 7 6 5 4 3

Year   2026 2025

All rights reserved. Apart from any use permitted under UK copyright law, no part of this publication may be reproduced or transmitted in any form or by any means, electronic or mechanical, including photocopying and recording, or held within any information storage and retrieval system, without permission in writing from the publisher or under licence from the Copyright Licensing Agency Limited. Further details of such licences (for reprographic reproduction) may be obtained from the Copyright Licensing Agency Limited, www.cla.co.uk

Cover photo © Michael Stroud/Express/Getty Images

© Album / Alamy Stock Photo

Illustrations by Aptara Inc. and Marcus Duck

Typeset in India by Aptara Inc.
Printed and bound by CPI Group (UK) Ltd, Croydon, CR0 4YY

A catalogue record for this title is available from the British Library.

CONTENTS

Part 1: Migrants in Britain, c.800–present

Chapter 1	The big story of migration, c.800–present	2
Chapter 2	Migration in medieval England, c.800–1500	10
Chapter 3	Migration in early modern England, c.1500–c.1700	32
Chapter 4	Migration in eighteenth- and nineteenth-century Britain	52
Chapter 5	Migration in modern Britain, c.1900 to present day	78
Conclusion	The Big Story of migrants in Britain: change and continuity in the period c.800–present day	110

Part 2: The historic environment: Notting Hill, c.1948–c.1970 — 112

Part 3: Writing better history — 140

Glossary — 155

Index — 157

1 The big story of migration, c.800–present

Why study the history of migrants in Britain, c.800–present day?

In the last thirty years concerns about immigration have reached extraordinary levels in Britain. National newspapers report on the topic almost daily, politicians from the two major parties ensure their positions on immigration are a key part of their platforms and the biggest political decision taken by the British public in the twenty-first century, the vote to leave the European Union was, in part, fuelled by the debate around immigration.

The issue of immigration is not one that we can avoid. As historians we strive to understand how societies develop, what their values are and what key moments initiate changes in how people think. How Britain came to be the country that it is today is, to a large extent, down to migration. People from all four corners of the Earth have come to Britain and in small and great ways have had an impact on the direction of the country. In an age where the debate around migration is poisoned with hate and misinformation, it is important for us to see how our society has been shaped by those people who fled persecution or saw an opportunity for themselves and their families and chose to make Britain their home.

A contemporary migration debate

In the summer of 2021 there was a media focus on the relatively small number of refugees making the dangerous crossing from France to Britain, across the Channel. The Royal National Lifeboat Institution (RNLI), which helps endangered people at sea, was targeted by some critics for rescuing refugees who could not complete their journeys. As these critics tried to turn the public against the RNLI, the opposite effect was achieved, and this charity received more in donations from the public than at any other time in its history.

The story of migration to Britain shows up many **xenophobic** people, but it is also full of people who in some small way have helped migrants and refugees find a home in Britain; this textbook tells the stories of both. But above all, this book reveals the resilience and determination of those men and women who often took great personal risks to start new lives in Britain throughout the centuries.

> **What do you know about the current debates around immigration?**
>
> 1 Draw a mind map with the word 'immigration' in the centre. Then write any words you associate with immigration around it. Try to put your words into context through explanation.
>
> 2 Why do you think immigration has been seen, and continues to be seen, as a controversial issue? Try to develop your answer with examples.

▲ **Source 1** A group of people thought to be migrants are brought into Dover, Kent, by the RNLI following a small boat incident in the Channel, September 2020

What words do we need to know to study migrants in Britain, c.800–present day?

There are always key words associated with particular historical topics and you will find a glossary at the back of the book to help you with terms that might be unfamiliar to you. Migration can be a controversial issue in Britain, as we have seen, and it is important to take care with the language that we use.

Migration terms

There are two basic terms to describe people who move themselves, and often their families, from one country, or place, to another. There is a very important distinction between the two:

> A migrant is a person who moves from one place to another, usually to find work and/or better living conditions, or to study. Migrants make the choice to move.

> A refugee is someone who is forced to leave their country to find safety from persecution and/or conflict. Refugees have no choice but to move to a safer country.

Migrants
Migrants can be:

> Economic migrants who want to move to another country for new job opportunities and/or to escape poverty and hardship in their homeland. Economic migrants do not necessarily want to settle in the new country. They usually have the option of returning home.

> Immigrants who migrate and do want to settle in a new country. Immigrants would become citizens of the new country and take up the rights of the existing population. They could eventually choose to return to their first homeland if they wanted to.

Refugees
Refugees have to ask to be accepted into a country they wish to flee to, and while they are waiting for a decision on their right to remain they are called asylum seekers. The process of recognition as a refugee can be very lengthy and challenging.

Although the Pearson course and this book include only the term 'migrants' in the title, refugees are considered to be a key part of its overall story of people who move to Britain. In the different sections of the course there will be information and discussion about groups of refugees alongside the accounts of migrants at the time. Be sure to make a note of any person or group who you would consider to be refugees.

Offensive terms

In the past, names have sometimes been used that are seen as abusive and disrespectful to certain groups of migrants and refugees. These terms do appear in some written sources from the past. The people who wrote the sources didn't necessarily understand that the terms were offensive, sometimes because their use was so widespread at the time. Where these words appear in sources in this book they have usually been printed as they were used. Your teacher will talk to you about the use of those words. Three common examples are terms that relate to:

- people of African descent, who were called 'negroes' until quite recently. You will see this word in some sources (pages 54, 67 and 83). This is not a word that we consider appropriate to use nowadays. There is also a highly offensive word that we have chosen not to print in full; where it is used in a source you will see it printed as 'n_____'. There is no need for us to use the full word today, when it is necessary we use the phrase 'the n-word' instead.
- travellers whose heritage is from the Romani nomadic people, who have been referred to as 'Gypsies' since the sixteenth century. The word was used because they were mistaken for people of Egypt because their skin was darker. The term 'Gypsy' on its own is now considered to be offensive, but people do use the terms 'Romani Gypsy' and 'Traveller'.
- people who were not white Europeans. The term 'coloured' was used up to the later twentieth century to refer to people who were not white Europeans. This is now considered disrespectful and offensive, but it appears in this book in some sources and in the title of some groups, as on pages 83 and 122.

> *Aliens*
> This was a Medieval term for someone who had migrated to England and was a citizen of another land. The legal term 'alien' was still in use in the UK in the early twentieth century, and it is still used in the USA.

> Negative attitude terms
> Two key words describe the negative attitude that some people have towards immigrants:
> - Xenophobia refers to hostility and prejudice towards people from other countries. There are records of xenophobic people in England from the Middle Ages, and they have been responsible for serious anti-immigrant disturbances and violence.
> - Racism is a different and much more recent term based on the idea that people in the world are separated into different racial groups and that some are inferior to others. These ideas of race developed through the eighteenth and nineteenth centuries and are still very influential in some people's thinking today.

PART 1: Migrants in Britain, c.800–present

How can we think historically about migrants in Britain, c.800–present day?

This GCSE unit examines more than a thousand years of history and a lot can change in a thousand years! There will be some aspects of migration that feature across the centuries; these will be referred to as 'continuity' in contrast to 'change'. General historical ideas like these are referred to as 'historical concepts'. You will use other concepts alongside **change** and **continuity** throughout the course:

- **Causation** will help you to understand *why* things happened and changed in the way they did. There will be different *causal* factors at work, such as government, religion, economics and business.
- **Significance** will help you to appreciate the impact and influence that particular people or events have had on Britain's past.
- **Similarity** and **difference** can help you to see how diverse groups and individuals experience things at the same stage in the past.

Migration is, in itself, a process of change, both for people who move and for those they settle alongside. You will spend a lot of time in this unit thinking about change.

Historical enquiries

Historians have to ask important questions about the past to learn more about how the world has developed over time. The specification for this examination course is presented in four time periods. For each period there are two strands of ideas connected to migration:

- **The context of migration:** This strand examines the attraction of Britain for migrants and the pattern of their settlement.
- **The experience and impact of migrants:** This strand examines how migrants settled into British society and how far they were made to feel welcome. It also examines how new settlers prompted aspects of society to change, particularly in terms of culture and the economy.

Each chapter of the book covers a specific time period, and within each time period we explore two enquiry questions linked to the strands from the specification:

- What was the attraction of Britain to migrants in the period studied?
- What was the experience and impact of migrants in Britain in the period studied?

Visualising change and continuity

When we are thinking about a complex idea like change, it can be helpful to visualise it in a simple way with a familiar image.

In this book we have chosen to use the image of a road or 'highway' to show change and continuity in migration (there are highway images at the start of each major section of the book, on pages 10–11, 32–3, 52–3, 78–9 and 80–1. Travelling is an essential part of migration, and we use the highway to mark the timescale of the centuries. There are aspects of change that are suggested on the highways (see below). The migrants featured in the highways, as well as many more, are highlighted in bold the first time they appear in the text.

The *direction* of change: there are particular events that have a major impact on the pattern of migration to Britain. These are often legal decisions that make it harder or easier for people to settle in the country. Historians talk about 'turning points' in the past, after which aspects of life are very different from how they were before. Turning points can be seen on the migration highways as sharp turns in the road: changes that assist migration are shown in green and those that deter migrants are in red.

The *extent* of change: there have always been migrants in Britain, but there are some periods when the volume of arrivals is much greater than others. On the highway, this idea is shown by the dots on the road surface. Periods of large-scale migration will appear as dense patches of dots.

The *pace* of change: this is harder to show on the highway, but you can get a sense of how quickly things were changing by looking at the patterns of dots in relation to the timescale of the highway.

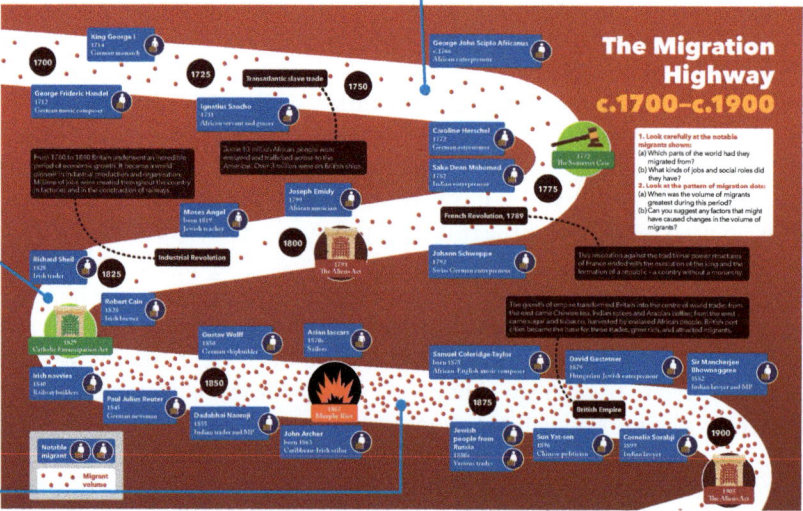

4

What are the key aspects of the attraction of Britain for migrants, c.800–present day?

There are two places involved in the movement of migrants and refugees: the place they are moving to and the place they are coming from. The motivation for their journey could be connected with one of these places, or both. We talk about 'pull factors' that attract people to the new place, and 'push factors' that force them to move from their homeland.

> 1 Remind yourself of the definitions of 'migrants' and 'refugees'. Which group is more likely to be driven by 'push factors'?

In this unit we will mainly focus on pull factors, because this is one of the British history modules of this GCSE course. However, you will want to acknowledge different push factors that affected particular groups. The first enquiry in each section of the course will focus on the attraction of Britain for migrants and refugees. This involves looking at the broad history of England as a nation up to 1707 and then of Great Britain when England, Wales and Scotland were officially united under one ruler from the eighteenth century onwards.

The economy, society and political nation of England, and then Britain, have changed immensely over the period of this course. However, there have also been significant continuities: from the time of the Anglo-Saxons, trading with England was seen as valuable and well-organised, and economic opportunities were generally protected by stable governments through the centuries. The four boxes below explain vital elements in the context of Britain that drew in migrants.

FACTORS INHIBITING OR ENCOURAGING CHANGE

There are four key aspects of British life and society that this course highlights as factors affecting change:

- institutions (Government and church)
- religion
- economic influences
- attitudes in society

The first three help to shape the context for migration (see this page). The fourth one is a very important part of the experiences of migrants (see pages 9 and 10). Attitudes in British society towards migrants can be positive or negative (see pages 2–3). Always note the impact of these factors throughout your studies in this course.

Economic influences: trade and jobs

Economic migrants could be wealthy merchants who came to England to organise their own city's participation in a particular trade, either in English exports, particularly wool throughout the Middle Ages, or imports, including wine and silks. They could also be ordinary workers finding jobs in activities that were short of labour, like the Irish men taking jobs in railway building in the mid-nineteenth century and the Irish women registering as nurses in the mid-twentieth century.

Religion: mission and sanctuary

There are two main ways in which religion can be the main factor in the movement of people. Some devout believers can decide to migrate to another country to spread their religion; these people are often called missionaries. In the twelfth century there were a number of European monks who came to England to reform the English Church. Religion can also be the factor behind the movement of refugees who face persecution for their beliefs in their homeland. Thousands of French and Flemish religious refugees came to England in the period c.1500–c.1700.

Institutions: Government

Throughout the centuries, monarchs and governments have on occasion introduced policies and laws that aimed to attract particular types of migrants to Britain. This was almost always to meet a specific economic need. Furthermore, immigrants who settle in a new country would want to be treated fairly and justly. Therefore the legal frameworks and the political authorities play an important part in the attraction of Britain. In the earlier centuries discussed in this course it was the monarch who had the most power to decide on the rights of English citizens. But in the seventeenth century Parliament became the principal political power in the country. It was King William I who first invited Jewish people to England in the 1070s, and King Edward I who expelled them in 1290. It was Parliament that decided to invite Jewish people back in 1655 and who passed the Act of 1858 that gave them the right to become MPs.

Education and culture

English universities always attracted some migrant scholars, including famous German Protestants in the sixteenth century. Well-known people from India, including Mohandas Gandhi and Cornelia Sorabji, came to study law in England in the nineteenth century. England has been home to many migrants who bring new cultural talents, including the German Renaissance painter Holbein in the sixteenth century, and the Trinidadian author Sam Selvon in the twentieth century.

PART 1: Migrants in Britain, c.800–present

How did Britain change its connections with the world from c.800?

THE WIDER WORLD

The British Isles were connected to the wider world during the years of the Roman Empire's occupation between 43 and 410CE. Peoples of different heritages from Europe and Africa were certainly present in England at that time. From c.800, there were changes in these global connections and five broad periods are described across these pages. The map shows the most common areas from which external migrants have travelled to Britain.

GLOBAL CONNECTIONS c.800–c.1150

This period saw England become united as a kingdom, under Kings Alfred and Athelstan, but it later became a part of the overseas empires of peoples of Scandinavian heritage. In the eleventh century, England was ruled by Danish kings between 1016 and 1042 and then was conquered by Normans in 1066. These foreign rulers brought migrants with them in the fields of trade and religion, and also as new landowners. Significant groups of Flemish, Jewish, and Norman French migrants arrived.

GLOBAL CONNECTIONS c.1150–c.1500

England was the centre of a small empire in these centuries, beginning with the lands of the Angevin kings covering half of France. In the thirteenth, fourteenth and early fifteenth centuries, the English kings fought to maintain power in France, with varying degrees of success. Migrants continued to come to England, mainly for economic purposes, including Flemish weavers and Italian bankers and merchants. This was also the period in which English control of Wales was firmly established. In 1485 the new English king was an Anglo-Welsh lord: Henry Tudor.

GLOBAL CONNECTIONS c.1500–c.1850

In these centuries the British became connected with more distant parts of the world, and this started to have a small impact on migration. The establishment of Caribbean and North American colonies was connected with Britain's leading role in enslaving African people and transporting them across the Atlantic. Other trades connected Britain to Asia, particularly the Indian subcontinent. Links with Europe continued, and the religious Reformation of the sixteenth century brought thousands of refugees to England, escaping Catholic domination. Significant groups of Flemish and French migrants arrived, and in 1655 Jewish people were allowed back after more than 300 years of exile.

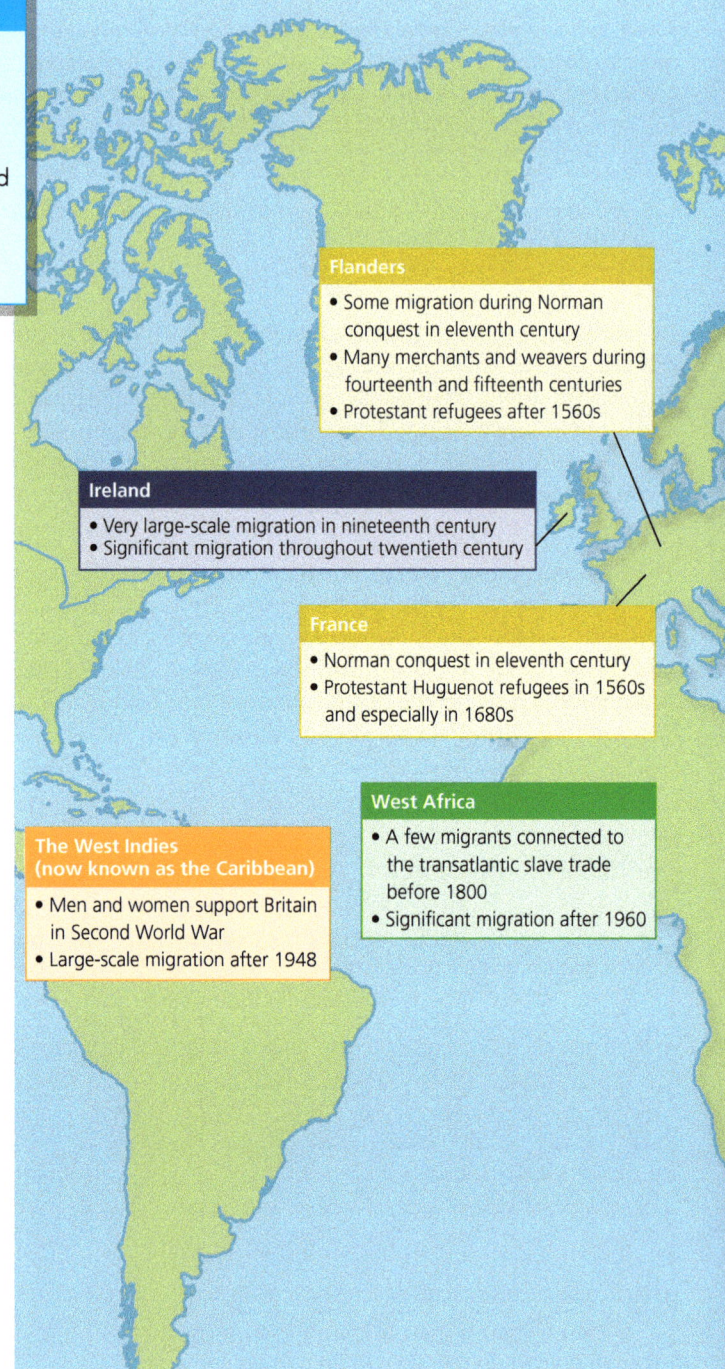

Flanders
- Some migration during Norman conquest in eleventh century
- Many merchants and weavers during fourteenth and fifteenth centuries
- Protestant refugees after 1560s

Ireland
- Very large-scale migration in nineteenth century
- Significant migration throughout twentieth century

France
- Norman conquest in eleventh century
- Protestant Huguenot refugees in 1560s and especially in 1680s

West Africa
- A few migrants connected to the transatlantic slave trade before 1800
- Significant migration after 1960

The West Indies (now known as the Caribbean)
- Men and women support Britain in Second World War
- Large-scale migration after 1948

---

1. Choose key words that sum up the state of Britain's global connections in each of the five phases described here.
2. If you were printing a world map to help people at the time of each phase make sense of what was happening in England/Britain at the time, what would your map show? Explain the changes across the five phases.

6

1 The big story of migration, c.800–present

THE BRITISH ISLES

People of the territories of England, Wales, Scotland and Ireland have been connected for centuries. As immediate neighbours, some of them travelled to and from their homelands for various social and economic purposes, and they continue to do that. This would be considered *internal* migration when the territories were under the same government, as was the case for all these lands in the nineteenth century. Nowadays, migration from the Irish Republic is considered *external*, but not from Northern Ireland because it is still part of the United Kingdom.

GLOBAL CONNECTIONS c.1850–c.1950

This was the century of British imperial dominance in the world. There were British colonies on all the continents and this was the basis of Britain's status as a world power in international affairs. There were more arrivals from Asia and Africa than before, but not many settled as immigrants. The World Wars of the twentieth century saw significant numbers of African, Caribbean and Asian people in Britain, and this was sometimes met with intolerance from British citizens. Europe continued to contribute a large share of total migration, particularly Jewish refugees from persecution in Eastern Europe and then Germany. There were also large flows of Irish migrants. During this period there were also high levels of emigration *from* Britain, particularly to parts of the empire.

GLOBAL CONNECTIONS c.1950–c.2020

Britain's status as a world power was fatally weakened by the Second World War. The decades afterwards saw a process of **decolonisation** of territories across the world. At the same time, there were shortages of workers in many industries and public services in Britain and migrants from many of the imperial colonies decided to come and fill them; as the Caribbean writer and scholar Stuart Hall declared:

> We are here because you were there!

Britain was transformed into a more multicultural society and this brought new challenges for British people to work through. Europe was briefly the major focus of Britain's global connections again, after some 500 years, when it became a member of the growing European Union (1973–2020). The whole world developed far more complex global connections by the twenty-first century, and this 'globalisation' is likely to continue to have major consequences for migration.

Eastern Europe
- Large-scale Jewish migration in late nineteenth century
- Large-scale economic migration in twenty-first century

Central Europe
- German cultural and intellectual migrants since Renaissance
- Some economic migrants in nineteenth and nineteenth centuries

China
- Sailors since nineteenth century
- Refugees from Hong Kong after 1990

India
- Lascars (sailors) and ayahs (nannies) in nineteenth century
- Large-scale migration after 1960

East Africa
- Some sailors from Somalia since 1870s
- Asian refugees from Kenya and Uganda in 1960s and 1970s
- Somalian refugees from 1990s

▲ **Source 2** Map of Britain's global connections and major sources of migration, c.850–c.2020

> 3 The popular television programme *Who Do You Think You Are?* investigates the ancestry of British celebrities. They are often surprised to find out how far their global connections reach. If you were the producer of the programme, what would you advise the celebrities to expect, using the information here?

PART 1: Migrants in Britain, c.800–present

a) Study Sources 3 and 4 carefully. We can assume that there are Somalis in the picture of the mosque in Source 3, since they are a Muslim people and the dress is consistent with what you would expect of them.

Make a table to record aspects of each source that show assimilation and autonomy. Research aspects of the background to Somalis who were living in Cardiff around 1950, and look at other pictures of people in Britain living in 1950 to help you assess the usual social appearance and activity at the time.

b) How far do Bert Hardy's pictures of Cardiff in 1950 suggest that Somali immigrants were integrating into British society?

c) What further questions would you need to ask to confirm your answer to Question b?

What has been the experience and the impact of migrants to Britain since c.800?

The second enquiry of each section focuses on the experiences and impact of migrants in Britain. Your enquiries will reveal that this varies from group to group. All immigrants will want to have a positive experience in their new home country and they will want to enjoy the attractions of Britain that encouraged them to migrate in the first place.

With time, most immigrants have wanted to see themselves as British, especially those who are the second and third generations of immigrant families. In identifying as British, they do not necessarily want to lose their connections with their birthplace. Many immigrants choose to have a sense of 'dual identity' and refer to themselves as 'British Irish' or 'British Asian', etc. There are two key terms that help us to discuss the experiences of immigrants and the ideas of identity:

- **Assimilation** refers to how far individuals or groups of immigrants adopt the culture, customs and values of the majority of people living in their new home country. This is often done to settle into a country more easily in order to be accepted.
- **Autonomy** refers to how far individuals or groups of immigrants hold onto the culture, customs and values of their homeland. Immigrants who maintain a high degree of autonomy have often been regarded with suspicion by the British majority.

In the last fifty years, as immigration has become a topic of national debate and research, people have moved away from assuming that immigrants should strive to thoroughly assimilate into British society. The idea of **integration** was conceived as a new vision of how Britain would be transformed through diverse immigration. The idea is of a new **multicultural** society built in Britain through immigrants sharing aspects of their home cultures, while maintaining aspects of their own identities.

Assimilation and autonomy – migrants in Cardiff in 1950

There were a number of immigrants in Cardiff in the mid-twentieth century, concentrated in a district near the docks called Tiger Bay, Butetown. The majority were sailors who had come from the edge of the Indian Ocean bordering on Africa, mainly from Somalia and Yemen, and also from parts of West Africa. A photographer called Bert Hardy visited Tiger Bay in 1950 and took a number of pictures of the immigrants living there. We have chosen two of them to illustrate these ideas of assimilation and autonomy.

▲ **Source 3** Muslims at an Islamic prayer meeting at a mosque in Tiger Bay, Cardiff, April 1950

▲ **Source 4** A group of Somalis meet in Tiger Bay, Cardiff, April 1950

1 The big story of migration, c.800–present

Assimilation and autonomy diagrams

Assimilation/autonomy circles can be used to reflect the extent of assimilation and autonomy in the lives and experiences of different immigrants. These circles are a simple version of a pie chart with only two segments in the circle. One segment represents assimilation and the other is autonomy. You should consider all you know about an immigrant or group of immigrants to decide on the appropriate share of the circle for each. You should then annotate your diagram to include key ideas that have shaped the decision that you made.

Here are two possible diagrams:

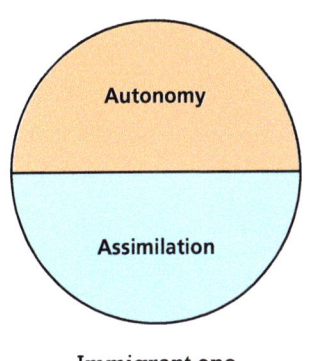

Immigrant one

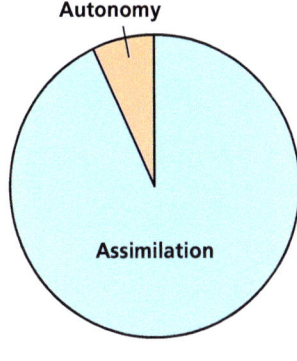

Immigrant two

> 1 How would you describe the possible experiences and identity of these two imaginary immigrants?
> 2 Can you think of characteristics and circumstances that may have led to these two very different profiles? You might consider these key factors when suggesting answers: religion, language, culture, employment, appearance and neighbours.

Making notes on the enquiry questions

To help organise your thoughts as you work through the two enquiry questions in each chapter, you can create two tables like the ones below. Make notes in your tables as you work through the information and sources.

For each enquiry there are different features of the period that are listed on the first page of the chapter. You can use these features to complete the first column of your table.

Enquiry question 1: What attracted migrants to Britain?

Feature of the context of England/Britain, *e.g. The wool industry*	Description of what was happening	How that attracted migrants	Examples of migrants and their destinations

Enquiry question 2: What were the experiences and impact of migrants?

Group of migrants, *e.g. Flemish people*	Relations with the authorities/institutions	Relations with ordinary people	Migrants' impact on public life

> **Notable migrants**
>
> As you work through the book you will meet different people who arrived in Britain as migrants. You can read about their migration stories in the 'Notable migrant' boxes. These are colour-coded to show in which country each migrant was born:
>
> Europe   Ireland   Asia
> Africa   UK (internal
> Caribbean   migration)
> Canada

At the end of each enquiry there will be a page called 'Communicating Your Answer' where you will be guided to complete a written task that is connected to the enquiry question and also to the kind of questions you will be required to answer in the examination.

The Migration Highway c.800–c.1500

The Kingdoms of the British Isles

England, Ireland, Scotland and Wales were entirely separate kingdoms during most of this period. English kings did attempt to have authority over the other kingdoms, but this was not always successful. Only Wales was united with England, under Edward I in the late thirteenth century.

Emma of Normandy
1002
Norman princess

1000

1050

1016 Cnut's invasion

Christendom

Most of Europe followed the Christian religion throughout the medieval era. Christendom meant the power of the religion over all aspects of people's cultural and social lives at the time. Christians were part of a single universal (Catholic) Church organisation that was led by the Pope in Rome. Some Christians devoted themselves to a religious life and became monks or nuns, living in monasteries.

1066 The Norman invasion

Lanfranc
1070
Italian archbishop

Cluniac monks
1089
from France

Flemings in Pembrokeshire, Wales
1108

1200

1150

1100

The Crusades

1190 The York Massacre

Aaron of Lincoln
born c1125
Jewish financier

Cistercian monks
1128
from France

Licoricia of Winchester
born c1210
Jewish financier

These were expeditions that armed themselves to fight against people who did not follow the ways of European Christendom. Crusades could be against heretic (non-Catholic) Europeans, or followers of Islam in the Middle East and in Spain. Most of the medieval Crusades were focused on securing possession of Jerusalem for Christians.

Notable migrant

 Migrant volume

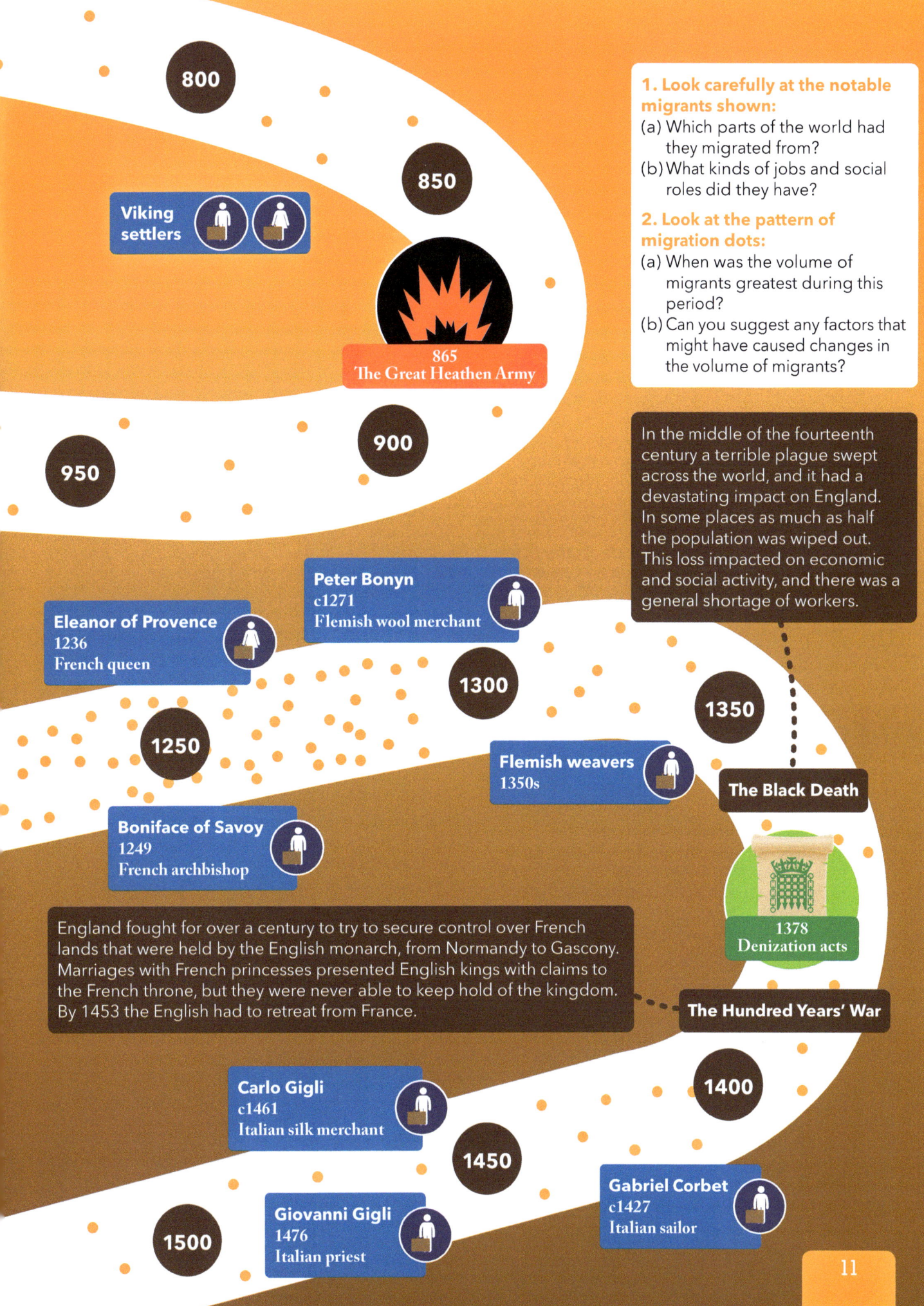

2 Migration in medieval England, c.800–c.1500

2.1 What was the impact of invaders on England c.800–c.1100?

This first enquiry in the book is different from all the others because the first major groups of people who we know came to England from overseas and made a new home here were invaders rather than immigrants. They are still part of the story of migration in England, but their motivation and use of military force in taking control sets them apart from the immigrants in later centuries.

The first groups of people who invaded England were the Romans and Anglo-Saxons. Here you are going to study the invaders who arrived between the ninth and eleventh centuries – the Vikings and the Normans.

Invaders are likely to have more of an impact than migrants on the existing society that they conquer. As you study the sections of this enquiry, you should gather information and ideas about the impact of the Vikings and the Normans on:
i) government
ii) religion
iii) culture
iv) trade
v) the built environment.

The Vikings settle in the British Isles

The Vikings were from Scandinavia. In the eighth century, they began to explore far from their homelands in search of people to trade with, land to settle in and territories to raid. The Vikings were expert ship builders, and their long ships could sail in the open sea and up rivers. England was an especially easy and attractive target for the Vikings because of its long coastline, many rivers, wealthy monasteries and large settlements. In 793, a band of Norwegian Vikings launched a devastating attack on a monastery off the coast of Northumbria on the island of Lindisfarne. The raid shocked people around Europe because of the ferocity of the attack; many holy items were taken, monks were killed and a vast number of treasures were taken away to Norway. The attacks increased in number and it seemed that nowhere in northern Europe was free from the threat of a Viking raid.

From raiders to settlers

The ambition of the Viking raiders grew throughout the ninth century until, in 865, a substantial army led by the brothers Halfdan and Ivar 'the Boneless' landed in the Saxon kingdom of Northumbria and attacked the city of York. Before this attack, invading Viking armies had been happy to raid and take their loot back to their Scandinavian homes. This time, however, the invaders rampaged throughout England and settled in the kingdoms of East Anglia, Northumbria and Mercia (see Source 1). Only the kingdom of Wessex was able to hold out. The Great Heathen Army, as the Saxons called this force of Vikings, became the rulers of a large part of England. The Danelaw, as the area was known, was where Scandinavian migrants to England chose to settle in the years that followed. The area was governed according to the laws and traditions of the mostly Danish Scandinavian settlers. However, they did not impose any change of religion on the English Christians in their territories.

Christian conversion

The Vikings conquered the kingdom of Mercia in 874, and then Guthrum, a leader of the Great Heathen Army, led Viking forces to attack Wessex. Guthrum's hope of conquering all of southern England ended when King Alfred of Wessex defeated him in 878 at the Battle of Edington. Alfred's peace treaty insisted Guthrum convert to Christianity in exchange for being allowed to rule as a king within the Danelaw. Many of the Danes then became Christian and there are a number of traces in stone relics of the integration of ancient Danish myths and their new religion.

The Vikings' conversion to Christianity is an example of assimilation (see page 9) because the invaders adopted the religion of the natives in the land where they chose to settle. However, many of them would have kept connections with their traditional Scandinavian gods alongside their new religion (see Source 2). There were traces of these gods in Anglo-Saxon culture, and they have remained with us to this day: some of the days of the week are named after them, such as Wednesday, named for Woden, god of war, magic and poetry, and Thursday, named for Thor, god of thunder and sky.

2.1 What was the impact of invaders on England c.800–c.1100?

▲ Source 1 A map showing the Danelaw after the Treaty of Alfred and Guthrum in 879

Culture

In the area of the Danelaw, there are still signs of the Vikings in place names and other aspects of language:

- Many towns and villages have names that end with letters that have Scandinavian meanings: -by means 'village', as in Grimsby; -thorpe means 'new village', as in Scunthorpe; -beck means 'stream' as in Holbeck.
- Dialects in northern England still use particular Scandinavian words, such as dale (for valley) and fell (for hill).
- There are common words in the English language that originate from Scandinavia, such as club, ransack, muck, snub, dollop and glove.

> 3 How was the Great Heathen Army different from the previous groups of Vikings who had come to England?
> 4 Explain the impact of the Danelaw on English culture.

St. Brice's Day, 1002

England renewed its struggle with Denmark in the tenth century, and by 954 the Danish forces had left England. However, Viking raids began again around 980, and ten years later years later the English king, Aethelred II, was paying large sums of gold and silver to the people of Denmark to get them to return home.

In 1002, Aethelred decided to strike a blow against Danish people who had settled and assimilated in the English kingdom over the years. On 13 November 1002, which was St Brice's Day, Aethelred ordered the massacre of all Danish people living in English territory. Two of the victims are believed to have been the sister of the Danish king, and her husband, a Danish noble in Aethelred's service. This this provoked renewed, fierce Viking attacks.

> 1 What might have driven Aethelred to order the St Brice's Day Massacre?
> 2 Compare the way that King Alfred and King Aethelred II handled the Viking challenges.

a) Describe the aspects of the Middleton Cross that show
1) Christianity and
2) Viking culture.

▲ Source 2 The Middleton Cross from St Andrew's Church, north Yorkshire; probably made in the early tenth century

PART 1: Migrants in Britain, c.800–present

Case study: The Viking city of Jorvik

There had been a significant settlement on the site of York since the Roman occupation of England. The Romans used it as an army base, and the Anglo-Saxons established a Christian site there and made it the capital of the northern kingdom of Northumbria. The site was an internal port town on the River Ouse, which was deep enough for sea-going ships to sail right up to it, even though York was over 50 miles from the Humber estuary coastline. It was therefore an ideal centre for the Viking invaders and their long-ships. They took control of the city in 866 and changed its name to Jorvik. Beginning with Halfdan, Danish leaders kept control in Jorvik for most of the next 100 years.

Vikings and economic activity in Jorvik

Evidence of the impact of the Vikings on York has come from archaeological digs, particularly one in the area of Coppergate in 1976–81. Excavations revealed the careful layout of Jorvik's streets and the trades of its residents. The archaeologists found wooden bowls and cups, and items made from metals and animal bones. These materials would have been traded from other parts of the British Isles and from Europe: tin from Cornwall, gold and silver from Europe and Ireland, and amber, a semi-precious stone for making jewellery, from Scandinavia. They also found objects including combs, rings and pins that were carved from reindeer antlers which must have come from the Arctic (see Source 3) and silk, which must have come from somewhere in Asia.

▲ **Source 3** A comb made from a reindeer antler found in Coppergate

> **a)** What evidence is there that the Viking migrant-invaders had connected Jorvik in England with the wider world?

Vikings and Anglo-Saxons in Jorvik

Although the Danish Vikings had come as invaders to York, it does not seem that they drove the Anglo-Saxons away. Jorvik was not an exclusively Viking city. There is also evidence that the Vikings accepted the Christian religion of the local people, which shows they did assimilate into the society in some ways (see Source 4).

▲ **Source 4** A coin made in Jorvik for the Danish ruler Olaf Guthfrithsson, c.940. The name on the coin reads Anlaf Cununc. Anlaf is the Saxon version of Olaf and Cununc is the Norse word for king. The bird on one side of the coin is a raven, which is associated with both the Viking god Odin, and the Christian Saint Oswald

> **a)** Describe two symbols on the coin that suggest the Vikings supported Christianity.
>
> **b)** How far does Olaf's silver penny coin suggest that Jorvik was an **integrated** city?

Place names

The city of York still has place names that are connected to the Viking town, for example, Coppergate. 'Gate' was the Norse (Vikings' language) name for a street and it remains in many parts of York, and 'copper' came from 'cupmaker', which was the job of many people on that street.

Emma of Normandy and Cnut the Dane: immigrant rulers

Emma of Normandy and Cnut the Dane both migrated separately to England early in the eleventh century. Between them, they ruled in England for 33 years, during which time the country was peaceful and prosperous.

Emma, the Peaceweaver of Normandy: Queen in England, 1002–35

It is difficult to tell whether the teenage Emma, sister of the Duke of Normandy, was a willing migrant when she came to England in 1002. Her mission was to have an arranged marriage with the Saxon King of England, Aethelred II, who was more than twice her age. The Normans had migrated to northern France as Viking raiders, but settled down to create a strong French duchy in the tenth century. The Normans had been helping the Viking invaders of England with supplies, and Aethelred wanted that to stop. His marriage to Emma was designed to help, so she was called a 'peaceweaver'. Unfortunately, her husband was no more successful in handling the Vikings after their marriage than before, and they invaded again in 1013.

Cnut, the Viking from Denmark: King of England, 1016–35

Cnut was also a teenager when he first migrated to England with his father, Sweyn Forkbeard, in 1013. His father's victory over Aethelred led to Sweyn briefly becoming King of England, but he died before he was crowned. Cnut headed back to Denmark, but in 1016 he returned with a new invasion force and beat the Saxons to become King of England himself. At his coronation in 1017, he married Emma, then Aethelred's widow. Cnut ruled England for nineteen years and his reign was generally a time of peace and prosperity. With Cnut as King of England, the Viking pillaging of the country stopped, and most of Cnut's Danish warriors were sent back to Denmark by 1020. He organised the English kingdom very well, putting reliable Saxons in control of new, large earldoms to run the country.

Both Emma and Cnut were Christian monarchs and gave a lot of support to the English Church. Emma had connections to leading priests, such as Aelfsige, who was Bishop of Winchester, and Stigand, who went on to be Archbishop of Canterbury under her son, Edward the Confessor. Cnut also maintained good relations with the Saxon Archbishop of York, Wulfstan, who helped the King draw up new codes of laws for England based on the Saxon laws of King Edgar.

Cnut also became both King of Denmark in 1018 and then Norway in 1028. With little fighting, Cnut had established an empire across the North Sea, with England at its centre. When Cnut visited the Pope and other rulers in Rome in 1027, he negotiated reduced payments for English travellers to the holy city.

▲ **Source 5** An eleventh-century picture of Cnut and Emma presenting a gold cross to the new church at Winchester

a) What does this picture suggest about Cnut and Emma as **1)** a couple and **2)** rulers of their new homeland?

1. Explain the similarities and differences in the migrant stories of Emma and Cnut.
2. Discuss how the ideas of assimilation and autonomy can be seen in the lives of Emma and Cnut. You could create diagrams to show your ideas like the ones on page 9.

PART 1: Migrants in Britain, c.800–present

The Normans and the transformation of England

William of Normandy, the descendent of Viking raiders who settled in northern France, and great-nephew of Queen Emma, invaded England in September 1066. He became King of England after the Battle of Hastings in October, when he defeated Harold II, who had taken the throne on the death of Emma's son, Edward the Confessor, at the end of 1065. William's victory over the Anglo-Saxon army paved the way for the Norman Conquest.

Changes to England's governance

The number of Normans who settled in England in the years following 1066 was relatively small, almost certainly fewer than 10,000, almost all of whom were men. The most noticeable change, therefore, was the widespread replacement of Saxon landowners with Norman ones. Land that had been owned by 4000 Saxons was seized by William and given to only 200 Norman nobles, bishops and monasteries. In order to manage his newly acquired territory, William introduced the **feudal system** to England. All of the land in England technically belonged to King William and he gave out parts of it to nobles who swore to supply him with a certain number of knights, depending on the size of their estate. This system gave William far more control over England than previous Saxon kings had had and allowed him to introduce even more changes.

Because King William believed he was the rightful successor to Edward the Confessor, his first written statements and proclamations were made in English, as had those of the kings before him. But, after a period of rebellion between 1068 and 1070, William began to rely less on the English for support and more on his close Norman advisers. It was only after 1070 that Norman culture dominated English society.

Most of the information historians have about England during this time teaches us about what life was like for the wealthy and educated. In these sources, it is clear that Norman French was becoming the main language used at court and in government. Justice, prison, constable, agreement, fine, court, debt and evidence are all words that were introduced into the English legal system by the Normans.

> 1 Why did William introduce the feudal system to England?
> 2 Explain why William waited to impose Norman French on the English legal system.

Changes to the built environment of England

The Normans were great builders who changed the physical landscape of England through the construction of castles and churches.

Castles

▲ Source 6 A reconstruction of a Norman motte and bailey castle at Totnes in Devon

> a) Make a list of the features of the motte and bailey castle in Totnes that helped the Normans control the Anglo-Saxon population.

Motte and bailey castles

The Anglo-Saxons built walls around towns and cities to defend them from possible invaders. When the Normans arrived, one of the first things they did was to build castles. They built 65 major motte and bailey castles between 1066 and 1100. The Normans used them to frighten the local population and to remind them of Norman power and authority.

Stone castles

Over time, the motte and bailey castles were replaced with stone castles, which were even more resistant to attack. Castles were powerful defensive structures but they also became the place that ordinary people associated with authority. They were important centres of administration and local government. Tax collectors, officers of the court and market traders could also be found within the walls of a castle. Because they were home to large garrisons of soldiers, castles eventually became the centre of local activity and their presence also created a sense of security for the town or village.

Churches

Anglo-Saxon churches were usually small wooden buildings in the villages of England. Even in towns, like Norwich, there were lots of small churches for small district communities, rather than large structures. The Normans wanted to show that they had authority in religion to match their military authority. They built larger stone churches, and constructed **basilicas** in major towns, like London, Durham and York, which could hold hundreds of people worshipping at one time. One of the key interior features of these large Norman basilicas was the rounded arches. The Norman churches were painted inside with religious art, like the church in Copford Green, Essex (see Source 7). This gave a clear message about the power of the Church in people's lives, and the leaders of the Church were usually Norman. (For more about William I's approach to the Church in England see page 22–23.)

▲ **Source 7** The painted interior of the Norman church at Copford Green, Essex, built c.1130 for the Bishop of London

Cultural changes

Norman French became the language of government as a result of the Norman Conquest. The Normans formed the new aristocracy of England and the words they introduced reflected the new power structure. Many French words relating to government entered the English language, such as crown, authority, minister and even the word government. The Normans also brought new words for everyday things, such as food, and these eventually became part of the English language. Many cooked meats came to be known by Norman French names, such as beef, mutton, veal and venison, although the animal names remained Anglo-Saxon, such as cow, sheep, calf and deer. For 200 years after the Norman Conquest, French remained the language of ordinary conversation among the upper classes in England. The language of the ordinary working people remained English.

Commercial changes

The Normans brought new people into the trade and finance of England. Breton and Norman merchants set up businesses in English towns, particularly places where they paid less tax, such as London, Southampton and Nottingham. New trade across the English Channel included English wool exported to Flanders and wine imported from France.

Another group who came to England from Normandy after 1066 were Jewish people. These were the first Jewish people recorded in England, and they first settled in London and Oxford in the 1070s. William particularly wanted these people to provide him with financial services, as they did in his Norman capital, Rouen. They helped the King with loans and currency deals for international trade. During the reign of William's son, Henry I (1100–35), the Jewish people in London were granted freedoms by a royal charter, including permission to travel around England and carry on their business.

> 3 How far did the Normans change the built environment of England after their conquest?
> 4 Compare the impact of the Norman invaders on the former elites of Anglo-Saxon England and the ordinary working people. How far did their lives change?
> 5 How did the Norman kings encourage immigration in England?

FLEMINGS IN WALES

Flanders had long been politically and economically close to the English Crown. After 1066 those ties grew even closer as William I was married to the daughter of the Count of Flanders and the invading Norman force included many Flemings. Those Flemings could be found throughout much of England and some acquired great wealth. In an attempt to limit their growing influence, William's son, Henry I, moved the Flemings to live in South Wales. The region of Flanders was devastated by floods during this time and the refugees who escaped to England were also sent to live in Pembrokeshire, South Wales. So many Flemings settled there that the Welsh language, for a time, disappeared in the area in place of **Flemish** and Norman French and later, English.

PART 1: Migrants in Britain, c.800–present

Communicating your answer

Now it's time to write your answer to the Enquiry Question and …

STOP! We have forgotten something very important.

Good historians usually start answering a question by suggesting an initial hypothesis – a first draft answer. A hypothesis helps you to stay on track as you continue working but remember that you can change it or add to it as you learn more.

1. Based on what you have found out using pages 12–17, what was the impact of migrant invaders on England between c.800 and c.1100?

The next step is to collect evidence that helps you to answer the Enquiry Question. We are going to use a Knowledge Organiser. This is to help you avoid the common mistake of making notes so detailed that you cannot see the main points you need.

2. Make a larger copy of the table below. Add detail to it from the information you have been given so far in this chapter for the years c.800–c.1100.

Government, including Danelaw, and Governance	
Religion	
Culture	
Trade	
Castles	

3. Compare the information in your Knowledge Organiser with your partner's. Make any necessary additions.

Now it's time to write your answer!

Now you're ready write an answer to our question.

What was the impact of migrant invaders on England between c.800 and c.1100?

Use the following plan to help you structure your answer:

Paragraph 1: Describe the Danelaw and Norman governance and explain how this changed people's lives in England.

Paragraph 2: As above but consider religion.

Paragraph 3: As above but consider culture.

Paragraph 4: As above but consider trade.

Paragraph 5: As above but consider castles.

Word Wall

A Word Wall identifies words that are useful for writing an answer. They also help you to think and talk about your answer. Add to your Word Wall each time you finish studying a new time period. This helps you to:

- understand the meaning of technical words and phrases
- communicate clearly and precisely when you describe or explain historical events – this definitely helps you do well in your exams
- spell these important words correctly (good spelling is rewarded).

Here are some words and phrases to help you think about the Enquiry Question and England between c.800 and c.1100. Make your own copy on a large sheet of paper and leave plenty of space so you can add to it.

Red – words related to the history of migration.

Blue – historical periods.

Black – words that make your arguments and ideas clear to the reader.

Golden – words that help you to use evidence, explain and link your answer to the question being asked.

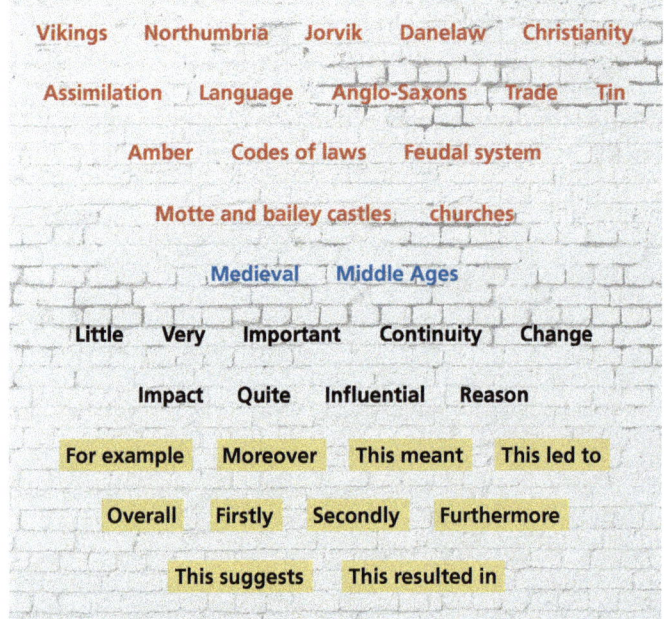

2.2 Why were migrants attracted to medieval England c.1100–c.1500?

The last successful foreign invasion of England came in 1066. After that, all those who came to settle in England were considered immigrants.

Our second enquiry question, for the second part of this chapter, is shown above. As you work through this part of the chapter, it will be helpful to gather important information in the form of notes, possibly in a table like the one on page 9. Remember the key questions for the 'attraction of England':
- What was happening in England?
- How did that attract migrants?
- Who came and where did they go?

There are four key features of this period: a) royal authority, b) trade, c) wool and d) the Church.

Medieval English monarchs and foreigners

The monarch had ultimate authority, but increasingly needed to consult with the most powerful nobles and clergy in the land. The first Parliaments were formed in the thirteenth century, and the monarch had to seek their support for raising taxes and funding wars. Peace and stability made England an attractive destination for immigrants wanting to do business, and possibly settle.

ENGLAND AND THE BRITISH ISLES

Most of the medieval migrants to England came from the neighbouring kingdoms of Wales, Scotland and Ireland. Those nations' rulers all battled against English attempts at supremacy; but they never conquered the English kingdom. Henry II (1154–89) firmly established Anglo-Norman forces in the east of Ireland in a region known as 'the Pale'. Edward I (1272–1307) put an end to any threats from the Welsh by conquering them in 1277–83, but ultimately failed to do the same with Scotland. The borderlands between these kingdoms would see the most mingling of peoples, but some Welsh and Scots migrated as far as London.

ENGLAND AND FOREIGN ROYALS

Royal marriages were an important way of creating and maintaining good relations with European nations. For 400 years following the Norman Conquest, almost all England's **queen consorts** were from France or Spain. These brides often brought large numbers of immigrant courtiers with them. When **Eleanor of Provence** married Henry III in 1236 she brought a lot of family with her. These powerful immigrants became integrated into the English establishment, and one uncle, **Boniface**, became Archbishop of Canterbury (1249–70). But they upset many English nobles, especially in London.

ENGLAND AND THE CRUSADES

The Crusades were military expeditions sent by the Catholic Church to defeat non-Christian Muslims and Christian **heretics**, especially in the Holy Land of Palestine. As Christian warriors, English kings were keen to join in. Richard I (1189–99) went on the Third Crusade against Saladin. His great-nephew, Edward, went on Crusade from 1270 to 1274. As king, Edward I spent his whole reign planning to return to the Holy Land, but never managed to do so. Funding the Crusades meant higher taxes on trade and immigrants. In the climate of the Crusades there was also open hostility in England towards non-Christian immigrants, particularly Jewish people (see page 26–27).

ENGLAND AND EUROPE

Medieval English kings had lands in France that they saw as highly important for their authority and prosperity. English power in France was at its height in the period 1154–1204 when the Angevin kings of England ruled over the western half of the kingdom of France. In 1204 King John (1199–1216) lost Normandy, but his successors clung on to Gascony in the south-west. His great-great-grandson, Edward III (1327–77) staked a claim for the French throne itself in 1340 and started the Hundred Years' War to secure it. England's continental connections opened up opportunities for alliances and migrations. However, wars could make life difficult at times, especially for French immigrants in England (see page 25 and 28).

1. What seem to have been the top priorities for England's medieval kings from c.1100 to c.1500?
2. How might immigrants be connected to each of the kings' concerns?

PART 1: Migrants in Britain, c.800–present

MATTHEW PARIS

Matthew Paris (c.1200–59) was a scholarly monk based at the Abbey of St Albans who specialised in writing histories. He also drew pictures to include in his manuscripts. He drew a full-page map of Britain in one work, which is shown in Source 1; it is not geographically accurate, but it does show the relative position of the main parts of the island. Paris used his map to show what he thought was most important in the thirteenth century.

Medieval England and European traders

▲ **Source 1** A medieval map of Britain drawn by the monk Matthew Paris, c.1250

a) Which two features of England did Matthew Paris emphasise most on his map of England? How would these features be connected to the economic life of English people?

b) How did Paris show Wales and Scotland in relation to England on his map?

c) What details on the map show that England was a good place for traders to come to?

English fairs

England had been a prosperous trading centre for many centuries, and foreign merchants were a regular feature in the country. Some of those foreigners would go straight back to their homeland when trading was finished, but others decided to settle down and make England their base for trade with Europe. From the twelfth century, England's rulers decided to encourage trade by issuing charters to towns that allowed them to hold an annual fair, or open market. Between 1200 and 1270, over 2200 such charters were issued. Some fairs became internationally famous, lasted several weeks and were organised to take place in sequence across the country:

- Stamford Fair (Lincolnshire), held at Lent
- St Ives (Cambridgeshire) at Easter
- Boston (Lincolnshire) in July
- Northampton (Northamptonshire) in November.

This plan meant that foreign merchants could visit all the fairs in turn.

English wool was the most important commodity that the immigrant traders wanted to buy.

1 Explain the part that the fairs played in migration to England in the thirteenth century and later.

2.2 Why were migrants attracted to medieval England c.1100–c.1500?

England's wool trade

Sheep farming was the most profitable activity for the majority of medieval English people. English sheep were kept mainly for wool, rather than meat. The cloth makers of Flanders (modern-day Belgium) and Italy thought very highly of English wool, and exports increased dramatically in the late thirteenth century. One group of immigrants became directly involved in sheep farming and wool production: monks, especially the **Cistercians** from France (see page 23). There were also opportunities for migrants from Wales and Scotland to work as labourers on English sheep farms, or to spin wool. The names of these workers were not usually recorded, unless they paid tax, like Alice Spynner, an Irish woman spinning wool in Leicestershire in 1440.

▲ Source 2 A medieval illustration of English men and women sheep farming

English monarchs used taxes on wool as a major source of revenue, and it was often foreign merchants who were taxed most heavily.

The height of the wool trade was in 1250–1350: in 1280, c.25,000 sacks of wool were exported from England; trade peaked at c.45,000 sacks in around 1305. Cloth manufacturing also brought some immigrants, and the skills of **Flemish weavers** in particular were a great boost to the growth of the English industry. Then, in 1351, the ruler of Flanders ordered the expulsion of hundreds of citizens of the major Flemish towns of Ghent and Bruges, because they had sided with England in the war with France (see page 29). King Edward III (1327–77) immediately offered protection for any of the *exiles* who wanted to immigrate to England, and many of them were weavers. (See page 29 for more about the impact of Flemish weavers on Colchester in Essex.)

> **a)** What jobs can you see the people doing in the picture?
>
> **b)** How does the picture show the importance of sheep to England's economy?

London guilds

The capital of England was the largest and most commercially active of England's medieval towns. From the twelfth century, London's many trades and craft industries became organised into *guilds*. Guilds supervised the quality of goods traded or manufactured, and also strictly controlled membership of trades, operating apprenticeships and collecting fees from all members. The most prestigious guilds, including the grocers, fishmongers and goldsmiths, became known as 'livery companies'.

This prosperous economic environment attracted merchants and craftsmen from other countries. When the population of England was drastically reduced during the Black Death, in the mid-fourteenth century, this immigration was welcome; skilled labour was in high demand. But by the fifteenth century, population numbers were recovering, and there were frequent complaints from guilds about the '*aliens*' who were competing for jobs in London's trades. Nonetheless, some guilds recognised the value of immigrants who brought skills to the crafts. The Goldsmiths' Guild regularly admitted alien craftsmen, although one regulation said that newly registered alien goldsmiths had to take on English-born apprentices.

> **2** Make a list of the ways that England's wool industry attracted immigrants in the Middle Ages.
>
> **3** How far did the guilds of London help make England an attractive place for immigrants?

PART 1: Migrants in Britain, c.800–present

The medieval Church and migrants

Religion was a major factor uniting people across Europe. Medieval Christians belonged to one Catholic (universal) Church, under the authority of the Pope in Rome. Church services and holy books were in Latin everywhere across Europe. William of Normandy was already a proud Christian leader when he took the English throne, and he brought migrant French religious reformers to tighten the organisation and moral life of the English Church. England became an attractive place to French monks who wanted English Christians to live their lives more strictly in their devotion to God and service to others.

Church leadership and 'alien' clergy

William I's key migrant church leader was **Lanfranc**, an Italian-born Benedictine monk who had earlier migrated to Normandy to lead William's new abbey at Caen in 1066. The King appointed Lanfranc as Archbishop of Canterbury in 1070. Lanfranc worked at removing corruption from the English Church, but also kept it quite independent from interference from Rome. He described himself as a 'novice Englishman' in a letter to the Pope in 1071. He didn't despise the English people, like some Normans, but he did prefer appointing immigrants to senior positions as bishops in the English Church. There was only one Englishman chosen to be a bishop in England between 1070 and 1140. Even Thomas Beckett, the famous Archbishop under Henry II, was born in London to French immigrant parents. Some English people were not happy about having so many 'alien' clergy.

Monastic immigrants: the Cluniacs

A **monastery** was a religious community of either men (monks) or women (nuns) who devoted themselves to the service of God. Some monasteries were totally isolated from the communities around them, but others were fully involved in serving them in education, health care and business. King William and Lanfranc were keen to recruit some of the new monks from the Abbey of Cluny in France, because they knew that **Cluniac** monasteries were much stricter in the way they followed God.

In 1089, Lanfranc succeeded in bringing four Cluniac brothers from the Loire area of France to transform a monastery (called a **priory**) at Bermondsey, just the other side of the River Thames from the City of London: the Priory of St Saviour. The monks were still governed by the leaders at Cluny, and all the Bermondsey **priors** were French immigrants until 1380. In 1268, Bermondsey priory was granted permission to host a Monday market at Charlton, as well as a three-day annual fair around Trinity Sunday. Cluniac monasteries were established all over England, and the ruling monarchs came to see them as a source of tax revenues. In 1294 Edward I temporarily seized all the alien priories and took their income for an emergency war with the French.

▲ **Source 3** A drawing of Archbishop Lanfranc from a manuscript of c.1100

1. Why did William the Conqueror and Lanfranc want to encourage immigrant monks to come to England in the late eleventh century?
2. Why might 'alien clergy' want to migrate to England?
3. How far do you think that Lanfranc was 'at home' in England?
4. How had the English kings' interests in monasteries changed by the thirteenth century?

THE HARRYING OF THE NORTH

The Harrying of the North was the Norman response to English rebellions in the north of England during the winter of 1069–70. King William ordered his knights to burn entire villages to the ground, destroy their sources of food, slaughter their livestock and kill their inhabitants.

Monastic immigrants: the Cistercians

An even stricter order of French monks was formed under St Bernard at Citeaux, about 60 miles north of Cluny. They were called Cistercians and they did all the work of the monastery themselves, at least in the early years, rather than paying local workers to do some of it for them. They searched for land that would be isolated from communities, usually in remote valleys, but they still served the poor and sick in their local areas. The first Cistercian abbey in England was founded in 1128 when the French Bishop of Winchester, William Giffard, recruited thirteen Cistercians from Normandy to come over to Waverley in Surrey. The north of England was also a good place for the Cistercians to set up abbeys, because there were parts of Yorkshire that had still not recovered from William the Conqueror's infamous 'Harrying of the North' in 1069, so they were deserted enough for the immigrant monks. Rievaulx, which was founded in the North York Moors in 1132, is one of the most famous of these Cistercian abbeys.

Rievaulx Abbey

The first Cistercian **abbot** of Rievaulx was William, who was born in Yorkshire, but left for France as a young man to become a monk under St Bernard. He returned as a Cistercian immigrant in 1132. Scottish immigrants then served as abbots for the rest of the twelfth century. The Cistercians at Rievaulx became heavily involved in wool production. Their remote valley was an area of moorland where sheep could graze, and the monks became skilled in breeding techniques. The monks used the profits from their trading in wool to expand their buildings to glorify their God, and to offer free hospitality to any visitors. The wool crop at Rievaulx, and other Cistercian abbeys, attracted Flemish, French and Italian immigrant merchants by the thirteenth century. The Riccardi house (see page 23) was dealing with Rievaulx directly by the 1370s.

◀ **Source 4** The historic site of Rievaulx Abbey

a) What aspects of the site can you see that would have suited the twelfth-century Cistercians?

b) The abbey is now ruined, but you can see the remains. What does the extent of the site suggest about the success of Rievaulx Abbey?

c) What does the nature of the area suggest about any economic activity that might have helped to fund the monastery's expansion?

5. Compare the development of the sites and opportunities for the immigrant monks at Bermondsey and Rievaulx in the twelfth century. How might the monks have been viewed by their local communities?

6. Why might these 'alien clergy' be an easy target for the authorities and ordinary people to blame if there were national or local problems?

PART 1: Migrants in Britain, c.800–present

Communicating your answer

Now it's time to plan your answer to the Enquiry Question.

Why were migrants attracted to medieval England c.1100–c.1500?

1. Look at the notes and the table that you were asked to create on page 19. Compare the work that you did with a partner.
2. Compare how important the following factors were for different groups of migrants in the years c.1100–c.1500:

    You could consider the impact on Jewish people, European traders and craftsmen.
    - Royal authority
    - Trade
    - Wool
    - The Church

Now it's time to write your answer to our question.

Use the following plan to help you structure your answer:

Paragraph 1 – Describe royal authority in England and explain who, and why, this attracted people to medieval England.

Paragraph 2 – As above but consider trade.

Paragraph 3 – As above but consider wool.

Paragraph 4 – As above but consider the Church.

Paragraph 5 – Your conclusion should weigh up which reason was the most significant in attracting migrants to medieval England in the years c.1100–c.1500.

Word Wall

Here are some extra words you can add to the Word Wall you made on page 18. They will help you write accurately and with confidence. Look over your notes for the period c.1100–c.1500 and see if you could add some **red words** of your own.

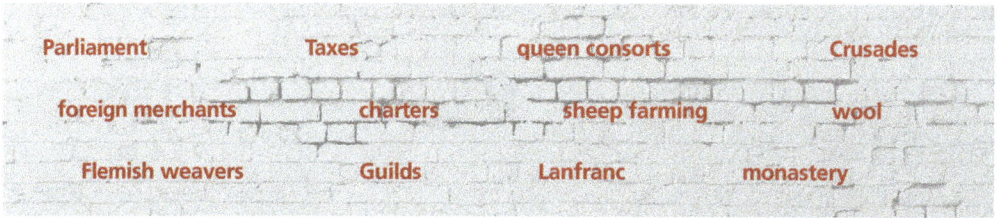

Parliament · Taxes · queen consorts · Crusades · foreign merchants · charters · sheep farming · wool · Flemish weavers · Guilds · Lanfranc · monastery

Practice questions

1. Explain why the migration of Vikings led to change in England in the years c.800–c.1100. **(12 marks)**

    You **may** use the following in your answer.
    - The wool industry
    - Normans

    You **must** also use information of your own.

2. 'Trade was the most influential factor that attracted migrants to England during the Middle Ages.' **(16 marks)**

    You **may** use the following in your answer.
    - The wool industry
    - Normans

    You **must** also use information of your own.

2.3 How far were immigrants welcome in medieval England?

> This is our big enquiry question for the final part of the chapter. As you work through the sections, it will be helpful to gather important information in the form of notes, possibly in a table like the one on page 9. Remember the key aspects for 'experiences and impact of migrants':
> - Relations with the monarch
> - Relations with local authorities and the Church
> - Relations with English people
> - Impact.
>
> There are four main groups for this time period: a) merchants from Italy and France, b) Jewish people, c) Flemish weavers and d) French monks.

English laws and medieval immigrants

Both national and local authorities were often concerned about the situation of foreigners living in their areas. There was a clear distinction made between the subjects of the monarch, who belonged to English families and owed the monarch their allegiance, and 'aliens' whose loyalty could lie with the place of their birth in a different land. English subjects of the monarch were sometimes termed **denizens** and they enjoyed particular rights in relation to property ownership and representation in courts of law, which aliens did not. So, new immigrants were aliens, and they could be taxed differently from the native English, which usually meant more heavily.

The monarch and their parliament did not always agree about immigrants. English merchants and craftsmen in parliament often saw immigrants as competitors who should be restricted, whereas the monarch often saw them as a source of prosperity and new ideas. In 1303, Edward I introduced the *Carta Mercatoria* (Charter of Merchants) that granted rights to foreign merchants, including freedom to trade and legal protection for any contracts and orders that they made. Later, in 1334, his grandson Edward III replaced this general agreement with a specific one for the rights of the German merchants of the Hanseatic League.

On the other hand, worries about national security could make English monarchs wary of aliens, and so expulsions of foreigners often occurred at times of war. In 1270, Henry III had a dispute with Flanders, and so he ordered the arrest of all Flemings in England. But the monarchs also wanted to protect particular loyal merchants who brought in a lot of public revenue. So, in 1271, **Peter Bonyn**, a Flemish wool merchant and friend of Queen Eleanor (Henry's wife), was given letters of protection by Henry III, which said he was to be 'reputed as a denizen and [the King's] merchant'.

Denization

A new process, called **denization**, was introduced from 1378, which enabled an immigrant in England to become fully accepted as a subject of the English ruling monarch. Again, this was prompted by a wartime crisis, when England was doing particularly badly in the Hundred Years' War. The young King Richard II (1377–99) ordered the removal of all foreigners from England. But his main concern was with foreign churchmen, not merchants. Denization allowed particular favoured aliens to swear an oath of **allegiance** to the monarch and secure the same rights in English law as English-born subjects. New denizens had to deny any rights they had in their native land. After the war crisis of 1377–78 was over, the **Chancery** decided to keep this process going, because the fees charged raised much needed cash. Denization was exclusively for wealthy aliens, and only 334 letters of denization were issued throughout the whole of the fifteenth century.

---

1. Why did both medieval monarchs and their parliaments treat aliens and denizens differently?
2. Why would Edward I want to issue the *Carta Mercatoria*?
3. How much of an impact do you think the denization process had on immigrants to medieval England?
4. Make a summary table of the things that medieval English governments did that **a)** attracted and **b)** restricted immigrants.

PART 1: Migrants in Britain, c.800–present

The persecution of Jewish people, 1189–1290

Jewish immigrants in medieval England were clearly different from English people in terms of their religion and language (they spoke French as well as Hebrew). Not all the Jewish people who migrated were wealthy, but there were a number who had sufficient funds with them to set up in trade and moneylending. For the monarch, these people were both a source of credit to borrow for warfare or construction projects like castles, and also a group who could be taxed more heavily.

The royal authorities tolerated these migrants as long as they were financially useful, but some English people could be very hostile towards Jewish people. Anti-Jewish attacks occurred for both religious and financial reasons. When there were particular Crusading expeditions against Muslim people in the Holy Land, English people at home could easily be whipped up into attacking any non-Christian group. Also, raising funds for Crusades could easily lead a knight or baron into debt with Jewish lenders, which made them even more unpopular.

The Jewish people in York and the riots of 1189 and 1190

Aaron of Lincoln (c.1125–86) was probably the wealthiest of England's Jewish people at this time. He was involved in financing building works at three cathedrals and nine Cistercian abbeys. In the 1170s he helped a group of Jewish people from Lincoln to migrate up to York and set up in business. Their leaders were Josce and Benedict and when the King died in 1189, they went to the coronation of his son Richard I.

Unfortunately, anti-Jewish riots broke out in London at the ceremonies, and Benedict was attacked and forcibly baptised by the mob. He **recanted** his conversion the next day, in front of the King, but on the return journey home, Benedict died of his injuries. Similar riots took place in other towns, such as Lincoln, where the Jewish people took refuge in the castle, and in Bury St Edmunds, where 57 were killed. The hysteria was almost certainly stirred up because King Richard was about to embark on the Third Crusade.

▲ Source 1 A modern representation of the siege at Clifford's Tower

A group of York's landowners, including Richard Malebisse and William Percy, then took advantage of the general hostility against the Jewish people to see if they could destroy the records of their debts to Aaron of Lincoln, which had actually passed to the King when Aaron died. In March 1190, they stirred up a mob to attack Benedict's family house, killing his widow and family, and went on an anti-Jewish rampage. Josce gathered the community together and took them to York castle, demanding royal protection from its constable. Local forces then got involved and they besieged the Jewish people in the castle's Clifford's Tower for several days, eventually setting fire to it (see Source 1). A visiting French rabbi, Yom Tov of Joigny, and Josce, persuaded most of the Jewish people to commit suicide rather than be forcibly baptised by the mob and possibly killed. The few who did surrender to the mob were in fact killed a few hours later. Altogether, about 150 Jewish people died that night. Meanwhile, Malebisse and the others went to York Minster to destroy their debt records.

> 1 What appear to be the main factors that decided whether Jewish people were welcome in the twelfth century?
> 2 Tell the story of how Josce's and Benedict's migration to York ended in disaster.
> 3 What appear to have been Malebisse's motives in the March 1190 massacre in York?

26

Consequences of the 1190 massacre

Richard I was outraged at the riot and 59 leading citizens of York were fined, whether they had actually been involved or not. Moreover, all debts to Jewish people were automatically transferred to the Crown on the moneylender's death, so there would be no more advantage in killing Jewish **creditors**. Malebisse fled York and had his lands confiscated. Jewish people only felt safe to return to York after a period of fifteen years. Meanwhile, Malebisse returned after a decade as a royal official, and is later recorded as borrowing again from the Jewish people of York.

> **4** What might a Jewish person at the time think about the royal response to the 1190 massacre?

Henry III and England's Jewish people

Henry III wanted the Jewish people in England to serve the purposes of the Crown and increased tax demands. However, he also responded to anti-Jewish hostility, especially from the Church, by introducing more restrictions on how Jewish people could function in England. A special badge was introduced in 1218 that all Jewish people had to wear: an image of the tablets of the Ten Commandments in yellow felt, called a **tabula**, but it was not rigidly enforced.

One of the wealthiest Jewish people in England at the time was **Licoricia of Winchester**. She became well known as a moneylender to England's **nobility** after the death of her first husband in the 1230s. Licoricia appealed to Henry III in 1242 to authorise her second marriage to David of Oxford, another wealthy Jewish financier, who wanted a divorce from his first wife. Two years after the marriage, David died and King Henry imprisoned Licoricia in the Tower of London until she paid him 5,000 marks (about two and a half million pounds today) in **death duties**. This money, along with other sums taken from Jewish people, was used to rebuild Westminster Abbey.

Henry III did, however, still allow social mixing, and there is evidence that English Christians and Jewish people drank beer together, which shocked other Europeans, especially clergy. Then, in 1253, Henry issued a new order banning all social interaction with Jewish people and enforcing the tabula. When the King demanded more funds from them in 1254, the English Jewish people asked to leave the country, but Henry refused to give them permission.

The expulsion of Jewish people in 1290

By the time Henry's son Edward I became king, new foreign sources were available for royal finances (see page 28), and in 1275 Jewish people were ordered to stop charging interest on loans in England. Financial ruin forced some Jewish people to engage in illegal **coin-clipping** and hundreds were hanged for the crime in 1279. Archbishop Peckham of Canterbury led a major attack on Jewish people in 1287, and most of them ended up in prison for failing to pay new tax demands. Finally, in 1290, Edward ordered the expulsion of all Jewish people from England by the end of November. This was a very popular decision with the members of the upper classes who had been indebted to Jewish people.

> **5** Consider the situation of Jewish immigrant communities in England in the period 1180–1290. How far would you agree with the following interpretation: 'The king decided whether Jewish people were accepted as immigrants or not, and their fate depended on him.'?

▲ **Source 2** A cartoon image of Aaron of Colchester in a legal document of 1277; its title is 'Aaron Son of the Devil'. (This is not the same Aaron as Aaron of Lincoln.)

> **a)** What can you find in Source 2 that shows the increasingly hostile environment for Jewish people in the thirteenth century?

PART 1: Migrants in Britain, c.800–present

Prosperous migrants in medieval England

Not a great deal is known about most medieval English immigrants. Many were farm labourers or servants in wealthier households so do not appear in official records of the time. A few do appear in records but with little detail, only their trade, such as Alice Josip, a Flemish hat maker in Ipswich. A very small number of immigrants were prosperous and made a clear impact on their new homeland, and some became denizens (see page 25). The impact of immigrants was usually in local towns, but sometimes they did affect national affairs.

Italian bankers: the Riccardi company and Edward I

In the thirteenth century, there were major changes in the way that European trade was carried out; some historians have referred to it as the 'commercial revolution'. Powerful merchants no longer travelled vast distances, carrying bags of coins for transactions. Instead, they stayed in their city and operated through networks of agents using bills of exchange in place of metal currency. Some merchants became bankers, especially in Italy where they were connected to the finances of the Pope and Catholic Church. Italian bankers also financed Crusading expeditions crossing the Mediterranean.

The Riccardi company of bankers came from Lucca in northern Italy, and they began contact with England by selling fine cloth to King Henry III. His son, Prince Edward, also asked Lucasio Natale of the Riccardi firm to help raise the funds he needed to go on Crusade in 1270–74. When the prince became King, the Riccardi then became one of his main sources of income for his many wars. The Riccardi company set up a base in London, with about a dozen staff, with smaller offices in York and Dublin.

▲ **Source 3** A fourteenth-century Italian painting of bankers at work in their counting-house (top) and with customers (bottom)

Unfortunately, in the mid-1290s the Italians failed to meet Edward's demands for emergency funds for an unexpected French war. So, in 1294 Edward turned on the Riccardi, confiscated their property, took away their rights to collect certain customs duties, and had them put under arrest. The Riccardi relationship was permanently broken, but the practice of connecting royal finances with immigrant bankers reappeared in later years.

The Giglis from Lucca: trade and the Church

Carlo Gigli came to England in the mid-fifteenth century as a highly successful silk merchant. This Italian immigrant, originally from Lucca and then Flanders, took denization for himself and his wife and family in 1460. Carlo also taught French and poetry in London. Eventually his trade took Carlo back to Flanders, but his son Giovanni, who had studied law and had become a priest, came to England in 1476 and was granted denization the next year. **Giovanni Gigli** was a tutor for the children of King Edward IV, and took important offices in the Church in England, including ambassador to the Pope in Rome from 1490. He was made Bishop of Worcester in 1497, but died the following year in Rome.

> 1 Compare the experiences of Jewish people and the Italian bankers under King Edward I in the 1290s.
> 2 What was the impact of the Riccardi bankers on England in the thirteenth century?
> 3 In what ways did the Giglis from Lucca assimilate into England? Why would that have been easier for them than for many other migrants?

2.3 How far were immigrants welcome in medieval England?

The Flemish weavers of Colchester

When King Edward III offered protection to Flemish immigrants in 1351 (see page 21), at least 27 Flemish weavers went to settle in Colchester in Essex. Essex had been hit very hard by the Black Death from 1348 onwards, but Colchester saw the size of its population of about 3000 increase to around 5500 by 1577, mainly because of immigration. Overall, these Flemings provided Colchester's emerging cloth industry with manpower, expertise and financial resources.

The Flemings helped to develop a particular type of cheaper, standard quality, woollen cloth, called Colchester Russet. This cloth appealed particularly to the Franciscan friars (Greyfriars) who wanted a humble quality cloth for their robes, and there was a Franciscan friary at Colchester. Colchester's cloth industry prospered until the mid-fifteenth century, and the town's long-term economic future was transformed. Colchester had ranked fifty-third in English towns in the tax returns of 1334, but by 1524 it was thirteenth.

The merchants of Southampton

The port of Southampton, on England's south coast, played a key part in the medieval economy, particularly in the export of wool and the import of wine. Immigrant merchants, particularly Italians, played an important part in these trades. One of the most successful was **Gabriel Corbet**, a Venetian mariner in the English navy, who then settled as a merchant in Southampton from around 1427, trading in wheat, wine and other goods. In 1431, parliament approved Gabriel's denization. He made friends with a number of prominent Southampton officials, particularly William Soper, the keeper of the King's ships, and with their help, Corbet was given a number of public positions, such as 'water bailiff' in 1443, which meant he collected trade duties. The peak of Corbet's authority came in 1453 when he was elected Southampton's sheriff.

▲ Source 4 The Merchant's House in Southampton, now owned and maintained by English Heritage

Some people in Southampton were opposed to the migrants. John Payne was the leader of the anti-Italian faction, and when he was elected Mayor in 1462 he used that authority to pick on immigrant merchants. Payne confiscated wine from Filippo Cini, falsely claiming he had not paid the right customs duties. Walter Fetplace led the town's pro-Italian group, and exposed Payne's fraud. Payne was removed from office on the King's orders; Fetplace took over as Mayor. Payne moved to London and died a very wealthy man in 1467, but Filippo Cini ended up in financial trouble in 1470. Cini tried to sell his African Moorish servant, Maria Moriana, against her will, and the matter was taken to the royal courts. Maria appears to have been helped in her case by supportive Southampton citizens, although the final outcome is not known.

4. Compare the economic impact of the Flemish weavers in Colchester with the Italian merchants in Southampton.
5. In what ways was Gabriel Corbet of Southampton accepted in medieval England?
6. How far did England's courts deal fairly with Filippo Cini?
7. What sort of arguments might John Payne and Walter Fetplace have had in Southampton in 1460?
8. What can we learn from Source 4 about the importance of Southampton's merchants?
9. What could we possibly infer from the story of Maria Moriana of Southampton?

PART 1: Migrants in Britain, c.800–present

Visible learning: Revise and remember

Just when you thought you might relax, you discover there is something just as important still to do! The most successful students realise that revision is not something that you only do towards the end of the course and the start of your exams. By getting ready for revision now, you make life much easier for yourself later on. Here are some ideas that you can complete after each chronological period considered in this book.

Technique 1: Using memory maps

A memory map is another form of Knowledge Organiser that helps you focus on the key features without getting lost in too much unnecessary detail.

Step 1: Use plain A3 paper (or bigger if you have it). Turn it landscape to allow some space and to stop the whole thing looking cramped.

Step 2: Add information to the map using your notes and looking back at pages 12–29 if necessary. Use pencil so you can make corrections later.

Remember:
- Use key words or phrases. Do not write in full sentences.
- Use pictures/images/diagrams to replace or emphasis words. This helps the information to 'stick'.
- PRINT important words to make them stand out.

Step 3: When you have finished, redraft your memory map to make sure everything is clear.

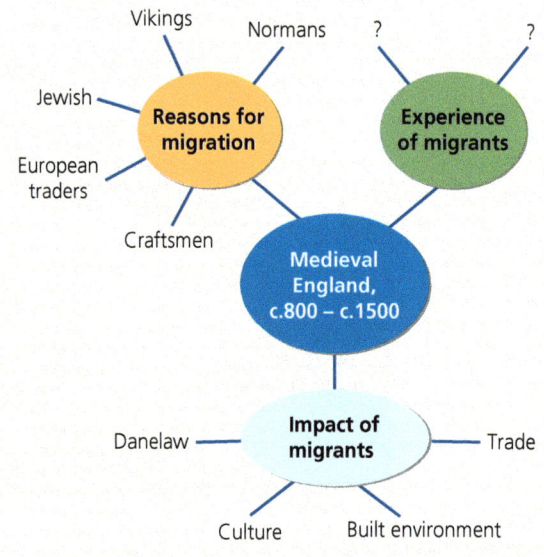

Technique 2: Test yourself

Making a memory map is itself a good way of revising, but you can also use it to test yourself. Try covering up parts of the memory map. Then try to draw that missing part of the memory map from memory. Check this against the original and see what you have missed.

Technique 4: Writing the Big Story

It's really important to keep the Big Story of migrants in Britain clear in your mind, as this is a great help in the exam. Use the notes in your book or look back over pages 12–29 and write a brief story of migrants in medieval England. You should include the words used in Technique 3 as well as the following:

Change – Vikings – This meant that – Continuity

Technique 3: Playing a game

In this game the contestant is given an answer and their task is to come up with the matching question. We have provided some answers below but it is your job to come up with suitable matching questions. Try to make each question as detailed as possible so that you are using your knowledge to help you word it.

Danelaw	Jorvik	Archaeological digs	Norse	Stone castles
Charters	English wool	Flemish weavers	'aliens'	Denization

30

2.3 How far were immigrants welcome in medieval England?

The big picture of migrants in Britain: what changes happened in the period c.800–c.1500

In the seven hundred years covered by this section there have been some dramatic changes, especially with the invaders who came to England in the early centuries, and there have also been aspects of migration that have remained the same for long periods. Each time you finish a section of this course, it will be valuable to look carefully at this concept of change and develop ideas and vocabulary that you can use in writing about it in the examination.

We are going to consider two main aspects of change or continuity in the past: timing and extent of change. Within each of these there are certain things to look for:

- The **timing** of change:
  - its pace could be gradual or rapid
  - its start could be abrupt or anticipated.
- The **extent** of change:
  - its social scope could be comprehensive or niche: who was affected by this?
  - its geographical scope could be localised or widespread: where was this happening?
  - its longevity could be short lived or long lasting: how long did the impact last?

> **Migration Highway**
>
> Use the highway diagram on pages 10–11 to help your thinking about the 'big picture' of migration.

We have only given two choices for describing our features of change that could stand as points on a scale. There are other words that you could use that represent another situation on that scale; for instance, *regional* could come between localised and widespread.

Consider these situations in this medieval period. Change is a process that happens over time, and these events could represent that process. Look at what was happening before and after the event, and decide how far they indicate *change* or *continuity* in the history of migrants in England.

It is quite likely that you will decide there are aspects of change and aspects of continuity in a situation. Make sure you describe the balance between change and continuity each time, as well as the timing and extent of change.

Look at the example that has been written for you on the Cistercians monks. Work out what aspect of change is being discussed in the parts that are underlined. Each example will not focus on all the aspects of change explained above.

An example: The arrival of Cistercian monks in 1128

> This group of French religious men were <u>part of the revival of Christianity</u> that had come to England after the Norman Conquest, which was a <u>major change</u> to society. They were part of a <u>fairly gradual change</u> that began with the Italian-French priest Lanfranc being made Archbishop of Canterbury and then the Cluniacs coming over in 1089. There were Cistercian abbeys <u>all over England</u>, but there were particularly large ones <u>in the north</u> where they had sheep farms. They boosted the woollen industry, which had been a key part of England's economy for a long time. The Cistercian abbeys were part of English society for <u>about four hundred years</u>.

The Great Heathen Army arrives in England in 865	Eleanor of Provence arrives to marry King Henry III in 1236	Flemish weavers encouraged to migrate to England in the 1330s
The Norman Conquest after 1066	Jewish people were expelled from England in 1290	

You could work on this activity in groups, and also come up with other situations you have studied that represent change and continuity. Your groups could devise ways of displaying this knowledge to the whole class.

Desiderius Erasmus
1499
Dutch philosopher and priest

1500

1517 Evil May Day

The Renaissance

Wynkyn de Worde
1481
German printer

John Blanke
c1501
African trumpeter

Hans Holbein
1532
German painter

Once England had finally abandoned her interests in France, people started to look much further afield for new ways of prospering. Large powerful trading companies were formed from c1600 that would exploit the spice trade with the East and the transatlantic slave trade. England's navy became a major asset. These links were associated with opportunities for colonies overseas.

An era in which European culture and learning thrived on the rediscovery of classical arts and philosophy. Renaissance thought encouraged new understanding in science and arts alike. The movement began in Italy, but it soon spread all over Europe, and by the sixteenth century England was exploring new art, architecture and science.

Manasseh Ben Israel
1655
Portuguese-Jewish rabbi

1650

Global Trading Companies

1600

Huguenot settlers

Anne Tanqueray
1685
French silversmith

Abraham de Moivre
c1686
French mathematician

The Glorious Revolution

1689 The Bill of Rights

John Theophilus Desaguliers
1692
French priest and scientist

Sir Solomon de Medina
1688
French Jewish army supplier

1700

William of Orange
1688
Dutch prince and English king

Joshua Kochertal
1708
German Palatine pastor

32

The Migration Highway c.1500–c.1700

Martin Bucer
1549
German-Protestant scholar

1550

The Reformation

1559 The Elizabethan Settlement

Flemings in Sandwich
1561
Weavers

Walloons in Canterbury
1575
Weavers

Mary Fillis
1584
Moroccan servant

1711 The Repeal of the Naturalisation Act

1. **Look carefully at the notable migrants shown:**
   (a) Which parts of the world had they migrated from?
   (b) What kinds of jobs and social roles did they have?
2. **Look at the pattern of migration dots:**
   (a) When was the volume of migrants greatest during this period?
   (b) Can you suggest any factors that might have caused changes in the volume of migrants?

This reformation of Christian beliefs and practices started in Germany led by Martin Luther, and then spread to other parts of northern and western Europe. The Protestant Reformation held that individual Christians could work out their own salvation directly with God, using the Bible written in their own language.

The Glorious Revolution involved the overthrow of the Catholic King James II, who was replaced by his Protestant daughter Mary and her Dutch husband, William of Orange. England's Parliament secured a settlement that guaranteed the rights of the English people to a Protestant monarchy and the freedom to avoid all-powerful European-style kings.

Notable migrant

Migrant volume

33

3 Migration in early modern England, c.1500–c.1700

3.1 How did the attraction of England for migrants change, c.1500–c.1700?

> Gather your knowledge for this enquiry in a table like the one on page 9. Use three key headings for the Early Modern period: (a) Religion and ideas (b) Economy and trade (c) Liberty.

▲ **Source 1** A portrait of Erasmus by Hans Holbein, 1523

Desiderius Erasmus was an expert in the study of Latin and Greek writings, and first came to England in 1499. After teaching at Oxford University, and making friends with important English scholars, such as John Colet and Thomas More, Erasmus went back to Europe to study more Greek. In a second migration from 1510 to 1515 he was Professor of Divinity at Cambridge University. He produced a version of the New Testament in both Greek and Latin, which was used by English scholar William Tyndale when he produced an English bible in 1526.

?
1 In what ways did European migrants help to bring the ideas of the Renaissance and Reformation to England?

New ideas in England: Renaissance and Reformation

The sixteenth century was a time of great change in the religion and culture of Europe, and migration brought new ideas to England. The Renaissance was a time of cultural changes in art, architecture, literature and music that flourished in Italy in the fifteenth century. New 'Protestant' ways of believing and worshipping came from changes known as the Reformation, which began in 1517.

Renaissance thought and Erasmus

The Church had been the single source of thought and belief for most people throughout the Middle Ages. However, fresh ideas were being gathered by scholars who went back to the texts of ancient Greece and Rome. Many of those works were rediscovered in Arabic translations found in Muslim Spain. These ideas celebrated the potential for humans to be creative and improve their own lives, which became known as humanism; this idea was at the centre of the Renaissance. One of the leading Renaissance humanists was a Dutch scholar and priest called **Desiderius Erasmus**, who was a temporary migrant in England.

Printing

The invention of mechanical printing by Johannes Gutenberg in Germany in around 1440 spread the new ideas of humanism across Europe. Printing was brought to England in 1476 by William Caxton, an English merchant, who learned it on visits abroad. In 1481, Caxton invited **Wynkyn de Worde**, a German immigrant, to join him in Westminster to improve his printing works. Worde got the business to print less expensive books for wider sales, such as books on Latin grammar for schools. When Caxton died, Worde took over the press and moved it to Fleet Street in the City of London in 1500, as the first of many famous printers on that road.

Reformation

In 1517, a German monk called Martin Luther published a public protest against the corruption of the Catholic Church and challenged the authority of the Pope in Rome. Humanist ideas were encouraging people to respond as individuals rather than accept papal authority without question. Luther's ideas spread through printed pamphlets and books, some of which came to England. A new branch of Christianity was being formed, which became known as Protestantism.

When King Henry VIII (1509–47) made himself the supreme head of the Church of England in the 1530s, so he could divorce Queen Catherine of Aragon, the path was opened to an English Reformation. It was his son Edward VI (1547–53) who made England fully Protestant, and his Archbishop, Thomas Cranmer, invited migrant scholars to help him draw up a new English prayer book. Two of the most important immigrants were **Martin Bucer** from Germany, and **Peter Vermigli** from Italy. They both arrived in 1549, and became Professors of Divinity at Cambridge (Bucer) and Oxford (Vermigli).

Renaissance art: Hans Holbein

Most of the iconic images of Tudor history were painted by a German immigrant called **Hans Holbein** the Younger, or by English artists who followed his style.

One of Holbein's portraits was of a German scholar called **Nicolas Kratzer**, who migrated to England in 1516 and became an astronomer and clock maker to Henry VIII, specialising in making complex sundials. Kratzer also tutored Thomas More's children, and taught mathematics at Oxford University.

Possibly the most famous of Holbein's paintings is of two other migrants in London in 1533 (see Source 2). They were Jean de Dinteville, an ambassador from the French king, and Georges de Selve, a French Catholic bishop. They were both young men who wanted an imposing record of their London visit.

Hans Holbein was born in Augsburg, Germany, in around 1497 and settled in England in 1532. He became Henry VIII's court painter in 1535. He painted Erasmus (see Source 1) and Thomas More, as well as royalty and nobles. Holbein's Renaissance-style portraits were much more life-like than medieval religious art. Holbein died of plague in England in 1543.

▲ Source 2 Holbein's painting of Dinteville and Selve, known as *The Ambassadors*, painted in 1533

a) How has Holbein shown the spirit of the Renaissance in this picture?

b) The book on the lower shelf is a book of **hymns** by Luther, and the musical instrument next to it (a lute) has a broken string. What might this be suggesting about the Reformation?

c) Can you find a reference to the work of Holbein's friend Kratzer in the painting?

England's final Reformation settlement

The new Protestant Church of England was smashed when Edward VI died aged fifteen and was succeeded by his Catholic older sister Mary (1553–58). But she only lived for five more years, and in 1558 her Protestant sister Elizabeth (1558–1603) became queen and reigned for more than 40 years over a Protestant England.

On the continent of Europe, struggles to decide whether a country was to be Catholic or Protestant were often difficult and violent, and sometimes caused wars. People who lost the battle for their kind of Christianity often sought refuge in a foreign country that followed their faith. Protestant refugees began arriving in England from the start of Elizabeth's reign. The Queen did not want a very rigid interpretation of Protestantism in England, and so different groups of foreign Protestants were able to set up their own churches.

2 Explain how and why England became a destination for Protestant refugees from Europe in the late sixteenth century.

Case study: Protestant refugees in Sandwich and Canterbury

About 50,000 Protestant refugees arrived in England in the sixteenth century. Most of them settled in London and the south-east of England. They tended to be poor, skilled workers seeking job opportunities as well as the freedom to worship in the way they wanted. As a large group of alien immigrants, they were called 'Strangers' and usually kept to their own part of a town or city and had their own churches.

Sandwich and the Flemings

Sandwich had been an important port on the coast of the English Channel in Kent from the fourteenth century, with Italian merchants trading in wool to Flanders. However, by the end of the fifteenth century, its river mouth had silted up, making navigation difficult, and foreign ships went elsewhere. The economy of Sandwich went into decline. Early in Elizabeth's reign, Protestant, Dutch-speaking migrants arrived in London from Flanders, seeking religious freedom from their Catholic Spanish rulers.

The Sandwich migration

- In 1561, officials in Sandwich asked permission to establish a Stranger community in the town consisting of 'men of knowledge of sundry handicrafts'.
- William Cecil, one of Elizabeth's leading political advisers, saw these migrants as an opportunity to revive the town's economy with new Flemish textiles techniques, making unique cloth called 'baize and say'.
- About 400 **Flemish Strangers** settled in Sandwich, including master weavers, and the town's business and trade increased: the number of trading vessels in the port went from 11 in 1561 to 36 by 1571.

Hostility towards the Flemings

The English residents of the town welcomed the Strangers and the economic revival they brought. However, resentment developed when the Flemings took on jobs outside of the textiles work to which they were officially restricted. This became a serious problem after 1567 when many more Protestant Flemings arrived in Sandwich after the Spanish King Philip II sent troops into Flanders to crush Protestant rebels. Groups of French-speaking Protestants called **Walloons**, who lived in a region next to Flanders, also started to settle in Sandwich.

Nearly 2000 Flemish and Walloon Strangers were settled in Sandwich by the end of the 1560s, working as tailors, bakers and builders, and in many other trades. The Town Council issued an order in 1570 forbidding Strangers from working outside of the cloth and fishing industries, but it seems to have had little impact, because they had to issue another similar order in 1581.

In the 1590s, the baize industry went into decline, disturbed by wars and plagues. Many of the Flemings decided to migrate from Sandwich to other parts of England, or to the new rebel Dutch Republic that declared independence from Spain in 1581.

1. What had attracted the Flemish refugees to Sandwich in 1561?
2. How did English people's response to the Flemish Strangers change between 1561 and 1581?

3.1 How did the attraction of England for migrants change, c.1500–c.1700?

▲ Source 3 St Peter's Church in Sandwich, which became the Flemish Strangers' church in around 1564. The special feature on the right-hand side of the picture is a Dutch gable roof that was clearly inserted by Flemish bricklayers

> a) How did the Flemish Strangers show their identity in St Peter's Church?
> b) Why might the English residents of Sandwich have been annoyed by the Dutch gable?

Canterbury and the Walloons

Canterbury had been a centre of Christianity in England for centuries, and from the thirteenth century it was the most famous **pilgrimage** site in England. Pilgrims had visited the shrine of St Thomas Becket, the murdered Archbishop of Canterbury, but the Reformation had put an end to shrines of saints, and Becket's was destroyed. The monasteries were also shut down and their lands confiscated by royal authorities. All of this upheaval in the Church led to economic decline for Canterbury. Houses that had been used by visiting pilgrims were now empty and the Canterbury authorities decided that they would be suitable for Strangers to rent and that these migrants could help the city's economy to prosper again.

The first major Walloon community was established in Canterbury in 1575, and some of the migrants were from Sandwich. Canterbury took French-speaking Walloons and they were given their own church where they could worship in French and conduct their own affairs. After a year or so, they were given a small part of Canterbury Cathedral in which to hold their services. The church membership was around 2500 in 1600, which was at least two-fifths of the total population of the city.

Walloons and silk weaving

The Walloons, like the Flemings, were particularly skilled in weaving cloth, and their speciality was silk. When they first arrived, the Walloons were not allowed to sell silks directly to the public, but by 1580 they could set up their own retail shops. They had around 800 **looms** in the 1580s. The Walloon weavers played a significant part in the economic life of Canterbury; they paid taxes and attracted traders to the city.

There was not as much hostility towards the Canterbury Strangers as was seen in London and Sandwich. However, the Walloons did face opposition from London silk weavers, who complained that the immigrants were working too hard and producing less cloth for the same price. The Canterbury weavers formed themselves into a trade union, called the Drapers' Union to defend themselves against these London rivals.

> 3 Why were the Walloon refugees welcomed in Canterbury in 1575?
> 4 Compare the experiences of the Flemings in Sandwich and the Walloons in Canterbury. Was religion as important as economic factors in their stories?

England's global connections: trade and empire

As well as being a time of change in Europe in terms of thinking and religion, this period was also a period of competition between rival nations to seek out and colonise land beyond Europe.

- From the late fifteenth century Spain and Portugal led the way with their colonisation, first of Africa and then the Americas. Portugal colonised Brazil and Spain took control from Mexico to Peru.
- The Ottoman Turks took over eastern Mediterranean trade after conquering Constantinople in 1453 and Venice in 1479.

At this time, English traders were looking for new markets further away. The wool trade with western Europe had been a major source of England's revenue and wealth for centuries, but wool exports had declined considerably by 1550 and woollen cloth was also less popular than previously.

Privateers and trade

England's sea power grew under the Tudors, with a larger navy, and trading boats that were also used for attacking and robbing enemy ships. This was called '**privateering**', rather than 'piracy', because it had some official support from the monarchy as 'revenge'. Following the Reformation, England's biggest enemies were Catholic Spain and Portugal. French Huguenot (Protestant) privateers encouraged English sailors to join their attacks on Spanish traders in the English Channel.

The transatlantic slave trade

Portugal and Spain built up a trade in enslaved African people who were taken to work on plantations in the Americas. John Hawkins, a merchant and sea captain from Devon, started England's involvement with this enslavement of African people in 1562, making three slaving voyages altogether. He was deliberately breaking the exclusive control that Portugal and Spain had over the emerging transatlantic slave trade. That trade lasted for centuries and became the largest forced migration in history.

> 1 Explain how England made a bid for greater global power and wealth under Elizabeth I.
> 2 How was religion connected to England's new global ventures?

> a) The land shown is supposed to be North America. How does Dee suggest England could build an empire there?
> b) Look for images in Dee's picture that show connections with religion. What does he infer about England's overseas mission?
> c) How might Dee's ideas lead to migration to England in the future?

◀ **Source 4** The title page of a book by John Dee, published in 1577: *General and Rare Memorials Pertayning to the Perfect Arte of Navigation.* Dee wanted England, under Queen Elizabeth I, to expand and build an empire. He was using this picture to show how the riches and opportunities of the New World across the Atlantic could make England a great world power in the future

Joint-stock companies and empire

New overseas enterprises needed a lot of financial backing to get started. Ships were expensive to build and supply for long voyages, and traders had to buy goods to exchange for precious metals, silks and spices. A new type of organisation was formed to bring a group of **investors** together to fund these ventures: a **joint-stock company**.

THE LEVANT COMPANY

- These were originally merchants who were trading in the Middle East, buying spices, textiles and other goods.
- The Queen negotiated access for these English merchants in the Ottoman Empire in 1580 as part of new diplomatic relations with the Turks.
- The Levant Company was then formed in 1592, bringing together existing businesses into a large **monopoly** organisation.
- The company prospered until 1750 when it lost its power.

THE EAST INDIA COMPANY

- This new venture was formed in 1600 and started exploring direct trading connections with the spice markets of Asia by challenging Dutch and Portuguese people in the East Indies.
- By 1630 the East India Company (EIC) merchants had changed tactics and set up trading centres on the mainland of India, with permission from the Mughal Empire (the dominant authority over India).
- Their major bases were in: Surat (1619), Madras (1639), Bombay (1668) and Calcutta (1690).

THE ROYAL AFRICAN COMPANY

- England's involvement in the transatlantic slave trade was brought under the control of a royal monopoly under King Charles II (1660–85). His brother, James Duke of York (the future King James II between 1685 and 1688), was the company's governor for many years.
- The first company was set up in 1660, and then the Royal African Company took over in 1672.
- The company built forts along the coast of West Africa. It was from here that enslaved African people were transported across the Atlantic to England's new plantation colonies in the West Indies.

Colonies in the Americas

More risky adventures involved the establishment of **colonies** of settlers in the New World of the Americas. Colonists were usually looking for resources to exploit, like gold or furs or plantation farming, but could also be motivated by a search for religious freedom. Some joint-stock companies were formed to help set up a colony, such as the Virginia Company, which was started in 1606. After several attempts, the Virginia settlers started to export tobacco as a major cash crop.

Other colonies were founded by individual efforts, like the one on the Caribbean island of Barbados, established by Sir William Courten, a wealthy London merchant. Courten's grandfather had been a Protestant immigrant from Flanders in 1568.

The overseas connections that were set up by these trading and colonial companies laid the foundations for a British empire, much as John Dee had wanted in 1577. These enterprises did lead to some new immigrants in England, like the Native American princess Pocahontas who arrived in England in 1615 as the wife of the Virginia colonist John Rolfe. People from India and parts of Africa also came to England, particularly as members of ships' crews. However, there were no major immigration movements into Britain from its empire until the twentieth century.

> 3 How did English businesses expand their global connections in the seventeenth century?
>
> 4 How did an English empire emerge by 1700? How far did that impact on immigration?

PART 1: Migrants in Britain, c.800–present

THE DUTCH AND AGRICULTURE

The Dutch influence on English agriculture became significant in the late sixteenth century. They introduced more nutritious crops, including new varieties of carrots and other vegetables, as well as techniques to make the land more productive. The Dutch brought a superior form of crop rotation and they also pioneered the draining of the Fenlands of East Anglia. They also introduced gin distilling to England in the mid-seventeenth century. When the new Dutch King William III started to heavily tax imported spirits, especially French brandy, in the 1690s, cheap locally produced gin became wildly popular.

A Dutch king and England's liberties

Religion remained a vital issue for England throughout the seventeenth century, and the possible return of Catholicism disturbed Church leaders and politicians. After a brutal civil war over issues of Catholic influence and royal power in the 1640s, England was quite peaceful and securely Protestant until the 1680s.

Protestant suspicions

By the 1680s many people believed that Catholics were part of a great conspiracy to get rid of the Church of England and bring England under the rule of a European-style Catholic monarch. These fears began to be realised during the reign of James II (1685–88), who was the first openly Catholic ruler of England since Mary I (1553–58). His attempts to grant Catholics greater equality were seen as a real threat to English Protestantism. James' daughter, Mary, was a Protestant. She was married to the Protestant Dutch prince, **William of Orange**. Many Church leaders and aristocrats began to look to William as a preferable alternative to James.

The Glorious Revolution

Fully aware of the distrust of much of the establishment towards James II, William launched an audacious invasion in November 1688 that was four times larger than the Spanish Armada of a hundred years before. When his forces landed in the East of England they were met with little resistance. It was the first successful landing of a foreign army on the shores of England since 1066. Seeing his position as hopeless, James II escaped to France and William and Mary were crowned as joint monarchs in 1689.

William claimed to be a liberator not an invader. He didn't officially seize the crown of England; it was offered to him by Parliament. Parliament stated the terms under which William and Mary would rule, and the Bill of Rights of 1689 was the cornerstone of that settlement. It guaranteed Protestant supremacy in England, the independence of parliamentary elections, freedom of speech within Parliament, and other rights of English citizens.

Rights and liberties

The idea that England was a place that guaranteed certain rights and liberties was firmly established at this point. In 1695 existing controls over what people could publish were removed, marking the start of a genuinely free press. Over the next two centuries England developed a reputation for being a refuge for migrants fleeing political or religious persecution.

Reactions to the Dutch king

Some English people did not welcome the arrival of a Dutchman as England's king, and particularly attacked William's foreign advisors. One critic wrote in a pamphlet that:

> we may soon have not only Dutch bishops, Dutch presbyters [church ministers] and Dutch commanders, but Dutch lords, Dutch commons and Dutch everything.

In fact their influence was limited. There were no Dutchmen in the House of Commons and only a few in the Lords. The anti-Dutch propaganda was as much to do with political squabbles as hatred of foreigners.

---

1. Explain how and why a Dutch migrant became King of England in 1689.
2. Why did English people describe the arrival of William of Orange as a 'glorious revolution'?

---

a) What seems to be the aim of Daniel Defoe's poem 'The True-Born Englishman'?
b) Use evidence from your studies to support what Defoe said about English people.

> **Source 5** The writer and journalist Daniel Defoe (c1660–1731) wrote a satirical poem in 1701 called 'The True-Born Englishman'. He ridiculed English xenophobia and defended the Dutch king
>
> an English Man ... ought not to despise Foreigners as such ... since what they are to Day, we were yesterday, and to morrow they will be like us ... we are really all Foreigners our selves.

3.1 How did the attraction of England for migrants change, c.1500–c.1700?

Communicating your answer

You know that the reasons for migration to England changed in the years c.1500–c.1700, beginning with the Reformation in the sixteenth century. However, knowing the events of the Reformation is only part of the story. You must also consider the reasons why groups and individuals migrated to England. Just describing these reasons is not enough. You must be able to 'prove' why that reason was important by explaining the effect it had. Try answering the following question by using the steps below.

Explain why the reasons for migration to England changed during the years c.1500–c.1700.

Step 1: Describing and explaining

Usually you would organise your answer into paragraphs – each paragraph describing a reason and explaining the effect it had. To help you do this, make a copy of the table and use the statements below it to fill in the blanks.

Reason	Describe reason	Explain how reason led to a change
Changes in religion led to new ideas		Therefore, individuals migrated to England to share the new ideas.
Changes in religion forced migration	Protestants were no longer welcomed in European countries such as Flanders which was ruled by Catholic Spain.	This led Protestant Flemings to migrate to England because it was a Protestant country during the reign of Elizabeth I.
England's trade increased		
England became involved in the transatlantic slave trade		

New ideas, such as Humanism, were at the centre of the Renaissance. During the fifteenth century these new ideas were spreading across Europe.

This introduced the forced migration of some enslaved African people to England as a result of the transatlantic slave trade.

England's involvement in the slave trade began in 1562 by a merchant and sea captain from Devon, John Hawkins. Under King Charles II England's involvement was brought under royal monopoly and by 1672 the Royal African Company took over all transportation of enslaved African people to England's colonies in the Caribbean.

England's sea power grew under the Tudors and English traders were looking for new markets as the export of wool decreased. By 1630, the East India Company had set up trading centres on the mainland of India.

This resulted in people from India migrating to England as part of ships' crews.

Step 2: Writing your answer

Make sure you mention specific groups of migrants and/or individuals. Remember that a good answer will link the description of the reason with an explanation of why this brought migrants to England in the years c.1500–c.1700.

You are now ready to answer the question. We have given you a good deal of help, but you will find more guidance in Writing Better History on pages 140–154. And remember – add to and use your Word Wall!

Word Wall

Here are some extra words you can add to the Word Wall you made on page 18. They will help you write accurately and with confidence. Look over your work for the period c.1500–c.1700 so far and see if you could add some **red words** of your own.

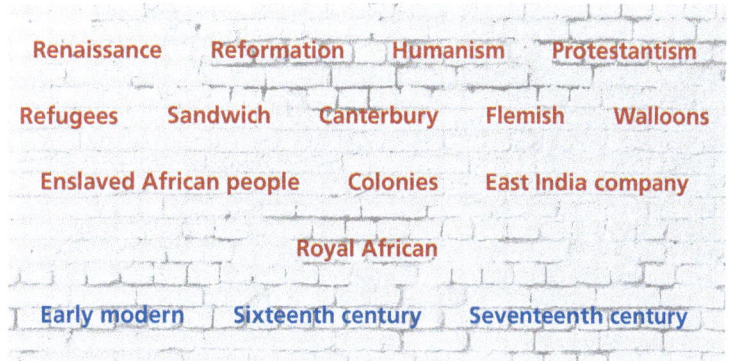

PART 1: Migrants in Britain, c.800–present

3.2 What were the experiences and impact of England's immigrants, c.1500–c.1700?

> Gather your knowledge for this enquiry on the experiences and impact of migrants in the Early Modern period in a table like the one on page 9. There are six key groups for this time period:
> a) African people
> b) Flemish people
> c) French Huguenots
> d) Foreign merchants
> e) German people
> f) Jewish people

Evil May Day, 1517

There were about 3000 foreign immigrants in London in the early sixteenth century, and their economic activity was highly visible; for example, Flemish weavers, and Dutch and German brewers. They were concentrated in certain districts, particularly the east of London and on the outskirts of the city walls. Royal authorities encouraged alien merchants because they brought in finances for wars and building projects. Aliens continued to be charged a special tax, or paid for denization (see page 42), as well as paying customs duties on trade.

Resentment of foreigners

There were two particular aliens whom the London crowds resented because of their close connections to King Henry VIII:

- Francesco de Bardi was an Italian merchant from Florence. Bardi exported English wool and sold satin and velvet to the King, who had given him exemption from paying customs duties. He was also having an affair with an Englishman's wife, who left her husband to live with Bardi. He then sued the husband for the cost of his wife's lodging!
- John Meautys was a French immigrant and a royal secretary working for King Henry. He had a house on Leadenhall Street in the City of London, where Frenchmen who were not supposed to be working in the woollen industry could shelter from the authorities.

Stories like this stirred up anger and resentment among people who were suspicious of foreigners in their city.

The build-up

John Lincoln was a second-hand goods dealer and hated foreigners. He persuaded Dr Bell, a priest from St Paul's Cathedral, to preach a sermon against aliens on 14 April 1517 (see Source 1). Lincoln then put up a notice calling people to meet at St Martin's Church, just north of the cathedral, on the evening of 30 April 30, to protest against foreigners.

The riot

A crowd of over a thousand met to protest, ignoring the curfew that the City of London authorities had imposed. Many of them were young apprentices, some just thirteen years old. The mob went on the rampage, attacking and looting the houses and business premises of foreigners. By the morning of 1 May there were about 2000 protesters on the streets. Meautys' home was looted and the Frenchman barely managed to escape with his life, apparently by hiding in the gutters of his house.

> **Source 1** Part of the sermon by Dr Bell, 14 April 1517
>
> The aliens and strangers eat the bread from the poor fatherless children, and take the living from all the artificers [skilled craftsmen], and the trade from all merchants, whereby poverty is so much increased that every man cries in misery.

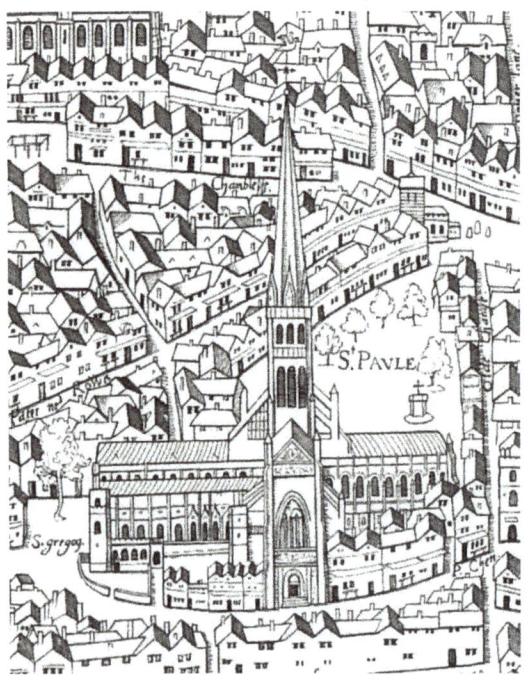

▲ **Source 2** St Paul's Cathedral on a map of c.1550, showing the preacher's cross for public sermons

> a) What is the specific accusation that Dr Bell is making against migrants?

1 How were the London apprentices encouraged to hate foreigners?

Aftermath of the Evil May Day Riot

The Duke of Norfolk led the response to the riot:

- He secured the city gates and sent his son onto the streets with 1300 armed men to arrest people and clear the city.
- About 300 people were arrested, and a small group of ringleaders was identified and quickly executed, even though nobody had died in the riot itself.
- The authorities decided to treat the riot as a really serious incident, and called it a rebellion against the King and government, not just against foreigners.
- Dr Bell could not be arrested because of his status as a priest, but John Lincoln was tried for treason and executed by being hung, drawn and quartered – a particularly gruesome death.

The King then decided to have mercy on the remaining prisoners. He staged an elaborate event at Westminster Hall on 22 May, in which hundreds of rioters were brought before him, tied with ropes. The king's chief advisor, Cardinal Wolsey, joined the prisoners in crying out for mercy, and Henry pardoned them all. The anti-foreigner riot had been turned into a test of loyalty to the King, and his people confirmed their obedience. The final public display of Henry's justice and mercy confirmed his position as a wise and honourable ruler. Evil May Day 1517 was the last major anti-foreigner protest for about 200 years.

2 Why would King Henry VIII want to punish an anti-foreigner riot so severely?

3 What could have been the reasons for the great show of mercy after the initial punishments?

◀ Source 3 A nineteenth-century depiction of the Evil May Day Riot of 1517

Romani Gypsies

Travelling people of Romani culture appeared in England from the early sixteenth century. They were referred to as 'Egyptians' because of their darker appearance, but they are likely to have originated in northern India. 'Gypsies' were nomadic and lived outside of settled towns and villages. Romani Gypsies soon attracted hostility from English citizens and authorities. The 1530 Egyptians Act ordered the travellers to leave England, but this was followed by a harsher act in 1554 that ordered execution as the punishment for being a Gypsy in England. A new law in 1562 allowed the Romani to become citizens of England if they settled down, but the anti-Romani Gypsy laws stayed in place for over 200 years.

African people in England, c.1500–c.1700

A major change took place in England's interaction with the continent of Africa in this period. As you found out on page 38, Portugal and Spain had established a system for enslaving African people and transporting them across the Atlantic Ocean region by 1550, but England was not involved for many years. There were African people in England during the time of the Tudors, but they were free men and women. By 1700, things had changed.

Black Tudors

References to about 350 African people living in England in the period 1500–1640 can be found in official records, including church books of baptisms and burials, reports of legal cases, and returns for the 'alien tax'. Recent research has revealed some of the individual stories of these men and women.

John Blanke is the most famous African man in Tudor England, mainly because his records appear in royal documents. He probably migrated to England from Spain in 1501 as one of the attendants of Princess Catherine of Aragon, who became the first wife of the future King Henry VIII. Blanke was a royal trumpeter, playing at Henry VII's funeral and the coronation of Henry VIII in 1509. The record of his successful request for his wages to be doubled has the new king's signature on the page, so we can assume he was a valued musician.

In 1512, John Blanke got married, presumably to an English woman, as there were very few African women in England at the time, and the King paid for his fine violet wedding suit as a present. The most striking record of Blanke is the image of the black trumpeter in the celebrations marking the birth of a son to Henry and Katherine in 1511 (see Source 4).

▲ **Source 4** John Blanke in the Westminster Tournament Roll of 1511

a) Compare John Blanke and the other trumpeters. How is he shown as a valued musician?

Reasonable Blackman was a silk weaver who lived and worked in Southwark, just across the River Thames from the city of London. This was an area of theatres and other entertainments, and Blackman possibly made costumes for actors. His name appears in the records of St Saviour's church for 1579. It is likely that he migrated to England with some of the Flemings and Walloons (see pages 36–37), as the Spanish rulers of the Netherlands had a lot of contact with Africa. Blackman got married in 1587 and there are records of three of his children being baptised in St Olave's church. Two of them died in an outbreak of plague in 1592, but his son Edward survived and became a silk weaver like his father. There is a record of Edward's marriage in 1614 in Spitalfields, where he probably worked.

?
1 Compare the contributions of John Blanke and Reasonable Blackman to Tudor society.
2 What do the stories of these two migrants suggest about the acceptance of African people in England at the time?

3.2 What were the experiences and impact of England's immigrants, c.1500–c.1700?

Moroccans in Elizabethan London

Trade between England and the North African kingdom of Morocco grew during Elizabeth I's reign, and included the import of Moroccan saltpetre for making gunpowder. Both nations were in conflict with Spain. Before 1492, Muslims of African heritage had ruled in southern Spain, and many had been exiled to Morocco when the Catholic monarchs Ferdinand and Isabella (parents of Catherine of Aragon) conquered them. Elizabeth I was visited twice, in 1589 and 1600, by an ambassador from Morocco named Abd-al-Wahid Al Annuri, to talk about an Anglo-Moroccan alliance against Spain. The ambassador's migration in 1600 lasted six months, but talks collapsed when Elizabeth tried to recruit the Moroccans as mercenaries.

> **Mary Fillis** was an African woman from Morocco living in London during Al Annuri's visit. She is referred to in the public records as a 'blackamoor', which was one of the terms used at the time to identify black African people. Mary was born in Morocco in 1577, the daughter of Fillis, a basket-weaver and shovel-maker. She arrived in London in 1584 and was a servant in the household of a merchant, John Barker. By 1597, Mary was working for Millicent Porter, a seamstress in Smithfield. Mary was baptised in St Botolph's church, Aldgate, on 3 June 1597 and Mrs Porter was a godmother. Two years later her mistress died and we have no further record of Mary Fillis.

▲ **Source 5** A portrait of Al Annuri, the Moroccan ambassador, 1600, painted when he was in London

3 What do the migrations of Al Annuri and Mary Fillis reveal about England's connections to Africa in Elizabethan times?

African servants in England, c.1700

By 1650, English merchants were actively involved in the transatlantic trade, enslaving and transporting African men, women and children to English colonies in North America and the Caribbean to work on plantations. As a result of the Transatlantic slave trade, there were black people in England who were treated very differently from people such as Mary Fillis. Although slavery was technically not legal in England, wealthy English families had unfree African people working for them. It became fashionable to include unfree African children in portraits to show power and status (see Source 6).

a) Compare the African child in Yale's picture with the image of John Blanke (Source 4). What are the similarities and differences in their migration story?

▲ **Source 6** A family portrait of Elihu Yale (centre of the table) with his sons-in-law (on his right, James Cavendish, son of the Duke of Devonshire, and on his left, Dudley North), and (standing) his cousin and heir, David Yale, painted in 1708. Yale's work in India for the East India Company (see page 39) made him very wealthy, and he wanted to marry his daughter into the Duke's family. Yale's name was chosen for a colonial college in Connecticut after he donated books in 1714 to the now world-famous American university

4 How did the experiences of African people in England change from 1500 to 1700?

Case study: Huguenots in seventeenth-century England

France suffered terrible religious conflict between the ruling Catholics and the minority of Protestants, known as Huguenots. Some Huguenots settled in England from 1550 onwards, as did the Flemings and the Walloons (see pages 36–37). Then, in 1598, the Edict of Nantes established religious freedom in France for Protestants, although it was still officially a Catholic country. However, nearly a century later, in 1685, the very powerful King Louis XIV decided to revoke the Edict of Nantes, and Huguenots became victims of aggressive persecution again.

Huguenot refugees

Thousands of Huguenots left France in the 1680s and between 40,000 and 50,000 settled in England, mainly in major towns and cities such as London. They enjoyed the protection of the monarch and parliament, especially after the Glorious Revolution of 1688 (see page 40). King William III and Queen Mary II raised £39,000 to help the resettlement of Huguenot refugees in 1689-93. Their official welcome was confirmed in 1709 when Parliament passed an Act to naturalise all Protestants aliens (see page 49). Although the Act was reversed in 1711, 2000 Huguenots had been naturalised by then. Huguenots generally lived in towns and pursued skilled crafts, such as textile weaving and watchmaking, and professions such as law and banking. London was the premier destination for them, and by 1700 there were about 25,000 Huguenots there out of a total population of about 600,000. The main areas for settlement were just outside the city: Spitalfields in the east, and Leicester Fields and Soho in the west.

> a) How does Hogarth compare the Huguenot community with working-class Londoners?
>
> b) How far does Hogarth's picture show that the Huguenots had assimilated into English society?

▶ **Source 7** *Noon* by William Hogarth, drawn in 1736, showing Huguenot churchgoers in Soho, London, on the right-hand side and ordinary working-class Londoners on the left-hand side

Huguenot crafts

Silk weaving was a major field of Huguenot activity, and they brought with them new French fashions and techniques for wealthy Londoners to admire and adopt.

There were also a lot of prestigious Huguenot gold- and silversmiths, including **Anne Tanqueray** (1691–1733), the eldest daughter of silversmith David Willaume, a Huguenot refugee in 1685. By 1724 she was a widow and running the family business, and in 1729 the Tanquerays were appointed to serve the monarch. Anne became one of the most famous female silversmiths.

Huguenots in finance

Many of the Huguenots had been very successful in business and finance, and brought their wealth with them. They had well-established contacts with merchants overseas, especially in Holland. Huguenots were used to taking risks in investment, and understood the value of putting their funds into new ventures, like the Bank of England, which was founded in the City of London in 1694. Over a hundred newly arrived Huguenots contributed £104,000 of the £1.2 million that set up the Bank. The Bank's first Governor, Sir James Houblon, was from a long-established English Huguenot family.

> 1 Why did some English people say that 'a drop of Huguenot blood is worth a thousand pounds a year'? Were they being complimentary?

▲ **Source 8** A sample from one of the silk cloth design books of James Leman, a Huguenot refugee, when he was a teenage apprentice to his father in Spitalfields

> a) How does the sample book show James Leman's contribution to English society?

Huguenot intellectuals

The seventeenth century was a time of great advances in knowledge, known as the Scientific Revolution. Some very important developments took place in England, led by Isaac Newton in mathematics and physics, and Robert Boyle in chemistry. A number of Huguenots were also part of this flourishing of science and were invited to join the Royal Society that had been founded in 1660 to 'improve natural knowledge' in sciences.

> **John Theophilus Desaguliers (1683–1744)** became an infant refugee when his Huguenot father was banished from France. He studied at Oxford University and also trained as a Church of England priest. In 1714, Newton invited him to lecture for the Royal Society and become a Fellow. He was also vicar of the Duke of Chandos' church in Stanmore, Middlesex, where Handel (see page 64) played the organ.
>
> Desaguliers was a great communicator of science, regularly giving public lectures, and also an inventor, making a blowing wheel to remove stale air from the House of Commons in Westminster in 1723. He was one of the first people in England to inoculate his children against smallpox, years before Jenner's vaccine. He joined the project to build Westminster Bridge, although it meant his own house had to be demolished in 1741. Towards the end of his life, Desaguliers lodged in the Bedford Coffee House in Covent Garden, where he continued to give lectures.

▲ **Source 9** A portrait of Theophilus Desaguliers, showing symbols of both his careers

> **Abraham de Moivre (1667–1754)** was the son of a Huguenot surgeon, and was studying physics in Paris when the Edict of Nantes was revoked in 1685. He and his family escaped to London and, in December 1687, he was made a denizen. He continued his scientific interests and met Newton and the astronomer Halley. De Moivre pioneered ideas in probability theory and became a member of the Royal Society in 1697.
>
> De Moivre joined the Church of England in 1705, but he failed twice to become a professor at Cambridge University, possibly because he was still seen as an alien. Without a top academic job, he had to rely on tutoring mathematics to the sons of aristocrats, usually in Slaughter's Coffee House in Soho. Slaughter's customers played games of cards and chess, and De Moivre advised them on their gambling chances, for a fee.

> 2 Compare the lives and experiences of De Moivre and Desaguliers.
>
> 3 How far had each of them assimilated into society in England?

PART 1: Migrants in Britain, c.800–present

> 1 How were both economic and religious factors significant in considering the return of Jewish people to England in the 1650s?
> 2 How far were the reasons for readmission fully respectful of Jewish people?

Jewish people return to England

After the English Civil Wars (1642–51) there was an increase in religious diversity in England. Some 350 years after their expulsion by Edward I in 1290 (see page 27), Jewish people were finally invited to settle in England. The reasons for this were complex but they fall into two broad categories:

- **Religious reasons**: Many Puritans believed that Jewish people returning to England could speed up the return of Jesus Christ to Earth. There was a widespread belief among them that Jesus' return would only happen once all Jewish people had been converted to Christianity, and that by re-admitting them to England this would happen sooner.
- **Economic reasons**: Jewish people had been facing persecution in Spain and Portugal since the end of the fifteenth century. They had been forced to convert to Christianity or face either exile or enslavement. Many chose to migrate to states in Europe that were more tolerant of Jewish people, with the Protestant Netherlands being the most common destination. The Jewish community in the Netherlands brought much business expertise with them and helped increase the prosperity of major cities such as Amsterdam.

Many English people observed the positive impact Jewish communities had had in the Netherlands and made the case for re-admitting Jewish people in the hope they would have a similar impact in England. Jewish people from the Netherlands also pushed for re-admittance because they believed it would allow them to avoid new restrictions that England had put on trade with the Netherlands.

Oliver Cromwell and the re-admission of Jewish people

Manasseh Ben Israel (1604-57) was a well-respected Dutch rabbi who was a key figure within the Portuguese Jewish community in Amsterdam. Ben Israel was deeply religious and believed that before the return of the Jewish messiah the Jewish people needed to be spread across the world. He therefore appealed to Oliver Cromwell to overturn the ban on Jewish people living in England.

▲ Source 10 A portrait of Manasseh Ben Israel

> 3 Compare the ideas of Cromwell and Ben Israel at the Whitehall conference in 1655. In what ways were they similar?

Cromwell invited Ben Israel to make his case at a conference held in Whitehall over two weeks in December 1655, before some of the most prominent English lawyers, clergymen and merchants of the day. There was significant opposition from English merchants who feared new competition, but there was enough support from others to make re-admission a possibility.

It was decided after the conference that there was no legal basis for excluding Jewish people from England since it was the King and not Parliament who ordered them to leave in 1290. The year after this legal ruling, Jewish people began to worship freely in London, but there was still opposition to their presence. After the death of Oliver Cromwell, and the restoration of the monarchy in 1660, the new king, Charles II, was petitioned by some people to withdraw the right of Jewish people to live in England. Instead, Charles II upheld the earlier decision, and even extended it to include formal protections for the security of Jewish lives and property.

A thriving Jewish population

As England became one of the most tolerant nations in Europe in the following decades, Jewish communities began to thrive. A symbol of the growing acceptance of Jewish people was the award of a knighthood by William III, in 1700, to **Solomon de Medina**, the first Jewish person to receive that honour in England. De Medina had arrived in England with William III and was a provider of supplies and services to the army. His military business was very successful, and he was the largest contributor to the construction of the Bevis Marks Synagogue in the City of London (see Source 11).

▲ Source 11 Bevis Marks Synagogue in the City of London

3.2 What were the experiences and impact of England's immigrants, c.1500–c.1700?

The German Palatines and immigration debates

The Huguenots made a good impression on many English people, with their skilled crafts and intellectual pursuits. England's population had become smaller since the civil wars, and there were concerns that more consumers were needed for the economy to grow. Huguenots seemed the ideal addition to society. However, not everyone agreed with encouraging immigration, and in 1709 a new group of German migrants created one of the most serious immigration crises that England had faced.

The Palatines

The Rhineland region of western Germany had been in the middle of European wars throughout the seventeenth century and the land was devastated. One of the worst affected parts of the region was the area known as the Palatinate. A small group from the Palatinate, led by a **Lutheran** minister, **Joshua Kochertal**, migrated to England in 1708, planning eventually to settle in the English colonies in North America.

Kochertal's transatlantic mission was sponsored by Queen Anne (1702–14) herself, and was so successful that Kochertal spread the news of colonial opportunities to the rest of the Palatines. By the summer of 1709 there were 6500 refugees from the Palatinate in London, hoping to be sponsored to settle in America. They were Protestants, but it was not religious persecution that caused their migration. These were poor economic migrants, and some were even found to be Catholic.

Britain was not prepared for the Palatine migrants (see Source 12) and very few ended up settling in England. About 3000 did make it to their chosen destinations in the American colonies. Another 3000 or so were taken to Ireland to boost the Protestant population there. Only a few towns in England, including Liverpool, agreed to take any of the Palatines, so many of the remainder went home to Germany in around 1712.

> **a)** How far does this pamphlet look as if it was sympathetic to the Palatines' situation?

The Naturalisation Act of 1709

As the Palatines were making their desperate journey to England, Parliament was considering an Act that would end the costly process of denization for Protestant immigrants who wanted to be British citizens. Its full title was the Foreign Protestants Naturalisation Act, and it stated, 'the increase of people is a means of advancing the wealth and strength of a nation'. By swearing an oath of loyalty to the British government, any Protestant churchgoer could become British.

The sponsors of the 1709 Act had been thinking of the Huguenots when they put it forward, and about 2000 Huguenots became citizens under the Act when it was passed. However, in 1711, politicians opposed to immigration took control in Parliament, and they repealed the Naturalisation Act in 1712.

> 4 How might the opponents of the Naturalisation Act have made use of the Palatines' crisis to justify the repeal of the Act?
> 5 Why did the Naturalisation Act of 1709 fail to end the denization process?
> 6 How do you think the Huguenots in Britain might have reacted to the repeal of the Naturalisation Act? Would any of them have been in favour of repeal?
> 7 Compare the reception of the Palatines in England with that of the Huguenots. Why was there such a difference?

Britain and the Act of Union, 1707

The separate kingdoms of Scotland and England (with Wales) were officially united in this act. They had had the same monarch since 1603, but now they were fully united with one parliament in the United Kingdom of Great Britain. The people were now British citizens.

Palatines' context

Although the experience of the Palatines fits into the next time period of the course, it has been included here to help the comparison with the Huguenots. Both of these groups impacted on the Naturalisation Act of 1709–11.

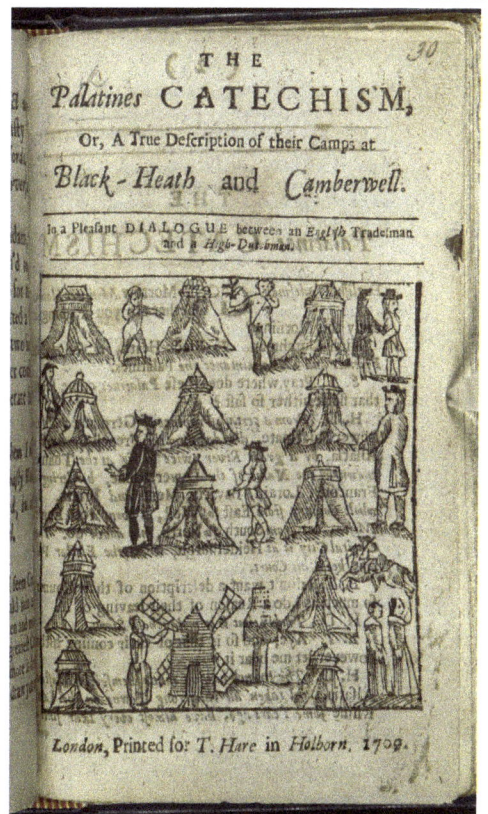

▲ Source 12 The front page of a pamphlet of 1709 called 'The Palatines Catechism'. It shows the tents on Blackheath Common in South London where some of the Palatines were placed.

PART 1: Migrants in Britain, c.800–present

Communicating your answer

It should be clear from this chapter that migration in England in the period c.1500–c.1700 shows both change and continuity when compared with medieval England. However, sometimes the exam will ask you to think about migration across more than just one time period. For example:

'Migrant relations with the authorities in England remained poor throughout the period c.800–c.1700.' How far do you agree? Explain your answer.

Answering a question like this requires you to select relevant information and to get a 'big picture' of the relations between migrants and the authorities in England.

Step 1: Recall – class sticky-note relay challenge

Split into small groups of no more than four. Your task is to work together and come up with a list of all of the ways migrants were treated by the authorities in England between c.800 and c.1700 that you have learnt about so far.

Write each action on its own sticky note and stick it to the board or an area allocated by your teacher. Everyone must take a turn writing a sticky note and sticking it up. Only one member of the group can be out of their chair at any one time. Your teacher will give you a time limit and the group with the most sticky notes (no repeats) wins!

Step 2: Knowledge Organiser – classifying the experience of different migrant groups in England

Next, you need to organise your knowledge to help you answer the question. If we stop and think about the actions of authorities towards migrants in England over time, we might come up with a list like this:

- Experience of Vikings
- Experience of Jewish migrants
- Experience of European traders
- Experience of Protestant refugees

1. Come together as a class and make a list of all of the experiences you came up with and write these in your books. Your list will be looking pretty long.
2. Now use the key to classify the actions experienced by different groups of migrants. Don't worry if you need to underline some in more than one colour and don't worry if you have used one colour more than others!

Step 3: Writing your answer

Make sure you mention the actions of authorities towards the different migrant groups. Remember that a good answer will make a judgement at the end – did migrant relations with the authorities in England remain poor throughout the years c.800–c.1700?

You are now ready to answer the question. We have given you a good deal of help, but you will find more guidance in Writing Better History on pages 140–54. And remember to add to and use your Word Wall!

Word Wall

Here are some extra words you can add to the Word Wall you made on page 18. They will help you write accurately and with confidence. Look over your work for the period c.1500–c.1700 so far and see if you could add some **red words** of your own.

Trade union   House of Commons   Resentment
Rebellion   Protest   Huguenots   Naturalisation Act

Practice questions

1. Explain one way in which the reasons for migration to Britain in the years c.1100–c.1500 were different from the reasons for migration to Britain in the years c.1500–c.1700. **(4 marks)**
2. Explain one way in which the experience of migrants in the years c.800–c.1500 was different to the experience of migrants in the years c.1500–c.1700. **(4 marks)**
3. Explain why the experience of migrants in England changed in the years c.1500–c.1700. **(12 marks)**
   You **may** use the following in your answer.
   - Anti-migrant protest
   - Huguenots

   You **must** also use information of your own.
4. 'The impact on culture was the most significant consequence of migration to England in the years c.800–c.1700.' How far do you agree? Explain your answer. **(16 marks)**
   You **may** use the following in your answer.
   - Language
   - Trade

   You **must** also use information of your own.

3.2 What were the experiences and impact of England's immigrants, c.1500–c.1700?

The Big Story of migrants in Britain, c.800–c.1700

We are now going to review the history of migrants to Britain from c.800 to c.1700. You should look over all of the enquiries in Chapters 2 and 3. We know that people always have some kind of opinion about immigrants. We have presented six different viewpoints, below, that could have been expressed at different times in this long period. For each quote, find evidence that could support the opinion expressed and also evidence that would contradict it. Copy and complete the table below and finally come up with your own judgement of the situation in each year.

> We single-handedly turned York into one of the most prosperous regions in Europe.

900 A Viking resident of Yorvik

> The many foreigners in London nowadays shows how open England is to the world under Queen Elizabeth I.

1580 A Tudor Londoner

> There hasn't really been that much change in my life since the Normans arrived over thirty years ago.

1100 An English peasant farmer

> What a blessing it is to live in a nation like England. The people are very tolerant.

1670 A Jewish merchant in London

> The new acts of denization are a great opportunity and show how the English welcome all foreigners as equals.

1400 A wealthy Italian merchant

> It's true what they say about those Huguenots: a drop of their blood is worth a thousand pounds a year!

1700 An English shopkeeper in London

Year	Quotation	Supporting evidence	Contradictory evidence	Your overall assessment of the opinion
900				
1100				
1400				
1580				
1670				
1700				

Timeline of Migration to Britain

1700 — **1725** — **1750** — **1800** — **1825** — **1850**

King George I
1714
German monarch

George Frideric Handel
1712
German music composer

Ignatius Sancho
1731
African servant and grocer

Transatlantic slave trade

Some 13 million African people were enslaved and trafficked across to the Americas. Over 3 million were on British ships.

From 1760 to 1840 Britain underwent an incredible period of economic growth. It became a world pioneer in industrial production and organisation. Millions of jobs were created throughout the country in factories and in the construction of railways.

Joseph Emidy
1799
African musician

Moses Angel
born 1819
Jewish teacher

Industrial Revolution

1793 The Aliens Act

Richard Sheil
1828
Irish trader

Robert Cain
1828
Irish brewer

1829 Catholic Emancipation Act

Gustav Wolff
1850
German shipbuilder

Asian lascars
1870s
Sailors

Irish navvies
1840
Railway builders

Paul Julius Reuter
1845
German newsman

Dadabhai Naoroji
1855
Indian trader and MP

John Archer
born 1863
Caribbean-Irish sailor

1867 Murphy Riot

Key:
- Notable migrant
- Migrant volume

52

The Migration Highway
c.1700–c.1900

George John Scipio Africanus
c.1766
African entrepreneur

Caroline Herschel
1772
German astronomer

Sake Dean Mahomed
1782
Indian entrepreneur

1772 The Somerset Case

1775

French Revolution, 1789

This revolution against the traditional power structures of France ended with the execution of the king and the formation of a republic – a country without a monarchy.

Johann Schweppe
1792
Swiss German entrepreneur

1. Look carefully at the notable migrants shown:
   (a) Which parts of the world had they migrated from?
   (b) What kinds of jobs and social roles did they have?
2. Look at the pattern of migration dots:
   (a) When was the volume of migrants greatest during this period?
   (b) Can you suggest any factors that might have caused changes in the volume of migrants?

The growth of empire transformed Britain into the centre of world trade: from the east came Chinese tea, Indian spices and Arabian coffee; from the west came sugar and tobacco, harvested by enslaved African people. British port cities became the base for these trades, grew rich, and attracted migrants.

Samuel Coleridge-Taylor
born 1875
African-English music composer

David Gestetner
1879
Hungarian-Jewish entrepreneur

Sir Mancherjee Bhownaggree
1882
Indian lawyer and MP

1875

British Empire

1900

Jewish people from Russia
1880s
Various trades

Sun Yat-sen
1896
Chinese politician

Cornelia Sorabji
1899
Indian lawyer

1905 The Aliens Act

53

4 Migration in eighteenth- and nineteenth-century Britain

> Gather your knowledge for this enquiry in a table like the one on page 9 under three key headings for the eighteenth and nineteenth centuries:
> a) Liberties and restrictions
> b) the Industrial Revolution
> c) the British Empire.

> 1 What do you think the author of the article in the *Gentlemen's Magazine* disagreed with: the practice of wealthy people having black servants or the general presence of black people in London?
> 2 What does the story of James Somerset tell us about how black people were treated in eighteenth-century England?

> ***Note on language**
> The quotes on this page use the term 'Negro' because that is what black people were called at the time – it is a term that comes from the Spanish word for the colour 'black'. Nowadays, it is not acceptable to use this term.

4.1 What was the attraction of Britain to migrants c.1700–c.1900?

Liberties and restrictions for immigrants: key turning-points

Liberty continued to be a core aspect of British identity after the turmoil of the seventeenth century, but it was not equally available to everyone in Britain, especially immigrants. However, there were some key legal and political turning-points in terms of the experience of British liberty for different migrant groups during these centuries.

Black African people in Britain: the Somerset judgment

Britain had been actively involved in the trading of enslaved African people across the Atlantic since the seventeenth century, and some were forced migrants in Britain. In 1764, the *Gentlemen's Magazine* stated that:

> The practice of importing *Negro servants into these Kingdoms is said to be already a problem that requires a remedy.

The 500 or so African people in Britain were becoming a very visible minority. They were not all servants but most had come to Britain as a result of the transatlantic trade. Attitudes towards them were frequently hostile, particularly among the wealthy class, many of whom profited financially from slavery.

In 1772, the status of black people in England became the focus of a sensational trial. An enslaved African man named James Somerset was brought to London from Virginia to accompany his 'owner'. He managed to escape in London but was soon re-captured and imprisoned on a ship to a Jamaican plantation. During his brief period of freedom in London, Somerset had been baptised as a Christian and found a community willing to defend him. He was freed from the ship and his case was brought before Chief Justice Lord Mansfield, who ruled that Somerset was held illegally because slavery was not recognised on English soil. This ruling gave some protection to black people if they were in England, and it also brought the issue of slavery in general to the forefront of political discussion in England.

Most black people in Britain at this time lived in poverty and had very few opportunities to become wealthy. In 1731, the Lord Mayor of London declared that 'no *Negroes shall be bound apprentice to any tradesman of this city'. This ban on doing skilled work forced black people either to remain as servants or to live outside the law.

Political refugees from France

When the rebels in the French Revolution overturned the traditional authorities of France after 1789, aristocrats and churchmen felt their lives were in danger. Many chose to migrate to Britain, because of its reputation for **tolerance** and **political stability**, and by 1792, 40,000 French refugees had arrived. The British government looked on these refugees sympathetically because they were mostly wealthy enemies of the Revolutionary government that was then at war with Britain. One of the refugees was a French Catholic priest called Reverend Gerardot, who set up a church on Scotland Road in Liverpool in 1806 (see page 76).

4.1 What was the attraction of Britain to migrants c.1700–c.1900?

Reactions of the British public to French migrants

Most British people were hostile to the French Revolution and they feared the spread of its ideas. Newspapers started to report that people in Britain were 'growing suspicious of Frenchmen' and demanded action against the migrants. They believed that the people fleeing were actually supporters of the Revolution and had come to England to spread its ideas.

▲ **Source 1** A British cartoon from 1792 representing what was happening in France during the Revolution. It depicts people involved in the French Revolution committing atrocities. Content like this often appeared in English newspapers at the time

a) How does the artist make it clear that the people shown in Source 1 are not the French refugees who had been welcomed in Britain from 1789 onwards?

b) Explain how images like Source 1 could have made the British public suspicious of French people living in Britain.

The Aliens Act

Eventually, the concern that spies and troublemakers were blending in with the refugees prompted the British government to introduce the first Aliens Act in 1793: the first law designed to control the entry of foreigners into Britain. Immigrants now had to prove why they wanted to enter the country and give personal details that would allow authorities to keep track of them.

Catholic emancipation and Irish migrants

The war with France also led indirectly to the largest flow of migration into Britain in the nineteenth century. After a failed French invasion of Ireland in 1796, and a rebellion against British rule by Irish republicans in 1798, the British and Irish parliaments passed the Acts of Union in 1800 to join Ireland fully with Great Britain. This allowed Irish people to travel to and live freely in Britain. However, England was not a very hospitable environment for most Irish people, because they were Catholic.

Catholics in England had not been allowed legally to own land, join the army or marry Protestants, but the Papists Act changed those laws in 1778. However, Catholics still could not vote. In the old Irish Parliament, Catholics had been allowed to vote in 1793, but King George III refused to approve such a reform for Britain. It was not until 1829 that the government persuaded the new king, George IV, and the House of Lords to pass a Catholic Emancipation Act giving Catholics the vote at last. Irish Catholic migrants were then able to take part in most of British political life on the same basis as Protestants.

LATER FRENCH POLITICAL REFUGEES

Following a devastating French defeat to Germany in 1871, the citizens of Paris rose in rebellion against the French government and occupied Paris for two months. When the authorities retook the city many of the people involved in the uprising, known as communards, were killed on the spot with thousands more imprisoned. Around 3500 managed to escape to Britain, with the vast majority settling in London.

3 Explain how the Somerset judgment, the Aliens Act and the Catholic Emancipation Act could be seen as turning-points in the history of immigration in Britain.

PART 1: Migrants in Britain, c.800–present

Industrialisation and urbanisation

These are the terms that are used to describe the enormous economic and social changes that took place in the nineteenth century. The two processes operated together to change the country.

- *industrialisation* refers to the change from an economy focused on farming to one dominated by large industries.
- *urbanisation* refers to the development of cities and towns as the centres for most of the country's population and activity.

Migration to Preston

One of the new industrial towns of the Lancashire cotton industry was Preston. The population census of 1851 shows that half of the adults in Preston had not been born there. Like other towns, the migrants came to Preston had not travelled far: 40 percent of Preston's immigrants in 1851 had walked less than ten miles to get there.

1. Explain why you think the Industrial Revolution made Britain attractive to potential immigrants.
2. How did the Industrial Revolution affect patterns of settlement within Britain?

The Industrial Revolution and migration to cities

The Industrial Revolution provided millions of new jobs in growing industries: cotton and woollen textiles; coal-mining; iron and steel production. The development of steam power, using Britain's supplies of coal for fuel, was a major factor in this Industrial Revolution. The new industries were therefore often developed in coal-mining areas in the North of England, the Midlands and South Wales. These areas needed workers for the new industries, and so attracted migrants from within Britain and from overseas. There was a lot of internal migration at this time, usually from rural to urban settlements, and sometimes between cities, but there were also more workers because of the overall growth in Britain's population.

Regional migration

By the beginning of the nineteenth century, all four of the British nations were united politically, and there was a good deal of regional migration from Ireland, Wales and Scotland into the industrial areas of England, particularly the North and the Midlands. Britain's population grew dramatically at this time, from c.15 million in 1800 to c.27 million in 1850 and then c.40 million by 1900. The highest rates of population growth were in Britain's cities, with industrial centres like Liverpool (see pages 58–9), Manchester and Birmingham leading the way. As in previous periods, London saw the greatest growth, and its population grew from just under 1 million people in 1800 to 6.6 million in 1900. London was the leading trading port, and so attracted migrants from home and abroad.

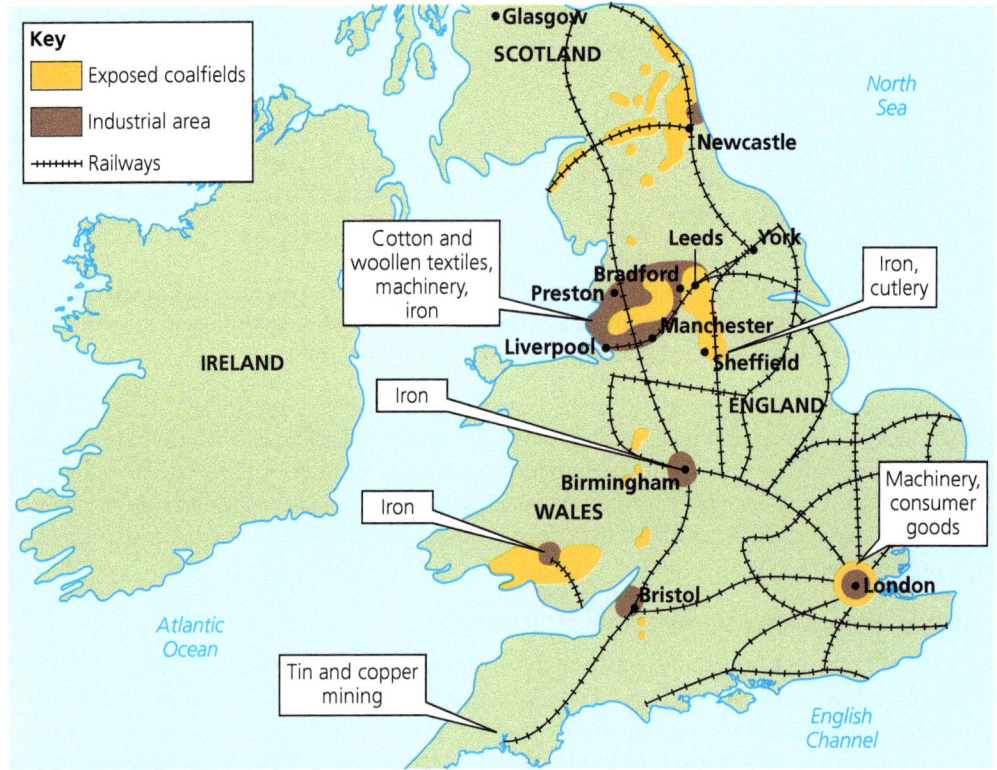

▲ **Source 2** British industries and rail links, c.1850

James Watt (1736–1819) was a famous Scottish engineer who migrated to Birmingham, England, in 1774 and contributed to the prosperity of the Industrial Revolution. Watt modified early steam engines to produce machines that would eventually transform the powering of factories, mines and transport. He set up a factory at Smethwick near Birmingham with Matthew Boulton to produce engines for sale that would be used all over Britain and abroad.

4.1 What was the attraction of Britain to migrants c.1700–c.1900?

St Katharine's Dock, London

One of London's first major industrial **infrastructure** projects was St Katharine's Dock, next to the Tower of London, built in 1827–28. The dock was designed by the Scottish engineers Thomas Telford, who had already built many roads and canals in Britain, and George Turnbull, a new Scottish migrant aged nineteen. Turnbull would go on to play a key role in developing railways in India in the 1850s as part of Britain's growing empire.

> **3** How were immigrants involved in the building of St Katharine's Dock?

▲ **Source 3** The new St Katharine's Dock in East London in the nineteenth century

> **a)** Study Source 3 carefully.
> What aspects of Britain's new prosperity in the Industrial Revolution can you see in the picture?
>
> **b)** How far does Source 3 reveal the attraction of London to immigrants in the nineteenth century?

Britain's railway revolution: engineers and 'navvies'

By the 1840s steam-powered locomotives were speeding up the carrying of products and people across the country, boosting trade. Migrants played a major role in the construction of these railways, as they had in the building of the English canal network. These groups of labourers were nicknamed 'navvies' (short for 'navigators' because the canals were sometimes called 'navigations').

Many of these navvies were Irish. In the 1840s, a serious potato famine had rocked Ireland. Millions of Irish people died, and millions more migrated. Although most wanted to go to the USA, many could only afford to reach Britain, arriving at port cities such as Glasgow, Liverpool and London. The arrival of the Irish sometimes caused aggravation with English and Scottish locals (see page 68). One of the engineers on Ireland's own railway projects, William Dargan (1799–1867), also migrated to England in 1846 to take the contracts for building the Liverpool and Bury Railway (opened in 1848) and for parts of the difficult Manchester and Leeds line.

> **4** How did the expansion of railways in Britain attract immigrants in the mid-nineteenth century?

PART 1: Migrants in Britain, c.800–present

Case study: Liverpool – a hub for immigrants in the nineteenth century

By 1800, Liverpool had become one of the most most prosperous city of Britain, and a lot of its wealth came from the transatlantic slave trade. After Britain abolished the trade in enslaved African people in its empire in 1807, Liverpool successfully developed other trades, and attracted thousands of immigrants. Liverpool's population grew rapidly, rising from c.80,000 in 1801 to c.350,000 in 1841.

Liverpool's economy in the nineteenth century

The American *Bankers' Magazine* declared in December 1851 that:

> Liverpool is now the greatest port in the British empire in the value of its exports and the extent of its foreign commerce. Being the first port in the British Empire, it is the first port in the world. … New York is the Liverpool of America, as Liverpool is the New York of Europe.

It went on to explain the advantages of the city's transport infrastructure, particularly canals and the new railways. Transatlantic trade was still very important, with imports of food and raw materials from the USA and exports of British manufactured goods in return. Trade provided thousands of job opportunities for dockworkers and sailors.

Liverpool's Africa trades

Liverpool's former slave traders maintained links with West Africa, particularly importing palm oil, used in lubricants and the manufacture of soap and candles. By the 1820s, the Liverpool area was the leading centre for soap production in Britain. Macgregor Laird introduced the first steamship service to West Africa from Liverpool in 1852, bringing faster and more regular voyages to places like the Niger River delta, the centre of palm oil trading.

Traders recruited Kru (a West African ethnic group) sailors on the coast of Sierra Leone to replace their English crews. European racist thinking argued that African people had a higher tolerance for the heat of the engine room, but more importantly, that African sailors should be paid less than white sailors. When they found themselves back in Liverpool after their journeys, some settled permanently there, because the pay for sailors leaving from Britain was much greater than it was from West Africa. Other Black and **Asian lascars** (see page 61) settled in Liverpool, and the city took on a **cosmopolitan** character. The *Liverpool Critic* stated in 1877:

> Unlike the dwellers in most English towns, all of us in Liverpool are, to a great extent, citizens of the world.

> **John Archer** was born in Liverpool in 1863, the son of a black sailor father from Barbados and an Irish Catholic mother. He became a sailor himself, living at times in North America. Archer later moved to Battersea in South London. He became active in local radical politics and served as Mayor of Battersea in 1913–14: London's first elected black politician.

▲ **Source 4** George's Dock, Liverpool in the 1860s

◀ **Source 5** John Archer

> a) Look carefully as Source 4. What features of the photograph support the statements in the *Bankers' Magazine* of 1851?
> b) How do Source 4 and the *Bankers' Magazine* suggest potential job opportunities for immigrants to Liverpool in the mid-nineteenth century?

> 1 Describe the change and continuity in Liverpool's connections with West Africa in the nineteenth century. How did these connections bring about changes in migration to Liverpool?
> 2 Research more about John Archer (see Source 4) and consider how far he was accepted in British society.

4.1 What was the attraction of Britain to migrants c.1700–c.1900?

Irish immigration to Liverpool

Thousands of Irish immigrants came to Liverpool throughout the nineteenth century. The number of Irish Catholics in Liverpool rose from c.5,000 in 1801, to c.24,000 by 1833. They took the insecure and poorly paid jobs, and many of the men became 'navvies' (see page 57). The proportion of Irish-born Liverpudlians in the population went from about 17 per cent (c.50,000) in 1844, to 22 per cent (c.84,000) in 1851, after the disastrous Great Famine. These Liverpool Irish could assimilate quite easily by appearance and language, and many even adopted the local 'scouse' accent. However, culturally and politically many of them remained distinct, holding on to nostalgic ideas of the 'old homeland' and the autonomy of their Catholic religion.

Here are two of the Irishmen who became well-known Liverpudlians in the nineteenth century:

> **Richard Sheil (1791–1871)** was born in Tipperary, Ireland, and spent many years trading in the Caribbean and Gulf of Mexico. He married a French woman, Josephine Faudre, on the island of Haiti, and migrated with his family to Liverpool in 1828. He continued his trading connections, but also became active in local politics. Richard represented the strongly Irish **ward** of Scotland Road as a Catholic **Liberal** on the city council. He proudly kept his Irish accent and was a leader of the Catholic Club, founded in 1844 to encourage Liverpool's Irish middle-class citizens to protect Catholic rights.

> **Robert Cain (1826–1907)** was born in poverty on Spike Island, County Cork. In 1828, his ex-soldier father migrated to Liverpool and the family lived there in dreadful slum conditions. By 1840 Robert was working as an **indentured sailor** to West Africa. After serving five years, he returned to Liverpool and eventually set up his own brewery in the Scotland Road area in 1848. He moved to a bigger site on Stanhope Street in 1858 and eventually owned around 200 pubs in Liverpool, becoming one of Britain's richest men. On official records, Robert Cain decided to state his birthplace as 'Liverpool'. His son, Charles, took over the brewery and went on to become Baron Brocket in the House of Lords.

3 Explain why Liverpool would have been such an attractive place for Irish migrants, especially after the disaster of the Great Famine in Ireland in the late 1840s.

Source 6 George Smyth, a successful Irish migrant and hat maker in Liverpool in 1848, wrote a report for an organisation back in Dublin, Ireland about the Liverpool-Irish. He said:

> The Irishmen in Liverpool perform nearly all the labour requiring great physical powers and endurance ... In almost every branch of trade Irishmen, notwithstanding the many prejudices with which they have to contend, have risen to the highest promotion ... Many Irishmen are distinguished for their ability as architects, draughtsmen, and clerks of the works.

a) Read Source 6 carefully. How does Smyth suggest that the Irishmen of Liverpool were doing well as migrants in England?

4 Compare the immigrant stories of Richard Sheil and Robert Cain. What was the balance of assimilation and autonomy in their experiences?
Do you agree with the autonomy/assimilation diagrams shown here? Look back to Chapter 1 to remind yourself about autonomy/assimilation diagrams.

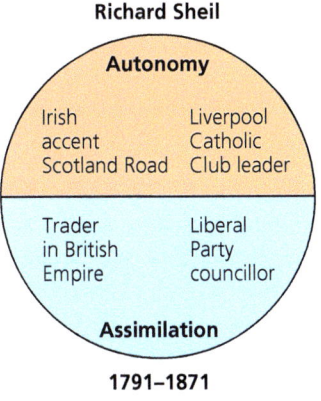

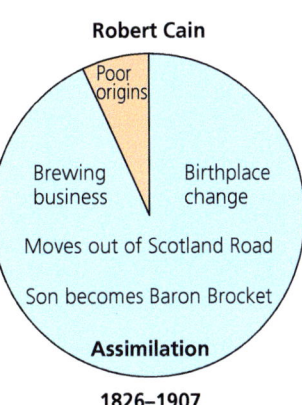

5 How far do Sheil and Cain seem to have benefited from the Catholic Emancipation Act of 1829 (see page 55)?

The British Empire and migration

The greatest growth of the British Empire in the early nineteenth century was in Asia. This was mainly as a result of the trade in tea, spices and cloth by the East India Company. Profits and taxes from these trades were used for military and naval expansion which gave Britain an advantage against other European and Asian rivals. In India, the company expanded from trading to ruling Indian territories. This growing presence in Asia eventually brought Indian and Chinese migrants to Britain (for more on the Indian migrants, see pages 70–71).

Chinese immigration

In the eighteenth and nineteenth centuries, the consumption of tea grew throughout Britain – as much as 5 per cent of annual household incomes was spent on tea in the middle of the eighteenth century. This tea came from China and the Chinese only accepted silver in exchange for their tea. In order to overcome this trade imbalance, British merchants connected to the East India Company began to sell the drug opium illegally in Chinese cities. In 1839, the Chinese emperor ordered British opium to be seized and burned. In response, Britain sent a fleet of warships and, in 1842, forced China to sign a humiliating treaty. China was forced to hand over Hong Kong to Britain and in the following decades the city grew into a populous and wealthy colony.

As a result of growing trade and the establishment of steamship routes between Britain and East Asia in the mid-nineteenth century, a small, steady stream of Chinese immigrants came to Britain. Most of these immigrants were sailors who settled in and around port cities such as London, Liverpool and Cardiff. Chinese sailors had little difficulty finding work in Liverpool in the late nineteenth century as the economic activity around the docks grew. Many went into business for themselves and opened small shops, restaurants and laundries. Widespread prejudice led to Chinese migrants being barred from any jobs that British people considered respectable.

Chinese communities

In London, many Chinese people chose to settle around the docks, specifically in Limehouse. Here, they set up a small but visible community. Although Chinese people had a reputation for honesty and hard work, some popular literature depicted them negatively and claimed that the areas in which they settled were home to opium dens and violence.

Due to a growing interest in its culture, Britain became an attractive destination to some **anglicised** Chinese people. The founder of modern China, **Sun Yat-sen**, spent time as a political refugee in London in the 1890s to generate support for his political movement. He wanted China to model itself more closely on technologically advanced nations, which the imperial rulers were resisting. Sun Yat-sen chose to live in London after meeting the Scottish surgeon, Dr James Cantile, while studying medicine in Hong Kong. Cantile had a residence in London.

▲ **Source 7** A plaque installed outside the former residence of the first President of China, Dr Sun Yat-sen, who lived in London between 1896 and 1897

1. How did the growth of the British Empire lead to an increase in Chinese migration to Britain after 1842?
2. What attracted Sun Yat-sen to London at the end of the nineteenth century?

4.1 What was the attraction of Britain to migrants c.1700–c.1900?

The British Empire: merchant shipping and lascars

The introduction of steam-powered ships in the 1860s removed the reliance on wind for ships to undertake voyages. This led to many more journeys from Britain to the countries in its empire. As trade with the empire grew, so the demand for overseas sailors increased: African, Chinese, Indian and Arab sailors, who were known as lascars.

Lascars

The opening of the Suez Canal in Egypt in 1869 cut the travel time in half from Britain to India, which led to even more ships making the journey. Many of the men who worked on these ships were from the Indian subcontinent, other parts of Asia and East Africa. Between 10,000 and 12,000 of these sailors visited British ports every year during the nineteenth century. Most of them made the return journey home, but a significant number chose to settle in and around the ports where they docked. The poor conditions on board the merchant ships were one reason why they avoided the return journey home and chose to settle in British cities. Others had no choice because it was not always possible to find ships to take them back, particularly in winter.

As a result, small communities of lascars sprang up in London and around other ports. These men performed music in public, swept streets and set up businesses, for example, selling spices and running restaurants mainly for other lascars. Many lascars could not make enough money to survive and lived off charity from Christian organisations. The Strangers' Home for Asiatics, Africans and South Sea Islanders was opened in 1856 in Limehouse, East London, with large donations from wealthy figures such as the Prince of Wales and Indian royalty, to provide for these needy sailors.

The port of Aden

When the Suez Canal opened, Britain's strategic port of Aden (acquired in 1839) at the junction of the Red and Arabian seas, became vitally important as a coaling station for steamships. Yemeni and Somali seamen were drawn to jobs in Aden, and many found their way from there to Britain. These men formed some of the earliest Muslim communities in Britain. They began to arrive in the late nineteenth century and settled in London, Cardiff and South Shields, with smaller communities in Liverpool and Hull.

▲ **Source 8** African and Asian sailors gathered in the Main Hall of the Strangers' Home in 1899

3 Explain how the expansion of Britain's trade and empire brought migrant sailors to British port cities by 1900.

4 Why would the life of a lascar be challenging and uncertain? How could settling in Britain have made their lives a bit easier?

a) How has the artist of Source 8 represented the different nationalities of the lascars in the East End of London in 1899?

b) Do you think the artist of Source 8 was sympathetic towards these men? Explain your answer.

PART 1: Migrants in Britain, c.800–present

Communicating your answer

We are going to look at a 12-mark style question to end this enquiry.

Explain why the attraction of Britain for immigrants changed in the years c.1700–c.1900.

We have been building your answers using paragraphs and topic sentences, with a range of linking terms. To help you improve your arguments further, we can build the writing with *linking phrases* rather than single words. This form of writing will help you to develop a clear line of argument through your answer, and each kind of phrase will direct your written arguments in a specific way.

In your answer, there should be three main paragraphs: one for each of the key ideas you are going to discuss. We will include one paragraph for each of the main points. The first is a model paragraph; the second has gaps for you to complete; and the third you will plan and write from scratch.

Paragraph 1: the attraction of British liberties (see pages 54–55)

Copy out this paragraph as an example in your notes. You should pay special attention to the way that types of linking phrase drive the sense of the argument forward. You could try writing your own paragraph, making the Irish Catholic issue the main example, and African people the additional case.

> **[Topic sentence]** Immigrant groups were given more of a share of British liberties during the period 1750 to 1850. **[Evaluating phrase]** Even though the British were still leaders in the transatlantic slave trade up to 1807, enslaved African people gained some liberty after the Somerset Case in 1773. **[Adding detail]** More specifically, the judgment said that nobody could force an enslaved African to leave England and return to slave labour overseas. **[Introducing new layers of evidence]** Going beyond this, former enslaved African people, like Francis Barber and Ignatius Sancho, were able to live more freely in English society. Not only African people, but also Irish people in England enjoyed more liberty, because after 1829 Catholics were allowed to vote in elections.

Paragraph 2: the connections with the British Empire (see pages 60–61)

Write this paragraph as an example in your notes. You should complete the gaps so that the whole paragraph makes sense. Look carefully at the meaning of the linking phrase, and in the fourth sentence you have to write your own.

> Britain's vast empire drew in different groups of immigrants during the nineteenth century. Once Britain had defeated the Chinese Empire in the war over opium in 1842, _____. In particular, they settled _____. As _____, they started up small businesses, such as _____. With more steamships coming across from Asia through the Suez Canal, _____.

Paragraph 3: the attraction of industrialised Britain (see pages 56–59)

Write this paragraph yourself, beginning with a topic sentence, and then include at least three more sentences that use linking phrases.

You can then write up the whole answer, possibly adding some examples from the case study of Liverpool to extend your work further.

4.2 How did the experiences and impact of immigrants vary, 1700–1900?

Immigrant entrepreneurs and British economic growth

The economic prosperity of Britain also attracted immigrants who wanted to develop new industrial and commercial ideas. Some of these **entrepreneurs** founded companies that became major businesses in modern Britain and some introduced ideas that became everyday practices.

George John Scipio Africanus (c.1763–1834) was enslaved in West Africa as a child, brought to England for the prominent Molyneux family and baptised in Wolverhampton. He was educated and became an apprentice in manufacturing brass metal. George left the Molyneuxs and married Esther Shaw, an English woman, in 1788. Around 1793, they set up an employment agency in Nottingham to place servants with high-class families.

> Gather your knowledge for this enquiry on the experiences and impact of migrants in the eighteenth and nineteenth centuries in a table like the one on page 9. There are six key groups for this time period:
> a) African people
> b) Chinese people
> c) German people
> d) Indian people
> e) Irish people
> f) Jewish people.

Sake Dean Mahomed (1759–1851) was a Bengali Muslim who worked for the East India Company in India and then migrated to Ireland in 1782. He married an Irish Protestant called Jane Daly and converted to her religion. The couple migrated to London and, in 1810, opened the first Indian restaurant in the capital. Then, in 1814, the Mahomeds moved to Brighton and opened up a new business: the Indian Medicated Vapour Baths, where Mahomed used a massage treatment called 'shampooing'. He was made 'shampooing surgeon' to both kings George IV and William IV.

▲ **Source 1** Mahomed's Baths in Brighton

Johann Schweppe (1740–1821) was a German-Swiss inventor of a process to carbonate water. He came to London in 1792 and set up the Schweppes mineral waters company. The firm failed at first, but the support of King William IV in 1831 helped it become world-famous.

Gustav Wolff (1834–1913) was a German Lutheran from Hamburg who migrated to Liverpool as a teenager in 1850. He worked for the Belfast-based shipbuilder Edward Harland, and, in 1861, they formed the Harland & Wolff Company, which became world-famous. Both men became Members of Parliament for parts of Belfast.

David Gestetner (1854–1939) was a Hungarian Jewish inventor and entrepreneur. While working as a copying clerk, he decided to design a duplicating method with stencils. He migrated to London in 1879 and then set up a business to make duplicating machines: the Gestetner Cyclograph Company. He settled in North London in 1898 and was a devout member of the Jewish community.

1 Copy and complete this table to show the similarities and differences between the five entrepreneurs described on this page.

Entrepreneur	Business/industry	Support in England	Religion	Impact
Africanus				
Mahomed				
Schweppe				
Wolff				
Gestetner				

2 Draw assimilation/autonomy circles (see page 9) to compare the experiences of Sake Dean Mahomed and David Gestetner. Explain the differences and similarities between them.

PART 1: Migrants in Britain, c.800–present

The influence of European immigrants on British culture

Many of the European people who migrated to Britain at this time were artists, musicians, writers and other intellectuals, who came for new opportunities or to escape repression in their own countries. Many assimilated into British society and some made a significant impact on national life.

Music and George Frideric Handel

In 1714, a German immigrant became King of the United Kingdom: **King George** was the first of the Hanoverian kings and all but one future British monarch over the next two centuries would marry a German spouse. As a result, Germans would be welcomed as migrants. This contrasted with the miserable experience of the Palatines from Germany at the start of the century (see page 49).

George Frideric Handel, born in Halle in central Germany, was already in London at this time, and continued to compose for the Hanoverians. He composed the anthem *Zadok the Priest* for the coronation of King George II in 1727. Handel successfully asked to become British by an Act of Parliament in 1727.

▲ **Source 2** In 1738 George Frideric Handel was so famous in London that the owner of the new Vauxhall Gardens pleasure park commissioned a statue of him from another European cultural immigrant, the French sculptor Louis-François Roubiliac

In the 1730s, Handel switched from Italian-style operas to composing English works for choirs called **oratorios**. The most famous of these was *Messiah* (1741), with its 'Hallelujah Chorus'. Handel was a significant supporter of charities and, in 1750, he started a pattern of annual performances of his *Messiah* to raise funds for the orphans' Foundling Hospital in London, whose supporters included the King.

The Herschels: sibling scientists

Two other eighteenth-century German immigrant musicians were William Herschel (1738–1822) and his younger sister, **Caroline Herschel** (1750–1848). William fled Germany to escape from war in 1758 and began as a musician in the north of England. He then settled in fashionable Bath in 1766, where his sister Caroline joined him from Hanover in 1772. Caroline learned to sing and performed several times in Handel's *Messiah*. But it was astronomy, rather than music, that made the Herschels famous.

In 1781, William discovered a new planet, Uranus, and King George III appointed him as a court astronomer. Caroline was his assistant in all his work and, in 1787, she was also given a royal salary, making her the first paid female astronomer in England. In 1786, Caroline began her own discoveries of comets, finding eight altogether. Both Herschels were acclaimed by the Royal Society, England's leading scientific organisation, but Caroline had to have her papers on new comets read out by male fellows of the Society, because it did not admit a woman fellow until 1945.

> a) How far does Maskelyn's letter show that Caroline Hershel was respected in English society?

> **Source 3** Rev Dr Nevil Maskelyne, Britain's Astronomer Royal, wrote about a visit he made to the Herschels in 1793:
>
> … I paid Dr & Miss Herschel a visit 7 weeks ago. She showed me her 5 feet Newtonian telescope made for her by her brother for sweeping the heavens. … She will thus sweep a quarter of the heavens in one night. The Dr has given her written instructions on how to proceed, and she knows all the nebulae.

> a) How did Roubiliac choose to show Handel in his statue shown in Source 2? What does it suggest about Handel's popularity with the British public? How easily had Handel assimilated into society in Britain?
> b) How did Handel's music contribute to British life in both **pageantry** and **philanthropy**?
> c) How important was the contribution of the Herschels to British **intellectual life**?

German business in Britain: sugar bakers and a news agency

While some German immigrants were professionals, like musicians, others were skilled working-class Germans who formed communities near the docks in London's East End. One such group was the sugar bakers, who refined raw sugar imported from the Caribbean plantations into white sugar loaves. By 1750, there were about eighty German-owned refineries in London. The working conditions were extremely hot and dangerous, and the young German male workers were given large quantities of beer every day to keep them hydrated. Many of them became sick, with their lungs coated in melted sugar, and a German hospital was founded for them in Hackney in 1845. The Germans wanted to practise their own Lutheran form of Protestant Christianity, and one of the churches they established was St George's, Whitechapel, built in 1762.

Two of the most notable services in that Lutheran church took place in November 1845, and involved a German Jewish immigrant, born Israel Beer Josaphat in 1816 in Kassel, Germany. He was the son of a rabbi, but in the autumn of 1845 he moved to London and converted to Christianity and then married Ida Magnus, daughter of a Lutheran pastor and banker, in St George's. At his baptism service as a Christian, he took the name **Paul Julius Reuter**. He became involved in publishing and news transmission, and in 1851 set up his own news agency near the London Stock Exchange. London brokers gave Reuter up-to-date information on their share prices in return for updates from the continent of Europe, and he was one of the first users of the telegraph cable across the English Channel. Reuter was made a British citizen by an Act of Parliament in 1857.

The 1848 Revolutions

Revolution erupted throughout Europe in 1848. Those calling for change demanded liberal constitutions that limited the power of the monarchy, expanded the right to vote to all adult men and guaranteed the freedom of the press. Although the revolutions led to change in some countries they mostly failed and many of those involved had to flee to escape imprisonment. A popular destination was Britain which was the only major European nation not to experience a revolution, mainly because it had long been the most liberal nation in Europe. The German economist and philosopher, Karl Marx, is the most famous political refugee from this time.

▲ **Source 4** A portrait of Paul Reuter painted in 1869

A close ally of Reuter in setting up his agency was Samuel Engländer, a radical Jewish migrant from Moravia in the Austrian empire. Engländer had been imprisoned several times for revolutionary activities. In 1848 he decided to migrate to England because, he said: 'I had never seen England and it was the land of the free'.

Arts and the Anglo-Italian Rossettis

In the nineteenth century, a family of Italian immigrants made a significant contribution to England's cultural life. Gabriele Rossetti was a poet and political activist, who was exiled from southern Italy in 1821 for supporting ideas of popular Italian nationalism. He came to London in 1824 and became a professor of Italian at the new King's College London. He married Frances Polidori, the daughter of another Italian exile, and their home in Fitzrovia became a haven for Italian refugees. Their four children contributed in different ways to Victorian England's cultural life:

- Dante and William Rossetti helped found the Pre-Raphaelite Movement in England. This aimed to revive an interest in realistic art scenes of nature and the late medieval world.
- Maria Francesca was an author.
- Christina Rossetti was a poet and also wrote the famous Christmas carol, 'In the Bleak Midwinter'.

> 1. How did Germans contribute to the economic and culinary life of the English in this period?
> 2. Why would England have been a good place for Reuter to set up as a news agent in the mid-nineteenth century? How did he contribute to English life and prosperity?
> 3. Research some of the artistic and literary achievements of the Rossetti family, and explain their contributions to English cultural life.

PART 1: Migrants in Britain, c.800–present

African people in Britain

The Somerset judgment (page 54) had been a small first step towards justice for enslaved African people. A movement followed that campaigned for the **abolition** of the slave trade and then slavery itself. This movement included some African migrants to Britain, particularly Olaudah Equiano (c.1745–97) and Ottobah Cugoano (1757–91). Although abolition did not happen until 1807 (slave trade) and 1833 (slavery), African people could live freely in Britain during this period, and some of them became quite famous.

Two African celebrities in eighteenth-century England

Joseph Emidy had been enslaved and taken from West Africa to Brazil in the 1780s. He learned to play the violin and, in 1795, was kidnapped by British Admiral Pellew, who took him to play violin aboard his ship. In 1799, Pellew abandoned Emidy at Falmouth in Cornwall. Emidy married a local English woman, Jenefer Hutchins, in 1802 and they had six children. He started teaching music and also played for local Cornish music societies; he played a concerto of his own composition at Truro in 1808, as well as works by Handel and others.

> 1 Compare the experiences of Joseph Emidy and George Frideric Handel (page 64) as immigrant musicians in Britain. How easy was it for each of them to *assimilate* into society?
>
> 2 What were the similarities and differences between the experiences of Emidy and Sancho in England?
>
> 3 What would have helped make Sancho and Emidy accepted in England? Why did some people fail to welcome them fully?

▲ **Source 5** A musical performance by Joseph Emidy and the Truro Philharmonic Orchestra, Cornwall, 1808

Johann Peter Saloman, a German immigrant **impresario** wanted to feature performances by Joseph Emidy in London, but the other leading musicians in London were against the idea, saying: '[Joseph's] colour would be so much against him, that there would be a great risk of failure.' When Emidy died in 1835, his **obituary** in the *Royal Cornwall Gazette* read:

> His talents may be said to have ranked under the first order while his enthusiastic devotedness to the science has rarely been exceeded.

Ignatius Sancho (1729–80) arrived in London in 1731 as an enslaved baby. The aristocrat Lord Montagu took an interest in the child's education and, in 1749, Sancho ran away from his owners to work for Montagu instead. While in Montagu's service, Sancho composed music and started writing letters to the novelist Laurence Sterne, including some about abolition. In 1774, Sancho left Montagu's service and set himself up in a grocery store in Mayfair, London. In 1780, he was the first African to vote in a British general election.

▲ **Source 6** A portrait of Ignatius Sancho from a book of his letters published shortly after he died

4.2 How did the experiences and impact of immigrants vary, 1700–1900?

The Committee for the Relief of the Black Poor

▲ **Source 7** A cartoon from 1821 by George and Isaac Robert Cruikshank, with the title: 'Lowest Life in London. Tom, Jerry and Logic among the unsophisticated Sons and Daughters of Nature at "All Max" in the East'

Most of the free African people in England in the 1780s were not prospering like Emidy and Sancho. Many of them were still servants, or they were reduced to begging. Some enslaved African people in the American colonies had fought for the British during the War of Independence (1775–83), so when they lost, the British had to find these black Loyalists a home. When some of these people found their way to London, they were abandoned by the government, and added to the numbers of poor, black people across the capital. Wealthy Londoners considered these poor immigrants a nuisance, and formed the Committee for the Relief of the Black Poor in 1786 to find a solution. A plan was made to take many of them to West Africa and start a new colony there, to be called Sierra Leone. After two attempts, the colony was permanently established in 1792.

Immigrants from Sierra Leone

Within forty years there was a college at Fourah Bay in Sierra Leone and some of its students became notable immigrants to nineteenth-century Britain. **Samuel Ajayi Crowther (1809–91)** came in 1841 to train as an Anglican priest, and returned as the first black bishop of West Africa in 1864. **Christian Frederick Cole (1852–85)** came in 1873 and enrolled at Oxford University as its first black student, studying Classics. Daniel Taylor came to study medicine and in 1875 fathered a son, Samuel, with a white woman, Alice Martin, who brought the child up alone when Daniel returned to Africa. **Samuel Coleridge-Taylor (1875–1912)** studied at the Royal College of Music as a violinist and composer, and became famous for his choral work *Hiawatha's Wedding Feast*. He was also the youngest attendee at the first Pan-African Conference in London in 1900, which campaigned against racism and the exploitation of Africa. In 1901, Coleridge-Taylor composed an overture entitled *Toussaint L'Ouverture*, after the leader of the Haitian Revolution.

> **Source 8** August Jaeger, a successful German migrant and music publisher in London in 1898, wrote a letter to the musical director of a famous cathedral choirs' festival, and said:
>
> ... a young friend of mine, S. Coleridge-Taylor, is most wonderfully gifted and might write your Committee a fine work ... He is only 22 or 23 but there is nothing immature or inartistic about his music ... Why not try him and make the '98 Festival memorable. I suppose you know that his father is a *negro. Hence his wonderful freshness ... believe me, he is the man of the future in musical England.

a) Sources 5 and 7 show two very different scenes that include African people in Britain in a musical gathering. Consider what each artist wanted the people who saw these images to think about the African people pictured.

b) Compare what the images suggest about how far African people were welcome in Britain at the time.

4 How far should the black Loyalists in London in the late 1780s have been welcomed in England? How far did this happen?

5 Explain the changes in the immigrant experiences of the black Loyalists and the Fourah Bay students. Why were the students more accepted in London?

6 Compare the immigrant lives of Joseph Emidy and Samuel Coleridge-Taylor. Use assimilation/autonomy circles to help you.

*Note on language

See page 54 for the use of the word 'negro' in Source 8.

a) Read Source 8 carefully. How far does Jaeger's letter show that Coleridge-Taylor was fully accepted in British society?

The experiences of Irish immigrants

By the mid-nineteenth century England had been a Protestant nation for three hundred years, but there were still fears of Catholicism in the minds of some English communities, particularly in areas with large numbers of Irish immigrants. There had also been hostility towards Irish labourers from English and Scots workers who felt they were a threat to jobs and wages.

Anti-Catholic/anti-Irish protest in Britain

The British press reported on anti-Irish ill-feeling when immigration increased around 1840. A Liverpool newspaper reported in 1839 that:

> [the Irish] flocked too numerously to their country, and by accepting of a rate of wages below the English standard, reduced their value in the labour market.

A Scottish newspaper reported in 1841:

> the swarms of Irish labourers who pour into this country … bring with them a moral and social plague.

However, some people had a very good opinion of the **Irish navvies** (see page 57). Samuel Morton Peto, an MP and a major railway contractor, said in Parliament in 1851:

> I know from personal experience that if you pay him (the Irish navvy) well, and show you care for him, he is the most faithful and hardworking creature in existence.

The idea of a tolerant approach to Catholics and their civil liberties led to more outspoken opposition to Catholicism and Irish immigrants in cities like Birmingham, Manchester and Liverpool. In 1850, the Pope **unilaterally** declared that Catholic bishops and cardinals would be appointed to serve in England for the first time since the Reformation. It was also a time when some priests in the Church of England were adopting habits of worship that were strongly influenced by Catholicism. All of this caused alarm in some Protestant circles. Matters were made far worse by the militant activities of Irish **nationalist** groups in England who wanted to secure independence for the Irish people. Acts of terrorism by the **Fenians**, including an assault on Chester Castle in February 1867, raised anti-Irish feelings to fever pitch.

> 1 Explain why some English workers were hostile to Irish navvies.
> 2 How did the media sometimes spoil the environment for migrants?
> 3 Why might some people in England have supported the idea of giving more liberty and rights to Catholics in the nineteenth century?

William Murphy

One of the most successful anti-Catholic/anti-Irish groups was the Orange Order, named after the Dutch Protestant William of Orange (see page 40). Orange Order lodges attracted lower middle- and working-class people who were hostile to 'aliens', particularly Catholic Irish immigrants. In 1867, the Orange Order in Birmingham joined other Protestant groups in inviting William Murphy to come and give his famous 'anti-**Popery**' lectures in their city.

William Murphy was himself an Irish immigrant to England. He was born a Catholic in Limerick in 1834, but converted to Protestantism as a young man. William became a missionary for the Irish Church Missions and migrated to England with his wife in the early 1860s. He started giving a series of public 'lectures' in 1865, which always ended with violent hate speech against the Catholics. Murphy used a notorious pamphlet called 'The Confessional Unmasked' to launch his attacks. The text alleged that Catholic priests exploited the women in their congregation by asking them sexually explicit questions in their confessions. On many occasions, he would declare: 'every Popish priest … a murderer and a criminal, a liar and a pick pocket', while waving a pistol on stage.

> 4 What do the activities of the Orange Order suggest about the extent of tolerance in English society?

4.2 How did the experiences and impact of immigrants vary, 1700–1900?

The Murphy Riot in Birmingham, 1867

The Birmingham authorities refused Murphy permission to speak at Birmingham Town Hall in 1867, but the Orange Order and others built him a wooden tabernacle (a temporary place for worship) on wasteland right next to the Irish district, to defy the authorities. Birmingham had the fourth largest Irish community in England, and the *Birmingham Daily Post* declared that Murphy 'cast a match into a powder keg'. Before the Court of Appeal eventually ruled against Murphy's work, riots had broken out in the city. A crowd of Irishmen had tried to disrupt the first meetings of Murphy's Tabernacle Week, but the police ended up siding with Murphy's supporters. His supporters then went on the rampage in the Irish Quarter, damaging all the houses and then smashing the front of the Moor Street Catholic church. The rioters also attacked a local synagogue. The Irish community were denied compensation for the damage that had been caused.

> **5** Why would William Murphy be considered a very divisive figure in nineteenth-century England?
>
> **6** Why do you think Murphy was allowed to continue his lectures after the 1867 riot?
>
> **7** How did Liverpool try to make the city a better place for immigrants?

The aftermath of the Murphy Riot

Catholic leaders appealed to the national government to curb William Murphy's activities. After more riots in the Manchester area in 1868, the Home Secretary, Gathorne-Hardy, noted that 'Mr Murphy is a positive nuisance and I think ought if possible to be stopped'. But the idea of free speech was important to English liberty, and Murphy continued lecturing, still using the contents of the obscene 'Confessional' pamphlet in his inflammatory talks. In 1871, he was badly beaten up by a group of six Irish labourers in disturbances in Whitehaven, and he died a year later, aged 38.

▲ **Source 9** A contemporary drawing of a scene from the Murphy Riots in Birmingham, 1867

Social welfare and Irish immigrants

Those Irish immigrants who made a new home in Liverpool usually found themselves in the most wretched parts of the city, sometimes living in cellars and doorways. In 1846, the city passed the Liverpool Sanitary Act that made the council responsible for drainage, paving, sewage and cleaning, and established a Council Medical Officer of Health. Liverpool was also the first English city to build council housing, in 1869. Despite these efforts, conditions for many Irish families remained very poor throughout the century.

▲ **Source 10** A photograph of the living conditions in part of the Scotland Road area of Liverpool in 1913

> **Father James Nugent (1822–1905)** was the son of a Liverpool Irish grocer, who went to Rome to train as a Catholic priest. He returned to his local parish in Liverpool, St Nicholas', and spent his life serving the needs of the local poor Irish Catholic community in many ways. He worked particularly with children and prisoners, setting up schools, colleges, a savings bank and a **temperance** society. The Archer family lived very near his church (see page 58).

> **a)** Study Source 10. How far does this photograph show that the efforts of people like Father Nugent had failed by 1913?

PART 1: Migrants in Britain, c.800–present

Indian immigrants in British society

Britain's imperial rule in India had brought a few Indian men like Sake Dean Mahomed (page 61) who prospered in early-nineteenth-century Britain, and some ordinary Indian sailors, or lascars, who settled in the port cities of Liverpool and London (see page 62). However, the numbers of such migrants were small. Towards the end of the century, there were a few highly qualified Indians who made an impact in politics and the law. There were also some Indian women migrants who came to look after the children of British families who were travelling as part of the Empire's administration.

Indian Members of Parliament

The Parsis, one of India's ethnic groups, of Persian heritage, lived mainly in the Gujarat province in western India. Parsis emerged as middle-men between the East India Company and local traders in Bombay (Mumbai), and took opportunities for both their sons and daughters to be educated by the British, who made this a requirement for securing respected jobs in their colonial administration. In the nineteenth century, some of these Parsis migrated to Britain in pursuit of business and education.

Dadabhai Naoroji (1825–1917) was a Parsi scholar and trader who migrated from Bombay in 1855 to join the first Indian-owned trading company in Britain. He left the business in 1858 because they were trading in opium, and started his own company, as well as becoming a professor of Gujarati at University College London. Naoroji entered politics and was chosen as a Liberal Party candidate for the 1886 British general election. After he lost, the Conservative Prime Minister, Lord Salisbury, said:

> however far we have advanced in overcoming prejudices, I doubt if we have yet to go to that point of view where a British constituency would elect a black man.

Opinion was strongly divided over Salisbury's remarks. Although many people accepted his reasoning, others were outraged at his racism. Naoroji was then successful in the 1892 election for the seat of Finsbury Central, and the *Manchester Guardian* newspaper reported:

> It is an honour in England because ... it has been proved possible for a popular constituency to disregard wide differences of creed and race, to recognise the political equality of our Indian subjects among Englishmen and on English soil.

As well as working tirelessly for his London constituents and also supporting the cause of Irish Home Rule, Naoroji saw himself as a representative of the people of India's interests in the British Parliament. He spoke out against the injustices of the British Raj, and supported other Indian immigrants, like Mohandas (Mahatma) Gandhi who studied law at UCL in 1888–90. Naoroji lost his seat in the 1895 election, and eventually returned to India in 1906.

▲ **Source 11** A photograph of Dadabhai Naoroji taken in 1888. He is wearing the traditional Parsi headgear

Sir Mancherjee Bhownaggree (1851–1933) was also a Parsi from Bombay who came to England to study law between 1882 and 1886, and then settled permanently in London in 1891. He joined the Conservative Party and stood for a Bethnal Green constituency in East London in the 1895 election. He always declared his support for the British Empire and said he would not 'advocate any claims for India' in Parliament. Bhownaggree was re-elected in 1900, but lost his seat in the Liberal landslide election victory of 1906.

◀ **Source 12** A photograph of Sir Mancherjee Bhownaggree, MP

> 1 Compare the assimilation and autonomy of Naoroji and Bhownaggree as Indian immigrants in Britain. Use circle diagrams to show the differences and similarities.

Indian women in Britain

Cornelia Sorabji

Cornelia Sorabji (1866–1954) was the daughter of Parsi Christians and became one of the first women graduates of Bombay University in 1888. She migrated to London in 1889 to complete her law education. Sorabji was supported by a number of notable liberal British people, including the Hobhouses and Florence Nightingale. They helped her gain permission to study at Somerville College, Oxford, and she became the first woman to take a law exam there in 1892, but she was only able to get her degree in 1922 after women were allowed to be awarded degrees at Oxford. In 1894, Sorabji returned to India to serve the people in various reforming projects, particularly to support women. She returned to Britain in 1929 and died in North London in 1954.

▲ **Source 13** This photograph shows the students at Somerville College, Oxford, in 1891. It was a college for women only, and there were three Indian women among that year's students. They are shown on the left-hand side of the picture. Bamba and Catherine, daughters of the exiled Sikh ruler Maharaja Duleep Singh, are on the front row. Behind them is Cornelia Sorabji

> a) What are the differences between the Singh sisters and Cornelia Sorabji in Source 13?
>
> b) What do those differences suggest about their assimilation and autonomy in Britain?

Ayahs in Britain

British people who settled in India employed many Indians as domestic servants in their households. They came to rely heavily on their nannies, known as **ayahs**, to raise their children and make life more comfortable for them. When these British people returned home, they often took their most valued Indian domestic staff with them, particularly their ayahs. Once in Britain, many ayahs were told that they were no longer needed and so many had to find other work in order to pay for their voyages home. Some even resorted to begging if work could not be found. Their plight was so common that in the late 1800s a home was founded for them to provide shelter and job opportunities.

> 2 How far do the lives of Naoroji, Bhownaggree, and Sorabji, show that Parsi immigrants were welcomed in nineteenth-century England?
>
> 3 How far did the Indian ayahs become victims of Britain's empire?

PART 1: Migrants in Britain, c.800–present

Case study: Jewish immigrants in London's East End

The persecution of Jewish people in Russia in the late nineteenth century began one of history's great human migrations. Jewish people travelled across Eastern Europe, by land and sea, to start new lives. Nearly 2.5 million set off to migrate to the USA, but the boat fare was too expensive for the poorest migrants who chose to settle in more tolerant parts of Europe, particularly Britain. Most Jewish immigrants settled in the area surrounding the port at which their boat had docked: the East End of London.

The arrival of Jewish people

The Jewish people migrating to Britain from Eastern Europe after 1880 were much poorer and less educated than earlier Jewish immigrants. There were also many more of them. This led to hostility from English working-class groups in London, as well as anxiety from some established Jewish communities. Some of the latter did, however, organise help for poor Jewish immigrants in 1859 by setting up the Board of Guardians for the Relief of the Jewish Poor.

The Board immediately became the chief source of support for Jewish people in need in the capital. As the numbers of Jewish Eastern Europeans arriving in London grew, the Board's funds dramatically increased. In 1861, it had spent £3,000 per year. This grew by about 800 per cent to reach £27,500 in 1908.

Although they could claim charity from the Board of Guardians, Jewish immigrants wanted to work for a living, and many took poorly paid jobs in trades they had worked in back in Eastern Europe, such as tailoring and cabinet-making. It was hard work, with long hours, overcrowded and insanitary conditions in small workshops, and irregular pay. Some of the Jewish women in the East End found jobs in the Bryant and May matchstick factory, alongside Irish women immigrants, and took part in the famous strike of 1888. These Jewish immigrants were distinctive in language, religion and often in the clothes they wore.

▲ **Source 14** An engraving showing Jewish immigrants in a Whitechapel sweat shop, sewing at a bench and sleeping in the same room. Printed in the *London Illustrated News* in 1904 alongside an article entitled 'The Alien in England: Scenes of the Foreign Invasion of the East End of London'

Study Source 14 carefully.
a) Identify at least three features of Jewish life in the source that suggest Jewish people experienced hardship in London.
b) Look carefully at the title of the article that appeared alongside this picture. What impact do you think the artist and the writer of the article wanted this to have on English readers?
c) How easily could Jewish immigrants from Eastern Europe assimilate into society in Britain in the late nineteenth century?

Support for Jewish immigrants

Leaders in the Jewish community set up organisations and premises to support the Jewish migrants in London's East End. Some aimed to help the immigrants assimilate into society, and others to help them maintain their autonomy within British society.

The Jews Free School

The Jews Free School (JFS) had been started in 1732, and relocated to the East End of London in 1822. JFS took on as many of the poor East European immigrant children as it could, which meant that the school became enormous. It may have been the largest school in Europe in 1900, with over 4,000 children attending. **Moses Angel** (1819–98) was a Jewish Londoner who began working at JFS in 1840 and soon became its headmaster. His main purpose was to educate the children for life in England and prepare them for assimilation. Angel discouraged the children at JFS from speaking the traditional Jewish language of Yiddish, which they would have spoken in Eastern Europe. The children were taught Hebrew and religious studies, but the language spoken and learned was English. An 1894 Board of Trade report described how the children 'enter the school Russians and Poles and emerge from it almost indistinguishable from English children'. Angel remained the headmaster of JFS until 1897.

The Jewish Lads' Brigade

The Jewish Lads' Brigade (JLB) was another institution started for Jewish children in the East End. It was founded in 1895 by Colonel Albert Goldsmid, who was descended from an important Dutch Jewish immigrant to eighteenth-century England. Although Albert's father had been born Jewish, he converted to Anglican Christianity because it gave him more opportunities in English society. Albert himself converted back to Judaism as an adult, and went on to become the highest-ranking Jewish officer in the British Army. Goldsmid's Jewish Lads' Brigade aimed to instil British values in Jewish boys, and in the First World War 535 of the JLB's 5,000 members died fighting for Britain.

The Russian Vapour Baths

Another leader of the Jewish communities in the East End was Benjamin Schewzik (c.1852–1915). He was a rabbi who fled from Russia, with other refugees, escaping persecution. Benjamin was a very successful preacher in the East End, and a professor of Jewish religious studies in Kent. He was also the successful proprietor of the Russian Vapour Baths, which stood opposite the synagogue in Brick Lane in the East End. An important part of the preparation by Russian Jewish men for the Sabbath is bathing on Friday nights before attending synagogue. By 1900, there were at least five baths for the exclusive use of the Jewish communities in the East End.

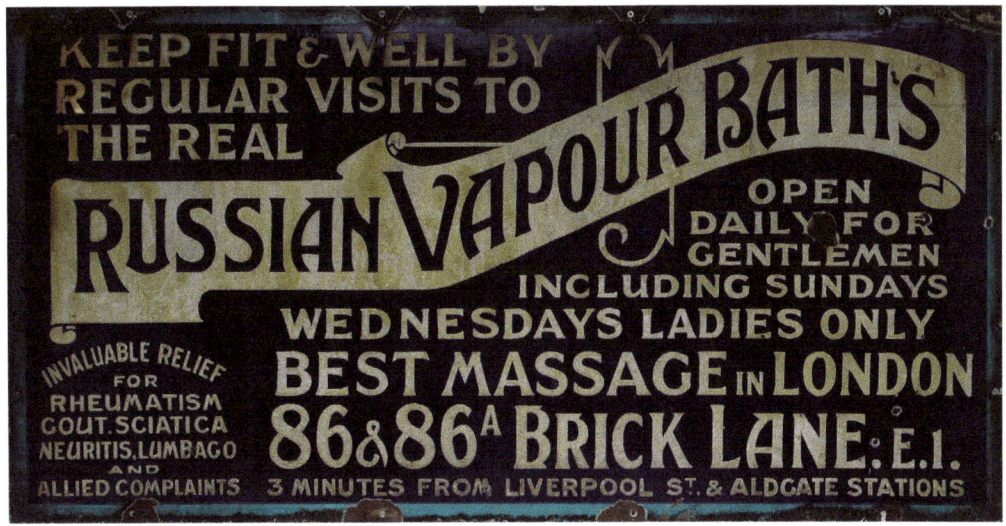

▲ **Source 15** A sign that was used to advertise the Russian Vapour Baths on Brick Lane, sometimes known as 'Schewzik's', after the owner

Jewish liberties

Britain did not officially persecute Jewish people in the nineteenth century, but there was still prejudice and hostility from some people and organisations. It was only in 1858 that Jewish people were able to become Members of Parliament, when the Jews Relief Act excused them from swearing the oath of office 'upon the true Faith of a Christian'. In 1871 Jewish people were able to take up fellowships at Oxford and Cambridge after the Universities Tests Act abolished the exclusive Protestant faith requirement.

1. Describe the challenges that Jewish people coming from Eastern Europe faced in their immigration to the East End of London.

2. Compare the impact of the three institutions: JFS, JLB, and the Russian Vapour Baths, on a) the assimilation and b) the autonomy of the East End's Jewish communities.

3. Who contributed more to the acceptance of Jewish people (from Eastern Europe) in Britain: Moses Angel or Benjamin Schewzik? Use assimilation/autonomy circles to compare the two men.

PART 1: Migrants in Britain, c.800–present

Hostile attitudes towards immigrants in the late nineteenth century

The attitudes of people in British society towards immigrants varied according to changes in the state of society and in the nature of the groups arriving. We have seen that throughout the centuries, Jewish people have suffered periods of serious hostility (see page 26–27).

Hostility towards Jewish migration to Britain

Unlike Russia, Britain did not officially persecute Jewish people in the late nineteenth century, but there was still prejudice and hostility from some people and organisations. The famous author Charles Dickens added to the anti-Jewish sentiments of the time with his portrayal of the child gangmaster, Fagin, in *Oliver Twist*. The character, who is involved in criminal activities, is referred to as 'the Jew' in the novel, published in 1837. Dickens was criticised by some people for this, and he said he regretted giving the impression he was anti-Semitic.

The Aliens Act, 1905

In the late nineteenth century, the newly arrived Jewish workers often took on jobs at lower rates of pay than British workers. This led to some strong pockets of resentment because the British thought the immigrants were taking their jobs. Captain William Stanley Shaw formed the British Brothers League (BBL) in 1902 to campaign in East London against immigration. The BBL was connected to the local Stepney MP, William Evans-Gordon, who led moves to pass an Aliens Act to restrict immigration, declaring:

> The Jewish emigrants do form a very large part of the whole, and in their case it may be said to take the form almost of a national migration. As things are, it is the poorest and the least fit of these people who move, and it is the residuum [the remainder] of these again who come to, or are left in this country.

The Aliens Act had the support of the Conservative Government and its MPs, including Bhownaggree (see page 70) and four Jewish MPs, who all wanted to restrict immigration into Britain. The Aliens Act was passed in 1905, and introduced categories of migrants who could be refused entry into Britain, including criminals and those who could not work to support themselves and their families. The first border control force was set up.

> **The Aliens Act as a Turning-Point**
>
> This important new law belongs with the next section of the course, 'Migration in modern Britain c.1900 to present day', and the information about its terms appears again on the Chapter 5 Highway on page 78, and on page 90. It appears here first as it marks the culmination of the debate about Jewish migration, at the turn of the century in particular.

> 1. How far did the end of restrictions on Jewish people being MPs in 1858 show that Parliament was shaping a tolerant Britain?
> 2. What kind of arguments were used to persuade British people that immigration had to be restricted at the end of the nineteenth century?
> 3. Why do you think that Bhownaggree (see page 70) supported the Aliens Act?

> a) What is the cartoon in Source 16 suggesting about the Aliens Act?

▲ Source 16 A cartoon in *Punch* magazine showing the impact of the Aliens Act of 1905

4.2 How did the experiences and impact of immigrants vary, 1700–1900?

Communicating your answer

You are now going to use your knowledge from this enquiry to answer two possible examination-style questions, one about the experiences of migrants and the other about their impact in Britain.

The experiences of migrants in Britain

To analyse the migrants' experiences, we will be using our key ideas of:
a) acceptance and rejection, to help consider the responses to migrants of the authorities and the existing population
b) autonomy and assimilation, to think about the responses of migrants to settling in Britain.

Our first question is:

> 'The relations between migrants and the authorities in Britain became more difficult in the years c.1700 to c.1900.' How far do you agree?

How the acceptance of groups of immigrants changed

We are going to use a diagram to show how the relations with migrant groups changed over time. Our example is of the Irish migrants, and the changes are shown for the nineteenth century. The box on the right tells you how these diagrams can be constructed.

> The Venn diagrams shown below will help to show how far a particular group of immigrants was accepted into British society. The bigger circle is British society and the smaller circle is the immigrant group. The further the smaller circle is inside the larger circle, the more the immigrant group was accepted into British society. Key developments and attitudes should be named in the different parts of the circles.

Irish migrants in England:

1801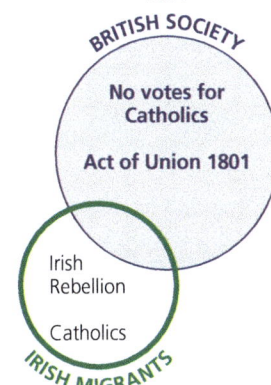

1830

1845

1867

1. Copy these diagrams into your notes. Underneath your diagrams describe and explain the **changes** in the acceptance of Irish migrants in British society between 1800 and 1900. You should refer to our key factors in your explanation:

   government | religion | economic influences | attitudes in society

   You should also comment on the **pace** and **extent** of the changes that you notice between these dates. Think about how long this period is, compared to the span of migration history in England.

2. Now draw similar diagrams for each of these groups: **African people – Jewish people – German people – Indian people**
   Decide which dates you think would be important to show change in the experiences of each group; the dates are likely to be different for each group.

3. Which groups had better relations with the authorities in Britain? What factors could explain the differences?

Writing your answer

The examination-style question is asking you to make a judgement about the particular viewpoint in the quotation. There will be aspects of the experiences of some migrants in Britain that show the relations with authorities becoming more difficult in this period, such as the hostility in certain cities towards Irish migrants in the 1860s (see page 68). However, there will be other things that show relations improving, such as the provision of a hospital for German sugar bakers in Hackney in 1845 (see page 65) and a home for Indian ayahs (see page 71). Plan your answer carefully so you arrange the evidence into paragraphs that agree with the quotation first, and then paragraphs that challenge it.

75

PART 1: Migrants in Britain, c.800–present

The impact of migrants in Britain

We will be using the key aspects of culture, trade and industry, politics and the urban environment in the two case study cities, Liverpool and London's East End, to examine the ways in which migrants made an impact in Britain in the years c.1700–c.1900.

Our second question is:

'The impact on the urban environment was the most significant consequence of migration to Britain in the years c.1700–c.1900.' How far do you agree?

The impact of different migrants groups on Liverpool and London's East End

The maps show different places connected with migrant groups. Complete a copy of the table using the information that you can find on the pages earlier in this section. (Note that not every cell of the table will have an entry.)

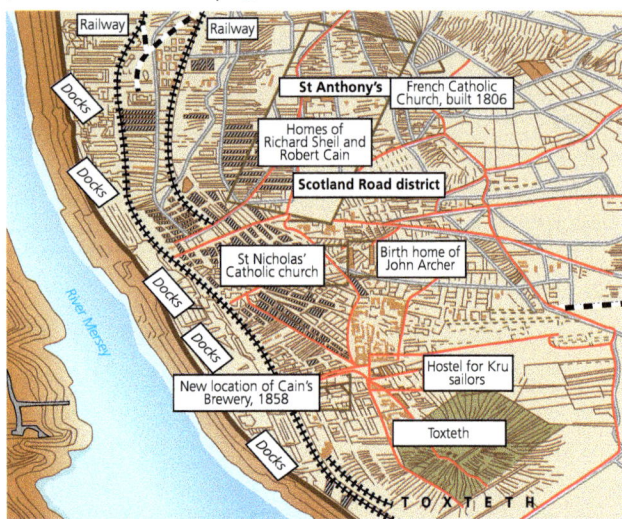

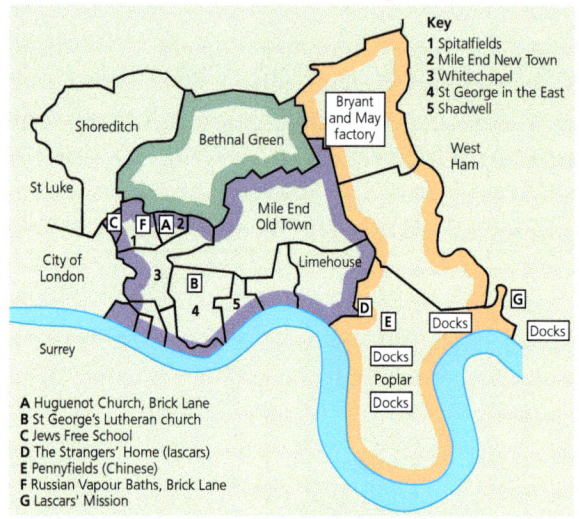

▲ **Map 1** Liverpool and key sites connected to migrants in the nineteenth century

▲ **Map 2** The East End of London and its migrant communities, 1690–1890

Group	Trade and industry	Urban environment	Culture	Politics
African migrants				
Chinese migrants				
German migrants				
Indian migrants				
Irish migrants				
Jewish migrants				

Writing your answer

Use the information in your table, and any other notes, to answer the question. You will have to think carefully about the phrase 'most significant'. Consider these further questions to help you make a judgement on which of the consequences of migration was *most significant*:

- How far did the consequences impact on the lives of *other* groups in the city?
- How *important* were the features that they changed?
- How far have the changes had a *lasting* impact on Britain?

Look at the ideas for improving your writing on page 62 and create four main paragraphs, one for each of the consequences of migration to Britain. Add an introduction and finish with a conclusion to complete your essay. The conclusion needs to have a clear judgement about what was the most significant consequence of migration to Britain in the years c.1700 to c.1900 and an explanation of the criteria you have used to come to this judgment. The best answers will not make a simple yes or no statement. It is important to show that you understand that change is a complex process and there are usually things that remain unchanged for some people, while others experience change.

The big picture of migrants in Britain: what changes happened in the period c.1500–c.1900?

We are now going to review the history of migrants to Britain from c.1500 to c.1900. You should look at all of the enquiries in Chapters 3 and 4 and particularly at the two migration highways (pages 32–33 and 52–53) for these two chapters.

We are going to think about how far Britain was '**open**' to migrants in these centuries. This investigation covers two important ideas of '**openness**':

a) the admittance of migrants across Britain's borders
b) how they were treated when they arrived and then settled.

We are going to use a scale of five levels to indicate the state of Britain's openness to migrants.

Openness level	Description of Britain and migrants
5	Migrants are invited to Britain and officially welcomed by the Government and the majority of people.
4	Migrants from a range of backgrounds are attracted to Britain by laws that promise tolerance, and some communities accept them.
3	Migrants from a range of ethnic and religious backgrounds are free to settle in Britain without official persecution, and some are accepted by local people.
2	Migrants from neighbouring countries are allowed to settle in Britain, and some are even tolerated.
1	Britain's doors are firmly closed to all but a small group of migrants. Migrants already in Britain face difficulties.

You have to decide which description best fits Britain in each of these years:

In deciding the openness level, you could ask these questions about the changes between the years:

- Did Britain change any of the laws about migration in the period?
- How far did freedoms change in the period, in relation to a) religion and b) enslavement?
- How far did economic opportunities change in the period?
- How did Britain's global connections change in the period, particularly in Britain's empire?
- How far did ordinary people change their responses to immigrants in the period?

> Choose any two of the years that you have worked with and explain the process of change for migrants that happened between the two years. You can repeat this with other dates to compare the degree of change.

Word Wall

Here are some words you can add to the original Word Wall you began on page 18. They will help you write accurately and with confidence. Look over your notes for c.1700–c.1900 and make sure that you know what all the words mean. Then add some **red words** of your own.

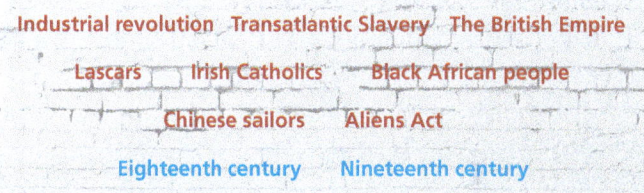

Practice questions

1. Explain one way in which the reasons for migration to Britain in the years c.1500–c.1700 were similar to the reasons for migration to Britain in the years c.1700–c.1900. (4 marks)
2. Explain one way in which the impact of migration to England in the years c.800–c.1500 was similar to the impact of migration to Britain in the years c.1700–c.1900. (4 marks)
3. Explain why there were changes in the experiences of migrants in Britain in the years c.1700–c.1900. (12 marks)
   You may use the following in your answer:
   - Jewish migrants
   - The media

   You **must** also use information of your own.

Aliens Act, 1905 The British Government responded to popular local unrest about migrants by passing this law to restrict their freedom to enter the country. The law said that 'undesirable immigrants', which meant criminals and poor people, would be refused entry. It was aimed at stopping further migration of Jewish people from Eastern Europe.

1900 · 1905 The Aliens Act · 1905 · 1910 · First World War 1915

Dr Harold Moody
1904
Jamaican doctor

Between 1914 and 1945 the world was caught in two huge military conflicts and Britain needed millions more soldiers to fight for them. Britain's imperial territories were drawn into both these wars against Germany and also Japan in the second. Subjects of the British Empire hoped that their loyal fighting would be rewarded with independence when the wars finished.

Guy Reid-Bailey
1961
Jamaican student and activist

Shanta Pathak
1956
Indian chef and entrepreneur

Roy Hackett
1952
Jamaican community activist

Olive Morris
1961
Jamaican activist

Claudia Jones
1955
Trinidadian-American activist

1955 · Decolonisation

Cyrille Regis
1963
Guianese-British footballer

1960

Dipak Nandy
1956
Indian lecturer and activist

1965

Beatrice Norman
1962
Ugandan nurse

George Odlum
1956
St Lucian politician

1965/68 Race Relations Acts

Wilfred Wood
1962
Barbadian priest

At the beginning of the twentieth century the European powers ruled over a range of colonial empires across the globe. The largest of these by far was Britain's empire. After the Second World War Britain had to begin reducing the expense of imperial control, starting with Indian independence in 1947.

78

The Migration Highway c.1900–c.1965

Charles Wootton
c.1918
Bermudian Royal Navy sailor

Learie Constantine
1929
Trinidadian cricketer and lawyer

1919 Riots in Liverpool and Cardiff

1920

1925

David Pitt
1933
Grenadian doctor and politician

1930

Ken 'Snakehips' Johnson
1929
Guianese bandleader

Leslie Thompson
1929
Jamaican trumpeter

1935

Paul Stephenson
born 1937
African-British activist

Una Marson
1932
Jamaican author and activist

Dr Joshua Bierer
1938
Austrian-Jewish psychiatrist

Elizabeth Anionwu
born 1947
Irish-Nigerian nurse and campaigner

Second World War

1940

1939-45 Second World War

1950

1945

Sam King
1948
Jamaican RAF engineer and postman

Carmen Beckford
1945
Jamaican nurse

Bea Green
1939
German-Jewish linguist

---

1. Look carefully at the notable migrants shown:
(a) Which parts of the world had they migrated from?
(b) Compare this highway to the previous ones (pages 10–11, 32–3 and 52–3). How far did the global spread of migrants change in the twentieth century?
(c) What kinds of jobs and social roles did they have?
(d) Again, compare this highway with the others and discuss how the range of roles has changed. Which is the most significant new role you can identify? Why do you think it has appeared?

2. Look at the pattern of migration dots:
(a) When was the volume of migrants greatest during this period?
(b) Can you suggest any factors that might have caused changes in the volume of migrants?

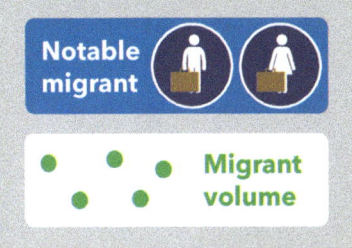

Notable migrant

Migrant volume

79

Notable migrant

Migrant volume

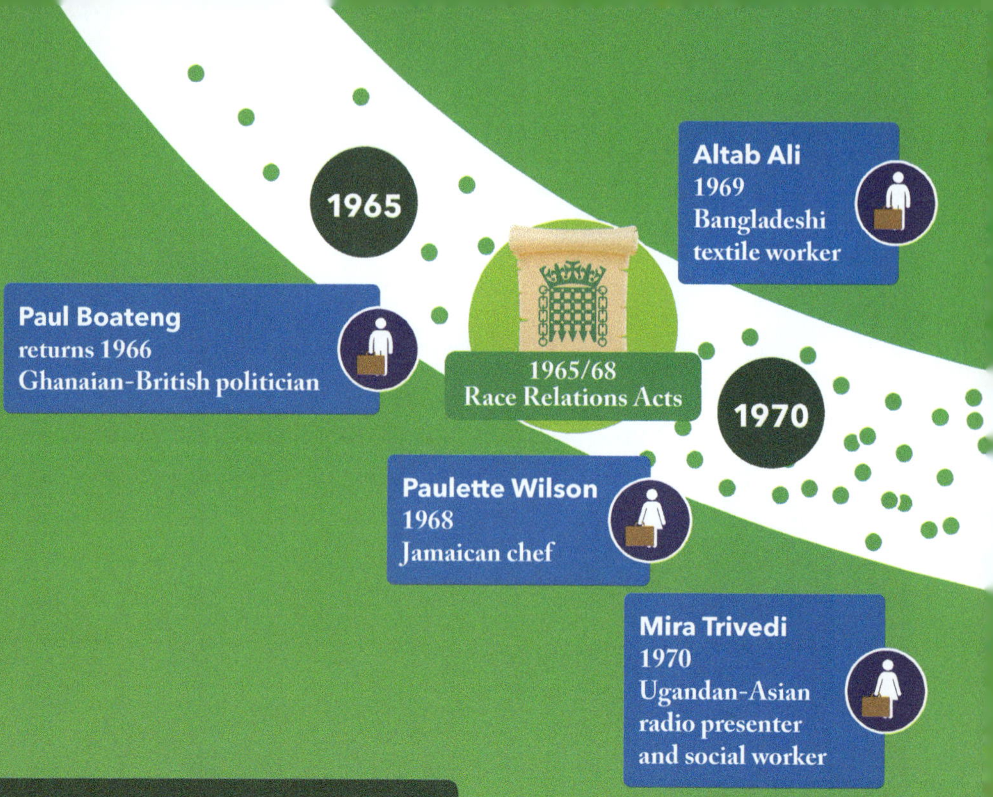

1965

Paul Boateng
returns 1966
Ghanaian-British politician

Altab Ali
1969
Bangladeshi textile worker

1965/68
Race Relations Acts

1970

Paulette Wilson
1968
Jamaican chef

Mira Trivedi
1970
Ugandan-Asian radio presenter and social worker

The European Union

After the Second World War the French and German nations decided to ensure future peace within Western Europe through close economic co-operation. Six countries formed the original European Economic Community in 1957. Others joined over the years, including the UK in 1973. Closer social and political unity developed in the 1990s, and many Eastern European countries joined in the early twenty-first century.

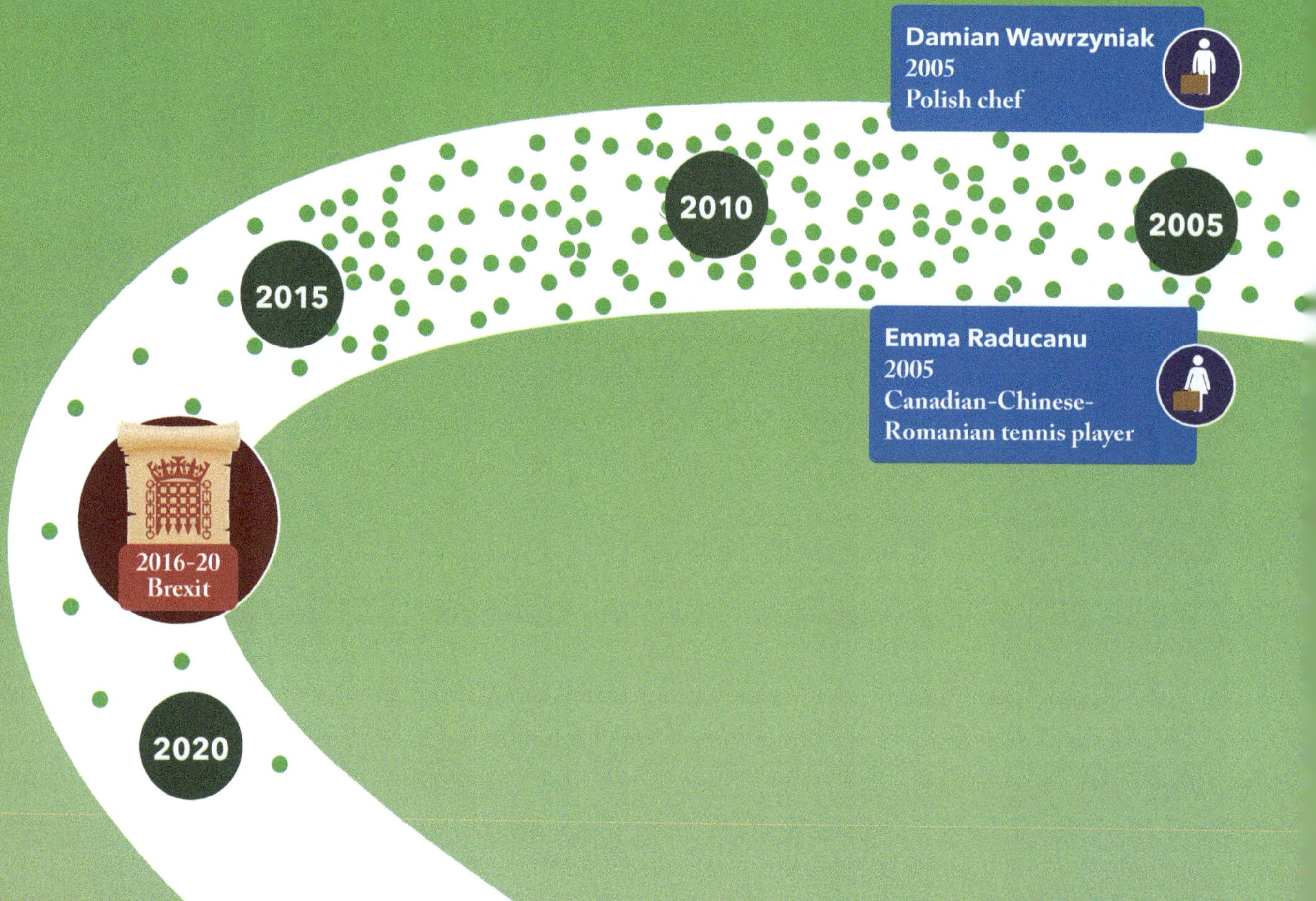

Damian Wawrzyniak
2005
Polish chef

2010

2005

2015

Emma Raducanu
2005
Canadian-Chinese-Romanian tennis player

2016–20 Brexit

2020

80

The Migration Highway c.1965–c.2020

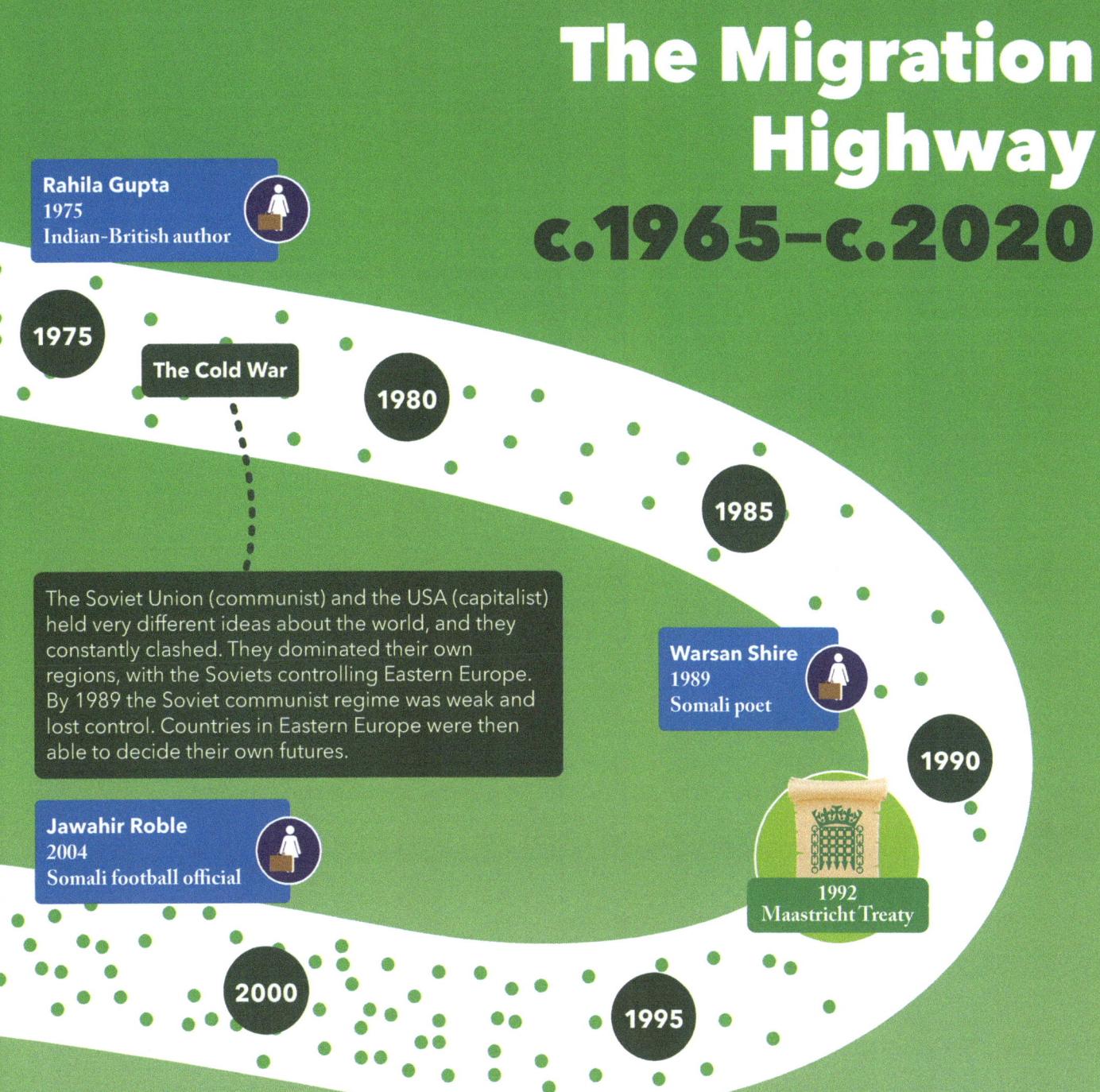

Rahila Gupta 1975 Indian-British author

1975

The Cold War

1980

The Soviet Union (communist) and the USA (capitalist) held very different ideas about the world, and they constantly clashed. They dominated their own regions, with the Soviets controlling Eastern Europe. By 1989 the Soviet communist regime was weak and lost control. Countries in Eastern Europe were then able to decide their own futures.

1985

Warsan Shire 1989 Somali poet

1990

1992 Maastricht Treaty

Jawahir Roble 2004 Somali football official

2000

1995

Look carefully at the two highways that cover the period c.1900–c.2020. Compare the changes that you can see in migration to Britain in this period with the previous three sections of the course, c.800–c.1900 (pages 10–11, 32–3 and 52–3). Consider the key aspects of our concept of historical change:

1. The extent of change: how far did the period c.1900–c.2020 see the greatest levels of migration to Britain since c.800? How far does the level of migration seem consistent throughout the twentieth century?

2. The pace of change: how far did patterns of migration change more quickly in the twentieth century than in previous periods? (You will need to consider the timescales shown on the highways very carefully.)

Key factors: consider how the key factors in our course have changed in importance over the whole period from c800–c2020. Draw a table, with a row for each of the following four factors: economic factors; institutions – government; religion; attitudes in society. Then create a column for each of the four time periods: c.800–c.1500; c.1500–c.1700; c.1700–c.1900; c.1900–c.2020. Use the highways to make notes in your table, to help explain the changes that you have identified.

5 Migration in modern Britain, c.1900 to present day

> Gather the information for this enquiry on twentieth-century Britain in a table like the one on page 9, under these key features:
> (a) Wars
> (b) Government immigration policy
> (c) End of the British Empire
> (d) European unity.

British ideas of racial superiority

There was no doubt in the minds of most British people in the late nineteenth century and beyond that they were vastly superior to the non-white peoples of Africa and Asia. They believed that this gave Britain the right to control those Asian and African peoples.

5.1 How far was Britain 'open' to migrants in the period 1910–2020?

The First World War and migrants from the Empire

When the First World War started in the summer of 1914, the British Empire was the largest in the world and ruled over millions of diverse peoples from Asia, Africa and the Caribbean. Britain was soon in need of more troops, and these colonies were asked to help. Over a million Indian people volunteered to serve in the Indian Army and c.140,000 went to the trenches on the Western Front in France and Belgium.

Indian soldiers in Brighton

Indian soldiers wounded on the Western Front were sent to England to be treated. Brighton was chosen as the centre for their care, and the Brighton Pavilion, a former royal palace built in the Indian and Chinese style around 1800, was converted into a main hospital. Over 4,000 wounded Indian men were treated at the Pavilion. However, the British authorities were very concerned about the possible mixing of the Indian men with white English women, so they did not want women nurses caring for them (see Source 1).

When the Indian soldiers first came to Brighton they were taken on trips to London and to local cinemas, but the authorities quickly put restrictions on their movements. They did not want these colonial migrants mixing freely and meeting English people as equals. By the end of 1915, the British decided to send the Indian troops to fight the war in the Middle East rather than in Europe.

> a) What does the photograph suggest about the care of the Indian wounded men in Brighton?
> b) What do you notice about the hospital staff looking after them?
> c) How did the British authorities change their attitudes to the Indian migrants in Brighton?
> Why did this happen?

▲ **Source 1** Indian soldiers at the Royal Pavilion in Brighton with their medical helpers

Race riots in 1919

When the First World War ended there were two million men 'demobbed' in Britain trying to find work at a time of economic hardship. In the major port cities there were black and Asian ex-service men, particularly seamen, looking for work. They became the focus of the anger of white British men who could use black and Asian men as scapegoats for their economic problems. Underlying feelings of white superiority and racist views towards black people were exposed in this time of hardship.

Riots in Liverpool

In Liverpool, hundreds of black men were unemployed in 1919, not only ex-seamen, but also workers in the city's sugar refineries who had been sacked because white workers refused to work with them. When trouble broke out in June between a group of black men and some Scandinavians, the police pursued the black men to a boarding house. A young Bermudian ex-Royal Navy sailor, Charles Wootton, ran from the house and was chased by two policemen

> 3 Consider why the 1919 riots broke out in Liverpool. What reasons were to do with a) racism and b) economic hardship?

and a mob of several hundred people to Liverpool's Queen's Dock. The police caught Wootton, but the mob snatched him, threw him in the dock, and then pelted him with stones until he drowned. The police made no arrests. Days of attacks on black people in the city followed.

The police blamed the black men, but the courts seemed to be a little less prejudiced: 12 out of the 29 black men arrested were found not guilty, but all the white people arrested were convicted. The response of the government was to try to get the colonial ex-seamen sent back to their colonies (repatriated) as soon as possible.

Riots in Cardiff

A similar riot erupted in Cardiff in June of the same year, with attacks on Somali and Arab seamen in the Butetown district (see Source 3). An Arab sailor was killed by a blow to the head, but the inquest could not decide whether it was caused by a chair leg or a police truncheon. Murder charges against six white men were dropped because of a lack of evidence. The police charged the Somalis described in Source 3 with major violent offences, but in court they were all found not guilty.

> 4 How far did Somali seamen get justice in the Cardiff riot of 1919?

British immigration controls after 1919

Although many of the black seamen and soldiers did return home to their colonies, some stayed behind and continued to seek work on British ships. By 1930, the total non-white* population of Cardiff was about 2,500, and two-thirds were Arab or Somali. The government, encouraged by the police and the white sailors' trade unions, did everything they could to prevent the settlement of non-white immigrants without having to pass new discriminatory laws:

- The 1925 Special Restrictions (Coloured Alien Seamen) Order made all non-white sailors carry a special registration certificate and report regularly to the police.
- In the 1930s, the Indian and UK authorities colluded to restrict the issue of passports to Indian workers.

> 5 Why did the British government prefer to restrict non-white immigration through regulations, rather than using new laws?

League of Coloured People

The League of Coloured People (LCP) was an organisation that challenged racial injustice in Britain. It was founded in 1931 by **Dr Harold Moody** (1882–1947), a Jamaican doctor with a surgery in South London. The LCP had its own journal called *The Keys* and spoke out against discrimination, including the 1925 Coloured Alien Seamen Order.

---

*The term 'non-white'

This term is used to distinguish migrants in Britain who were seen as different from the majority white population. It is not a term for describing an individual person.

Source 2 A Liverpool police officer commented on the 1919 riot:

The negroes* would not have been touched but for their relations with white women. This has caused the entire trouble.

*See page 3.

Source 3 A Somali named Ibrahim Ismaa'il spoke in 1928 about the 1919 Cardiff riot:

Seven or eight of us defended the house and most of them were badly wounded … In the end, the whites took possession of the first floor, soaked it with paraffin oil and set it alight. The Somalis managed to keep up the fight until the police arrived … some gave themselves up to the police, and we did not see them for a long time.

Covert regulations

British governments frequently operated restrictions in a covert way, especially when they were targeting particular groups of people. Legislation, like the 1905 Aliens Act (page 74) was very public and often attracted opposition. Until 1962, the British government chose passport restrictions as a hidden way of limiting immigration from non-white countries.

PART 1: Migrants in Britain, c.800–present

The Second World War and migrants from the Empire

As soon as war broke out again in September 1939, Britain welcomed back the lascars and other colonial subjects to help the war effort. Many more black and Asian men and women migrated to Britain during the Second World War, and this became a major turning-point in the development of Britain as a multiracial society.

Caribbean migrants

At this time, 10,000 Jamaicans joined the armed forces, particularly the Royal Air Force, and 1,000 Caribbean technicians were recruited for war work in Liverpool and Lancashire.

Learie Constantine (1901–71), a famous cricketer from Trinidad, first migrated to England in 1929 to play for a club in Nelson, Lancashire. When war started, he was given the role of Welfare Officer for West Indians, particularly in Liverpool. He helped migrants cope with racial discrimination. Constantine campaigned to help babies who had been born to white British women and black overseas servicemen, as many of them were abandoned.

On a trip to London in the summer of 1943 to play cricket, Constantine booked rooms for himself and his family at the Imperial Hotel in the West End of London. He had been told in advance that his colour would not be a problem, but when he arrived on 30 July, the hotel manager told him he could stay only one night. Constantine was told that other hotel guests, particularly a group of white American soldiers, would be offended by his presence. There was no law in Britain against racial discrimination at that time, but Constantine took the hotel to court for breaking contract. Constantine won the case.

After the war, Constantine trained in London as a lawyer, and spent over ten years in political and legal work in Trinidad. Between 1961 and 1964, he was Trinidad's first High Commissioner in London, and he then served on Britain's Sports Council and the first Race Relations Board (see page 97). He became the first black man in the House of Lords in 1969.

> **Migrants from India**
>
> Lascars from India quickly took jobs in the merchant navy; by 1941 there were about 600 Indians in the port of Glasgow. Indians also came to work in munitions factories, and there were 50 Sikh migrants in Coventry as a result. Wartime Indian settlers started to have an impact on society, and in London by 1946, there were twenty Sylheti (Bangladeshi) restaurants, compared to only one before the conflict began.

> 1 What do Una Marson's and Learie Constantine's experiences reveal about the openness of Britain to black immigration during the Second World War?

> **Una Marson (1905–65)** was a Jamaican author and activist, who migrated to London in 1932, and was a member of the League of Coloured People. She was recruited by the BBC in 1941 to host a radio programme called *Calling the West Indies*, reading messages from servicemen to their families. Marson became the producer of the programme in 1942, changed its name to *Caribbean Voice*, and used it to promote Caribbean authors.

▲ **Source 4** Una Marson in the BBC radio studio

Rebuilding Britain after 1945

After the wartime bombing, Britain had to rebuild a lot of its industries and cities, but there was a huge shortage of workers, possibly as many as a million. The government continued to believe that the permanent settlement of non-white people would cause social problems, and that only a small number could be assimilated into British society. The government chose instead to recruit white Europeans to fill the labour shortage. Immigration from the independent Irish Republic was encouraged, and hundreds of thousands came. About 200,000 white Europeans, particularly Poles and Italians, were also recruited in 1947-49, and a special act was passed in 1947 to allow Polish immigrants to have easy access to Britain (see Source 5).

> **Source 5** The Home Secretary of the Labour government, Chuter Ede, speaking in Parliament in 1947 about the value of Polish immigration to the UK:
>
> We have, nevertheless, had great experience in this country of the benefits that come from the assimilation of virile, active and industrious people into our stock.... a great part of our strength comes from the fact that we more than any other of the ancient nations of the earth, have been able to assimilate these people and get them into the mainstream of our civic life.

a) How far does your study of this course so far support Ede's claim?

The Nationality Act, 1948

The government was eager to welcome some citizens of Britain's overseas territories: the descendants of white settlers who had gone out to Australia, Canada, New Zealand and South Africa. But it would not have been acceptable to distinguish in law between British subjects according to ideas of race. Therefore, the Nationality Act of 1948 confirmed the right of all subjects of Britain's Commonwealth and Empire (and Irish people) to free access to settle in Britain. Britain would rely on collaboration with colonial governments to keep black and Asian subjects away. However, since 1945, Britain's colonies had started to become more independent so it became more difficult to control their actions.

> 2 Explain the British government's approach to meeting its shortage of workers after 1945.
> 3 What was the purpose of the 1948 Nationality Act? Why might it fail to achieve what the British government wanted?
> 4 Look back over this chapter so far and summarise the different ways in which the government tried to restrict non-white immigration before 1950.
> 5 How far do the sources and your knowledge support the interpretation that 'the voyage of the *Windrush* was an act of resistance'?

The *Empire Windrush*

Jamaica's colonial government refused to limit the issuing of British passports, because the Jamaican economy was in great difficulties and many Jamaican people needed better opportunities. The Colonial Office in London tried to directly discourage immigrants by sending information to Jamaica about misery in Britain. They sent a special film of the dreadful conditions in the British winter of 1947, one of the worst on record. But still the migrants came.

In June 1948, the famous voyage of the *Empire Windrush* carried about 1,000 migrants to Britain, including over 500 men, and a few women, from Jamaica. Many had been in England during the war, and most were skilled workers. The men who came to London and had no place to stay were sent to an old bomb shelter on Clapham Common in South London (see Source 7). They were quickly given jobs. They knew that some people expected them to give up and go home, but they were determined to meet the challenges. Some British employers, including London Transport and the new National Health Service, started to actively recruit from the Caribbean islands in the following decade, so the number of Caribbean immigrants increased.

> **Source 6** Sam King, an ex-RAF man, was one of the *Empire Windrush* passengers. He went on to be Mayor of Southwark in South London in 1983. This is from an interview in 1998:
>
> [The government] said they will not last one winter in Britain ... I'm here fifty winters; I'm among the living. They did not want us. And what's important for us to tell the nation ... we survive.

▲ **Source 7** Mr P Bulleid of the Colonial Office (holding his hand up on the right) welcomes Jamaicans to Britain in the Clapham Common shelter, 22 June 1948

Immigration controls, 1960s to 1980s

At this point in the course, it would be useful to consider some of the events that took place in the Notting Hill area of London at the end of the 1950s (see pages 120–21). The riots of 1958 played a part in the development of the British government's response to immigration of people of colour. More important to government policy was the rise in the numbers of black and Asian immigrants.

The Commonwealth Immigrants Act, 1962

This was the first of a series of laws that the British government used to try to prevent the immigration of people from Africa, Asia and the Caribbean, even if they held a British passport. It was clear by the late 1950s that the previous strategy of covert control (pages 83 and 85) was not going to be enough:

- The size of the black and Asian population in Britain nearly doubled in 1958–61, up to nearly 400,000. The Treasury was clear that 'the influx was economically beneficial' to Britain, but the Commonwealth Relations Minister said, 'most of the Indians and Pakistanis arriving here are quite unsuitable and cannot be absorbed'.
- The governments of independent ex-colonies were not prepared to stop their people from leaving for Britain.

After the 1958 riots, the Conservative government delayed the introduction of strict controls, because they didn't want such a move to be seen as a response to the violence. However, they were certain that social tension would only increase if black and Asian immigration rose further. A new system was announced in 1961 that ended the automatic right of entry for Commonwealth and Empire migrants. It set up a voucher system that divided potential immigrants into three categories and limited the number in the unskilled group (see box).

In the months before the Act came into force in the summer of 1962, there was a rush of arrivals 'to beat the ban'. The new act still allowed open access for dependents of settled immigrants, so many men from South Asia who had come on their own to Britain now sent for their wives and children. They did this as quickly as possible, in case further restrictions were introduced. Hence, the Act did little to reduce the numbers of non-white immigrants. Both Labour and Conservative governments in the decades that followed worked to make the controls tougher.

The categories in the Commonwealth Immigrants Act, 1962

A Those who already had a job to go to in Britain
B Those who had special skills that were in short supply in Britain
C Anyone else – unskilled workers, whose numbers were severely restricted

It was assumed that the white Commonwealth migrants would come under categories A and B, which would mean guaranteed free access.

The Act allowed families to enter the country to be with someone already in Britain, usually the fathers. Students were also admitted.

1 How far was the 1962 Act a turning-point in Britain's immigration policy?
2 Why didn't the 1962 Act put a stop to non-white immigration?

Tightening immigration controls, 1962–82

Year	Measure/Act	Government	Controls
1962	Commonwealth Immigrants Act	Conservative	All potential Commonwealth immigrants placed in three categories, and strict limits placed on unskilled category C arrivals.
1965	Tighter controls	Labour	No more category C immigrants. Only immediate family members as dependents. Time limits for student migrants.
1968	Commonwealth Immigrants Act	Labour	Any British passport holders could be subject to immigration controls, unless they, or a parent/grandparent, were born in the UK.
1971	Immigration Act	Conservative	Old categories of 'alien' and 'British subject' replaced by essentially racially defined 'patrial' and 'non-patrial': patrials had at least one British-born grandparent.
1981	Nationality Act	Conservative	Cancelled the 1948 Nationality Act. British citizenship was now only for patrials and people born in Britain.

▲ Table 1 Immigration legislation, 1962–81

3 How does Table 1 show that both major political parties in Britain did not support large-scale non-white immigration in Britain?

5.1 How far was Britain 'open' to migrants in the period 1910–2020?

East African Asians and British passports

Britain had brought large numbers of Indian people to its East African colonies in the early twentieth century. The British colonial authorities gave those Asian people a higher status than the black African people, and some Asian people built up businesses in the colonies. When Kenya and Uganda gained independence in the early 1960s, Asians, like the British, were seen as holding the African people back. Restrictions were introduced in Kenya and Uganda in the late 1960s that discriminated against Asian people.

Kenya

Most Asian people in Kenya had kept their British passports when independence was granted in 1963, and they used them to come to Britain in the late 1960s in increasing numbers: nearly 25,000 by 1967, and then another 12,000 in just the first two months of 1968. Labour politicians became increasingly anxious about this migration amid all the popular arguments of the time about 'overcrowding' and prejudice against other races. Despite the promise of security that they had previously said British passports offered, the British government moved swiftly to prevent any further Kenyan Asian migration. The 1968 Commonwealth Immigrants Act was passed as an emergency in days. The new 'patrial' restriction worked against any further Kenyan Asian migration to Britain (see Table 1), but those who had already arrived were allowed to remain.

> **a)** How has the photographer shown the plight of the Kenyan Asian migrants in this photograph?
> **b)** Could the photographer have been making a political point in this image?

▲ **Source 8** A Kenyan Asian migrant walks through customs at Heathrow airport, 1968

Ugandan Asians

In 1971, a military coup led by General Idi Amin removed President Milton Obote from power in Uganda. In August 1972, Amin declared that all Asian migrants who were not Ugandan passport holders would be expelled from Uganda in 90 days. The Conservative government was persuaded that it would be unacceptable to reject these migrants who held British passports, even though they were not patrials. About 29,000 Ugandan Asian people came to Britain in 1972. A Ugandan Resettlement Board was set up to try to disperse the immigrants around the country, rather than having them go to areas where Asian migrants had already settled. The majority of them ignored this and went to places like Leicester (see page 102) and the boroughs of Brent and Ealing in London, where existing Asian communities could give them support.

> **4** Explain why you think the Conservative government was prepared to override their 1971 Immigration Act for the Ugandan Asian people.
> **5** How far do you think the East African Asians were welcomed as immigrants to Britain in 1968 and 1972?

PART 1: Migrants in Britain, c.800–present

Racism in British politics, 1960–80

In the 1960s and 1970s it was a common belief that the assimilation of black and Asian immigrants to Britain was a major problem and that the only solution was repatriation. Both the 'problem' and the 'solution' were framed by the same racist ideas of white superiority that had been developed to justify the British Empire. These ideas survived the decolonisation of the British Empire that had been mostly completed by the end of the 1960s. There were a few English politicians who were ready to exploit some peoples' fears of non-white immigrants.

Smethwick, 1964

In the General Election of 1964, racist propaganda played a major part in Smethwick, a constituency near Birmingham. The Labour MP Patrick Gordon Walker, who had been the MP since 1945, lost to the Conservative Peter Griffiths, a local councillor and primary school headteacher. During the campaign, leaflets had been distributed that declared: 'If you want a n_____ for a neighbour, vote Labour' (see Source 9).

Smethwick was a shock to the new Labour government, whose overall national victory had been very narrow. Prime Minister Harold Wilson decided to continue, and extend, the Conservative policy of restricting immigration (see page 86), to avoid Labour being seen as 'soft on immigration'. Wilson's government did pass two Race Relations Acts to tackle discrimination but always alongside tougher controls (see page 97).

Enoch Powell

Another Midlands MP calling for the repatriation of immigrants in 1964 was Enoch Powell in Wolverhampton. Powell was a senior Conservative Party politician, who was horrified by the prospect of more large-scale Asian immigration from East Africa (see page 87) and wanted to have it stopped. On 28 April 1968, he gave a speech warning that immigration would lead to violence; it was called the 'Rivers of Blood' speech. Powell spoke out particularly against the Race Relations Act, arguing that white British people should be free to discriminate if they chose (Source 10).

> **Source 10** A section from Enoch Powell's 'Rivers of Blood' speech:
>
> The discrimination and the deprivation, the sense of alarm and of resentment, lies not with the immigrant population but with those among whom they have come and are still coming. This is why to enact legislation of the kind before parliament at this moment is to risk throwing a match on to gunpowder.

Powell's words shocked many in the political establishment and he was sacked the following day from his position in the Conservative leadership. However, opinion polls taken after the speech showed he had the support of 75 per cent of people in Britain, and there were large-scale demonstrations of support for Powell later in the year. However, in the following decades the government's response towards immigrants favoured integration rather than repatriation.

Right-wing extremism

The late 1970s and 1980s were politically, economically and socially challenging times for Britain and its diverse communities. Right-wing extremists were led by the National Front (NF), some of whose members then became part of the British National Party from 1982, under chairman John Tyndall. These groups would often organise demonstrations and march into areas with diverse ethnic populations and incite trouble, as in the August 1977 march into an area of Lewisham in south-east London. The NF opposed the European Community as well as **multiculturalism** and immigration of people of colour.

> **Source 9** From *The Times*, 9 March 1964
>
> Griffiths denied using the racist slogan, but said, 'I should think that is a manifestation of the popular feeling. I would not condemn anyone who said that. I would say that is how people see the situation in Smethwick. I fully understand the feelings of the people who say it. I would say it is exasperation, not **fascism**.'

> 1 Why do you think Harold Wilson called Peter Griffiths a 'parliamentary leper' when he joined the House of Commons in 1964?
>
> 2 Why were some non-white immigrants dissatisfied with Wilson's policies on race and immigration?

> a) How could Powell claim that it was the established British people who were facing discrimination because of the 1968 Race Relations bill?
>
> b) Why did some people think that Powell was being irresponsible in his speech?

> 3 Think back to previous anti-immigration protests and riots, such as the Evil May Day riot (see page 42) and the 1919 race riots (see page 83). What arguments do you think that the followers of Enoch Powell used to justify their hostile reaction to immigrants of colour?

Changes in Britain's role in the world, 1945–75

The Allied victory in the Second World War came at a great cost to Britain. The twin burden of rebuilding a nation and maintaining a sprawling global empire would prove to be too much and, in the decades following the war, successive British governments opted for reducing military commitments around the world to focus on home affairs.

The Commonwealth or Europe?

In August 1947, India and Pakistan gained independence from the British Empire after decades of nationalist struggles. Both countries joined the Commonwealth of Nations, the group of independent states made up of former British colonies. Many in Britain hoped that through trade with the Commonwealth, Britain would be able to remain in a position of international authority. However, after the Second World War, relations between the Soviet Union and the West developed into the Cold War (see the Highway on page 81). In this new climate, the USA pushed Britain into strengthening its relations with Europe, rather than pursuing its interests in the Commonwealth.

Decolonisation

Democracy was a principle that Britain was supposed to support in its empire when colonies became independent, which meant the black peoples of Africa would be in control of their countries. The new African states, like Ghana (1957) and Uganda (1962), accepted the democratic principle of 'one person – one vote'. These nations were outraged when the colony of Rhodesia refused that principle (see box). The sight of African and Asian nations pressuring Britain to take military action against a country governed by white British migrants made many people in Britain doubt the loyalty of much of the Commonwealth. The fact that those nations were increasingly associated with black and Asian immigration to Britain in the 1950s and 1960s further contributed to suspicions about the value of the Commonwealth to Britain.

The EEC

While the USA was pushing for Britain to focus on its European role, opinions within Britain were mixed. So, when West Germany, France, Italy, Belgium, the Netherlands and Luxembourg agreed to form the European Economic Community (EEC) in 1957, Britain declined the invitation to join. However, by 1960 the British economy was not growing anywhere near as fast as the French or West German economies, which prompted Britain to apply to join the EEC. But as the French were suspicious of Britain's motivations for joining, the application was not accepted until 1973. Britain would remain a part of this European network for over 40 years.

Rhodesian independence

In 1965, against the wishes of the British government, the southern African territory of Rhodesia (later renamed Zimbabwe) declared independence. The white-settler minority government there had been told to give greater political power to the black African majority, but they refused and instead cut all ties with Britain. Many Commonwealth nations urged Britain to take direct action against the Rhodesian government. The Labour government in London refused to use force, and the white rebellion continued until 1980.

4 Explain how each of these factors affected Britain's relations with the Commonwealth after 1945:
   ☐ The Second World War
   ☐ The power of the USA
   ☐ The Rhodesian crisis
   ☐ Immigration

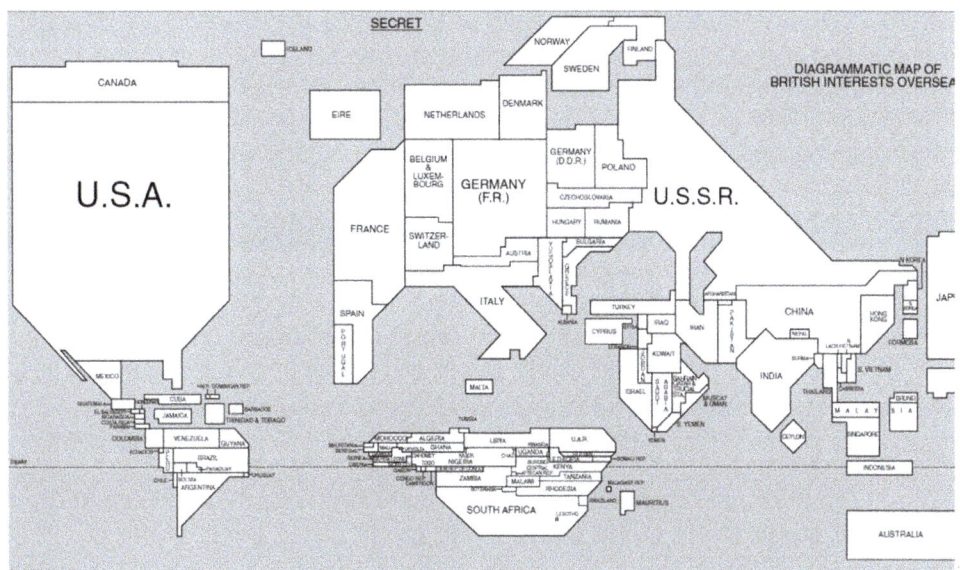

▲ Source 11 A world map produced in the Foreign Office around 1970 to show its view of the relative importance of countries to Britain's future

a) Compare the importance of these areas in the Foreign Office's ideas about the world in 1970:
   – the USA compared with China
   – Africa compared with Europe
   – India compared with the Netherlands

b) What does this map suggest about the way Britain might feel about Commonwealth migration from African and Asian nations?

PART 1: Migrants in Britain, c.800–present

> **Bea Green** was born Maria Beatha Siegel in Munich, Germany, in 1925. She left Munich on the *Kindertransport* in June 1939, after her father was viciously persecuted by the Nazis. Bea went to school and university in England, and then became a translator. She served as a magistrate in London.

Asylum seekers and refugees, 1900–2020

The Aliens Act of 1905 was the first British law to make a distinction between who was an immigrant and who was a refugee (see page 74). The Act stated that permission to land at British ports should not be refused to those seeking entry 'to this country solely to avoid persecution or punishment on religious or political grounds'. The power to decide who was avoiding persecution was left to the immigration officers at the ports and later to the Home Office. Therefore, the rules around who could successfully claim asylum changed according to public opinion and the personal views of the Home Secretary and other members of the government of the time. One of the first major groups of migrants welcomed to Britain after 1905 was from Belgium (previously known as Flanders). When Germany invaded the neutral country of Belgium in 1914, over 250,000 Belgians took refuge in Britain.

Kindertransport: Jewish refugees from Nazi Germany

After decades of restricting Jewish migration to the UK, the British government slightly eased restrictions in the late 1930s as Nazi persecution increased. Wide-scale anti-Semitism throughout Britain ensured that no government minister supported the idea of admitting large numbers of Jewish refugees. However, it became essential to admit some Jewish refugees in order to reinforce the idea that Britain was a liberal country that opposed the Nazis.

Kristallnacht

In November 1938, the Nazis carried out violent co-ordinated attacks against Jewish people and businesses throughout Germany, known as *Kristallnacht* (Night of Broken Glass). After this, British public opinion towards admitting Jewish refugees forced the government to ease restrictions. An unspecified number of unaccompanied refugee children were allowed to come to Britain on temporary travel visas. Private citizens or organisations had to guarantee payment for each child's care. Under 10,000 children came to Britain through this *Kindertransport* scheme out of the 500,000 who applied. Many of those who had their applications denied were murdered in the Holocaust.

▲ **Source 13** Bea Green in 1998 at home in London

> a) What appear to be the motives for the British government's policy on Jewish refugees in the 1930s?

> **Source 12** When the Nazi regime in Germany began persecuting Jewish people in 1933, the British Cabinet stated that:
>
> [The government should] try and secure for the country prominent Jews who were being expelled from Germany and who had achieved distinction whether in science, music or art. This would not only obtain for this country the advantage of their knowledge and experience, but would also create a very favourable impression in the world, particularly if our hospitality were offered with some warmth.

> 1 How far do you think the asylum and immigration laws became **(a)** tougher and **(b)** fairer from 1990 to 2010?

The growth of asylum applications and tightening restrictions

Following the end of the Cold War, increased political instability throughout the world led to increasing numbers of people fleeing war and attempting entry to Britain as asylum seekers. From the 1990s, public opinion on growing immigration was increasingly hostile, often stirred up by campaigns in the press. The period between 1990 and 2010 therefore saw the toughening of asylum and immigration regulations, as shown in Table 2.

▼ **Table 2** Asylum and immigration legislation

Year	Act	Government	Changes
1993	Asylum and Immigration Appeals Act	Conservative	A refugee had to have a well-founded fear of persecution for reasons of race, religion, nationality, social group or political opinion.
1996	Asylum and Immigration Act	Conservative	Increased the powers of arrest for immigration offenders, and made it a criminal offence for employers to hire any migrant without a work permit.
1999	Immigration and Asylum Act	Labour	Speeded up the processing of asylum claims. Reduced the provision of welfare to asylum seekers, giving food vouchers, rather than income. Gave no choice on place of settlement for refugees.
2002	Nationality, Immigration and Asylum Act	Labour	Reformed the regulations for immigrants to register as British citizens: strict requirements included an English literacy test, and a 'Life in the United Kingdom' test.
2006	Immigration, Asylum and Nationality Act	Labour	Introduced a tier system for entry to the UK, with skilled migrants given preference over unskilled migrants.

5.1 How far was Britain 'open' to migrants in the period 1910–2020?

Refugees in Britain, 1990–2020

The majority of applications for asylum between 1990 and 2010 came from countries that had been torn apart by devastating wars.

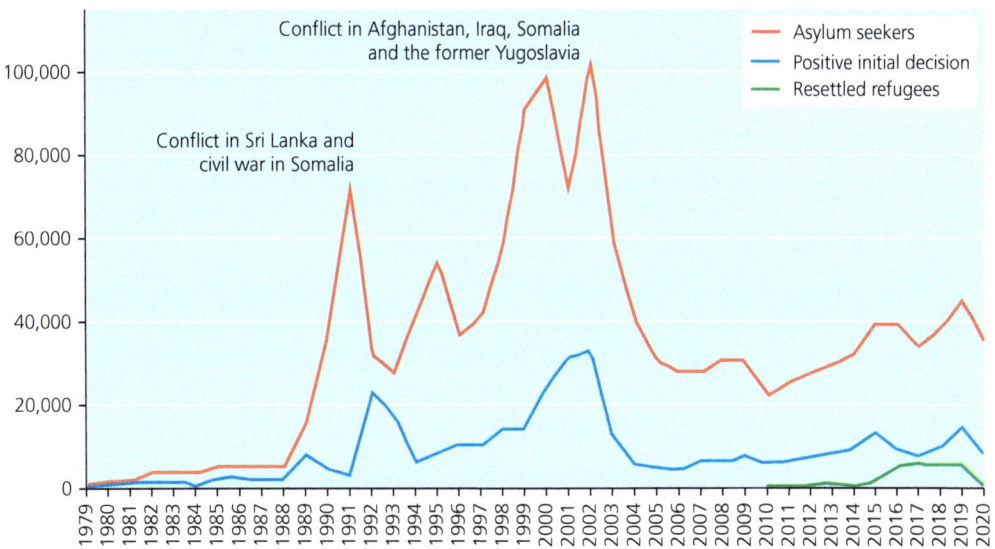

▲ Source 14 Number of people who claimed asylum, positive initial decisions and refugees resettled, per year, UK, 1979 to 2020 (main applicants and dependants; positive decisions are grants of asylum or other permission to stay)

Somalis

Between 1989 and 1991, a civil war raged in Somalia and thousands of civilians were displaced to refugee camps in bordering nations. For many Somali refugees, Britain was a favoured destination because of its well-established Somali communities and the country's reputation for being tolerant of people from different backgrounds. Many Somalis who had been granted asylum in other European countries after the civil war, undertook a secondary migration and came to Britain. For example, up to 20,000 left the Netherlands to come and settle in Britain between 2000 and 2010. The most common reasons for this, given by the migrants themselves, included a growing hostility to Muslim immigrants across Europe that was less pronounced in Britain, as well as better chances of getting work and establishing businesses in Britain. The total population of Somalis in Britain was 108,000 in 2018; the majority live in London, with other large communities in Birmingham, Leicester, Bristol and Liverpool among other cities.

Afghans

Afghans first began to migrate to the UK in 1979 after their country was invaded by the Soviet Union. The number of Afghans seeking asylum in Britain grew in the 1990s as law and order in Afghanistan broke down in consecutive civil wars. Between 1994 and 2006, around 36,000 Afghans claimed asylum in the UK but in the following years the numbers dropped as the UK government began to refuse more and more asylum claims from Afghans as it deemed the country to be safe. When violence engulfed Afghanistan again in 2021, Britain agreed to settle 20,000 Afghan refugees.

Syrians

In 2011, civil war gripped Syria. Over 6 million people were displaced, living in refugee camps in bordering countries. The aim of many of these refugees was to start a new life in Europe. Many paid smugglers to take them to European countries such as Germany. In 2015, during the height of the Syrian refugee crisis, the picture of a three-year-old Syrian boy named Aylan Kurdi lying lifeless on a Turkish beach appeared on the front pages of global newspapers. His death represented the desperation of those fleeing the Syrian civil war and it prompted the British government to relax its asylum policy and accept 20,000 Syrians directly from refugee camps to come to Britain.

Warsan Shire is a Somali poet born in Kenya in 1988. She migrated with her family to Britain at the age of one. In 2014, she was named the first Young Poet Laureate for London and has written many poems about the lives of refugees in Europe. Shire's verses have been used by activists and protestors to remind people of the humanity of refugees.

▲ Source 15 Warsan Shire

Source 16 An excerpt from 'Home' by Warsan Shire

i want to go home, but
home is the mouth of a shark
home is the barrel of the gun
and no one would leave home
unless home chased you to the shore
unless home tells you to leave what you could not behind,
even if it was human.
no one leaves home until home
is a damp voice in your ear saying
leave, run now, i don't know what
i've become.

a) How has Warsan Shire expressed the challenges of refugees in her poem?

91

PART 1: Migrants in Britain, c.800–present

1. Explain what was meant by the 'free movement of people' within the EU.
2. Why do you think that successive British governments publicly spoke against EU immigration while allowing for more migrants to settle in the UK?

The EU and the rise of anti-immigration politics

In 1992, twelve European nations, including the UK, signed the Maastricht Treaty signalling a 'new stage in the process of European integration'. The most controversial element of the treaty was the 'free movement of people', which allowed citizens of EU nations to travel freely to other EU states. Before 1995, annual **net migration** to the UK from the EU only went above 10,000 in two years. Even after 1995, EU migration was only a fraction of the total, until 2004.

Eastern European migration

In 2004, eight countries of central and eastern Europe joined the EU. Britain, Sweden and Ireland were the only members to completely open up to migrants from the eight new EU nations and all three experienced high rates of migration.

Successive British governments believed that immigration was essential to the growth of the UK. Many EU migrants came to do jobs in large British cities, working in hotels and cafés or in skilled trades as electricians and plumbers. The British economy grew rapidly between 2004 and 2008 but the financial crash and recession that took hold in 2008 led to a slowing of migration and many EU migrants returned to their country of origin.

a) Using the information in the graph in Source 17, make a timeline outlining how rates of migration from EU nations that joined in 2004 changed between 2004 and 2016.
b) Compare the volume of migration of the three different groups of migrants from the EU in the UK from 2006 to 2016.

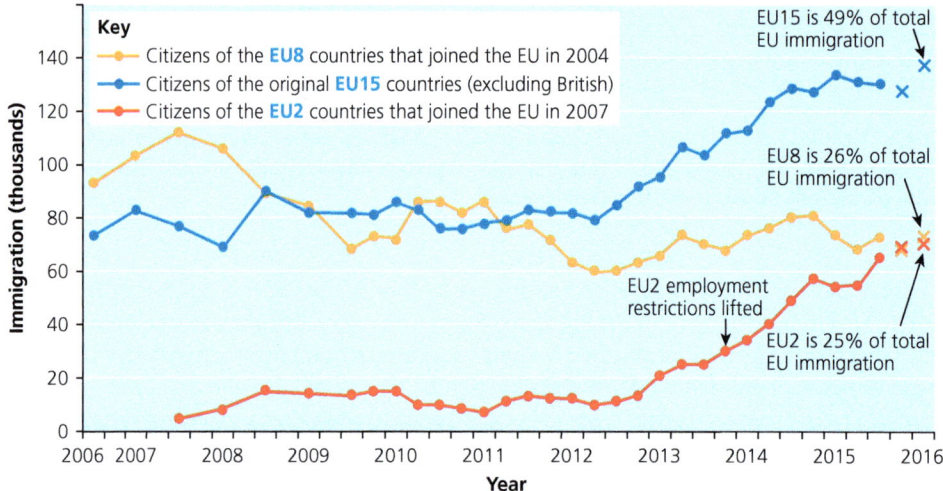

▲ Source 17 EU immigration to the UK, 2006 to 2016 (year ending June 2016), from countries that were in the EU in 1995, and joined later, in 2004 and 2007. See glossary

UKIP and Brexit

Between 2011 and 2016, popular right-wing newspapers carried over 300 negative stories about migrants. These newspapers openly supported the policies of the UK Independence Party (UKIP), which campaigned against immigration. Between 2014 and 2016, UKIP was the third most popular party in Britain. Its leader, Nigel Farage, stoked up anger about immigration levels in the UK. He offered a simple solution: a **referendum** on British membership of the EU. Prime Minister David Cameron agreed to hold a referendum in 2016.

The campaign to leave the EU was successful: the UK voted to leave by 52 per cent to 48 per cent, and in January 2020 the UK formally exited the EU (known as Brexit). Many migrant groups felt less welcome in the months after Brexit; a majority of police forces in England and Wales saw record levels of hate crimes in the first three months following the EU referendum.

Damian Wawrzyniak (1980–) was born in Poland and migrated to England in 2005. In 2012 he was appointed one of the head chefs for the 2012 Olympics. Wawrzyniak opened a top restaurant in Peterborough in 2017, and offered free meals to homeless people once a week. After Brexit he faced challenges in securing full settled status in the UK, despite all his work, and in 2019 he said, 'I feel unwelcome'.

> **Source 18** Ewa Lewecka, a Polish teacher of English as an Additional Language, moved to England in 2005. In 2019 she said in a newspaper interview:
> We were full of admiration for this country ... but everything changed in 2016. Now I feel disappointed, unhappy, unwanted ... The worst thing is the loneliness. I feel like everything collapsed, and I'm not alone in feeling that. ... I used to love it here.

a) Why did both Ewa and Damian become disappointed with England?

The 'Windrush Betrayal'

Britain's immigration policies from 1905 onwards showed a continuity of distinction between white European heritage peoples and people of Africa, Asia and the Caribbean (pages 83 and 86). Furthermore, concerns about immigration increased towards the end of the twentieth century, under both Conservative and Labour governments. The number of immigration enforcement officers employed by the Home Office grew from 120 in 1993 to 7,500 in 2009.

The 'hostile environment'

In 2012, the Home Secretary, Theresa May, introduced measures aimed at making life unbearably difficult in the UK for those who did not have the legal right to remain in Britain, so they would leave the country. May stated:

> 'The aim is to create, here in Britain, a really hostile environment for illegal immigrants.'

These anti-immigration measures were most likely to impact negatively on people who did not look or sound white British.

Doctors, landlords, police officers, employers and teachers were instructed to check the official status of people they were serving in their work, in case they might be illegal immigrants. The result was that it was usually black, mixed or Asian people, or those with 'foreign' names, who were asked to give proof of their status. Without documentary proof of immigration status, people faced going without medical care, and/or losing their jobs and their homes.

▲ Source 19 One of the vans that the Home Office sent into parts of London in the summer of 2013 to build up the 'hostile environment'

The Windrush generation

The *Windrush* generation are people who arrived legally in the UK from Caribbean countries between 1948 and 1973 (see page 85). They included many children, who arrived in Britain on their parents' passports. Their names were included on landing cards on arrival, but these were destroyed by the Home Office during an office move.

In 2012, as part of the 'hostile environment' policy, the Conservative government declared that the *Windrush* generation had to show an official document for each year that they had lived in the UK. These documents were needed in order to continue to work, get NHS treatment or even stay in the UK. It became clear from media reports in 2017 that people who had been unable to provide these documents had been wrongly detained, denied legal rights and even deported back to the Caribbean. These were innocent British subjects who had lived, worked and raised families in the UK for decades.

After widespread media coverage, the government apologised for the targeting of legal immigrants, and compensation was set up for those affected. In 2021 a lot of the victims were still waiting for that compensation.

> **Paulette Wilson (1956–2020)** arrived in Britain from Jamaica at the age of twelve in 1968. She became a chef and worked in the House of Commons canteen in the 1980s. By the 2010s, she was a grandmother, had moved to Wolverhampton to be near her family, and volunteered at a homeless centre.
>
> In 2015 the Home Office targeted Wilson as someone who had to prove her immigration status. After two years of struggling, in October 2017 she spent a week in the infamous Yarl's Wood Immigration Removal Centre, effectively imprisoned, awaiting deportation to Jamaica. Then, suddenly, media attention led to a government climb down. Wilson was freed. She then helped others trapped by the 'hostile environment' policy. She died, aged 64, on 23 July 2020.

---

3 To what extent did the 2012 'hostile environment' measures result in unjust discrimination?'

4 Explain why the immigration scandal of 2017–18 was described as the 'Windrush Betrayal'.

5 How far was Britain 'open' to migrants from 1910 to 2020?

Look back at the activity on page 77. Choose the Openness level that best fits Britain in each of these years:

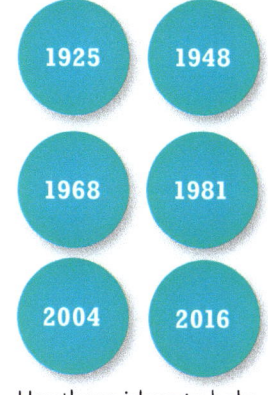

1925 1948
1968 1981
2004 2016

Use these ideas to help plan and write your answer to the enquiry question.

PART 1: Migrants in Britain, c.800–present

Communicating your answer

Now that you have completed your research on the period c.1900–present, it is time to answer an enquiry question. You will also need to use your notes from Chapter 4 to answer this question.

'The growth of the British Empire was the main reason for migration to Britain during the years c.1700 – present.' How far do you agree? Explain your answer.

Before answering this question you need to think about what to include in your answer. That's where the iceberg comes in. It is here to warn you that certain kinds of questions may contain hidden dangers lurking beneath the surface. On a first look, this question seems to be just asking you about the growth of the British Empire. However, the question also includes the key words 'how far'. This is always a sign that there is more to the question than meets the eye and that you need to consider other factors that are not mentioned in the question. Remember, you can find advice in the Writing Better History section on page 140–54.

Word Wall
Here are some final words you can add to the original Word Wall you began on page 18. They will help you write accurately and with confidence. Look over your notes for c.1900–present and make sure that you know what all the words mean. Then add some **red words** of your own.

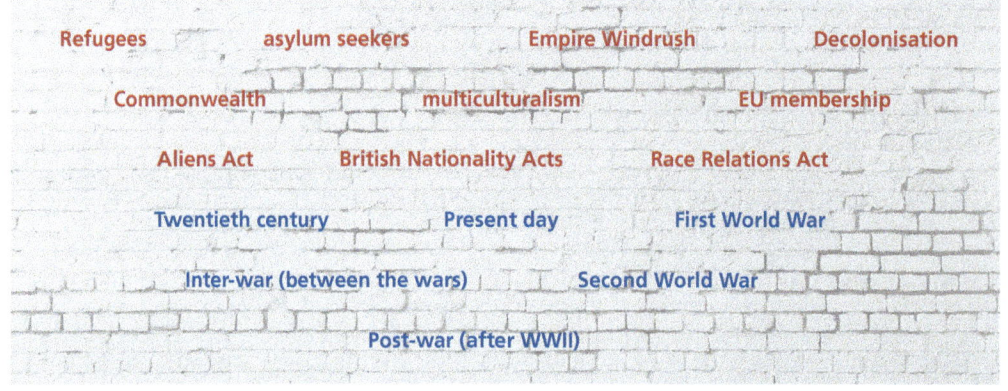

5.1 How far was Britain 'open' to migrants in the period 1910–2020?

Visible learning: Revise and remember

The experience pendulum

In the last two chapters you collected a lot of information about the reasons for migration to Britain since c.1700. Revision involves taking large amounts of content and slimming it down so it is easier to remember. One way is to make your revision visual. You could view the changes as a pendulum swinging from one side to the other.

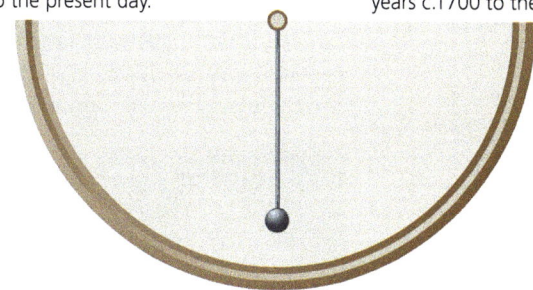

Change
Reasons for migration to and within Britain that were new in the years c.1700 to the present day.

Continuity
Reasons for migration to and within Britain that were present before and throughout the years c.1700 to the present day.

Making your own pendulums

'Over the last 200 years, the experience pendulum has swung back and forth, with the reasons for different groups of people migrating to and from Britain changing over time.'

1 Go back over your notes and decide how far the pendulum swung for each of the following:
   - Changing social structures and increased liberties (page 54)
   - Increased British political stability (page 54)
   - Catholic Emancipation in 1829 (page 55)
   - The Industrial Revolution (page 56)
   - Britain's economic growth (page 63)
   - The Trans-Atlantic slave trade (page 54)
   - The World Wars (page 82)
   - Rebuilding Britain after 1945 (page 85)
   - EU membership (page 89)
   - Seeking asylum (page 90)

   For each one, list some evidence in bullet point form for your decision.

2 You could use the pendulum idea to analyse the reasons for migration to and within Britain over time. Think about how you would draw a pendulum for each of the following periods. Make sure you add reasons below each one:
   - c.800–c.1500
   - c.1500–c.1700
   - c.1700–c.1900
   - c.1900–present

Practice questions

1 Explain one way in which the reasons for migration to Britain the years c.1500–c.1700 were different from the reasons for migration to Britain in the years c.1900–present. (4 marks)

2 Explain one way in which the reasons for migration to Britain in the years c.1700–c.1900 were similar to the reasons for migration to Britain in the years c.1900–present. (4 marks)

3 Explain why the reasons for migration to Britain changed in the years c.1900–present. (12 marks)

You **may** use the following in your answer:
- The World Wars
- EU membership

You **must** also use information of your own.

PART 1: Migrants in Britain, c.800–present

> Gather the information for this enquiry into the experiences and impact of migrants on modern Britain using a table like the one on page 9. There will be a lot of material under the 'impact' column. The key groups of migrants to structure your notes are:
> a) African people
> b) African-Asian people
> c) Caribbean people
> d) Irish people
> e) Jewish people
> f) South Asian people
> g) Polish people.

5.2 How did immigration transform Britain in the twentieth century?

Race relations and British politics

Negative thinking about non-white immigrants from governments, the police and trade unions throughout the century (see pages 83–85) was expressed very publicly by some individuals and businesses in the 1950s. Discrimination that excluded or separated people according to their race was seen around the world, in the USA and South Africa, and in many parts of the British Empire, including Rhodesia and Kenya. Racial discrimination was called a 'colour bar', and it operated across Britain, restricting people's access to accommodation, pubs and restaurants, and their employment opportunities on the basis of race (see Source 1).

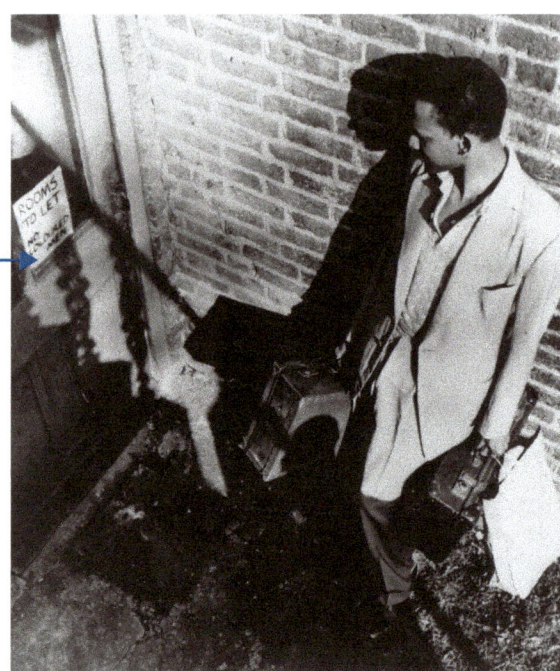

▲ **Source 1** The colour bar facing a Caribbean man seeking a place to live in 1958

> a) How far does this picture show the impact of the colour bar on black immigrants in the 1950s?

> **Source 2** Marion Glean in *Peace News*, September 1964:
>
> The truth is that race never is an issue until the discriminated against racially make it one ... It is time that we coloured people of Britain stop this nauseating begging for crumbs and behave like men (sic). We have a right to be ordinary citizens of Britain.

Campaign Against Racial Discrimination

Black and Asian immigrants organised their own protest campaigns against discrimination, including the Bristol Bus Boycott (see page 98) in 1963. **Claudia Jones** (see page 126) publicised such activism in the *West Indian Gazette* newspaper. **Marion Glean** was a Trinidadian, like Jones, who was studying at the London School of Economics in the 1960s and was part of a network of Caribbean and South Asian activists, which included **Jocelyn Barrow (1929–2020)**, a Caribbean pioneer of multicultural education. Glean arranged a meeting for her network with Rev. Dr Martin Luther King, Jr in December 1964 when he visited London. The meeting inspired them to set up the Campaign Against Racial Discrimination (CARD) and Barrow became its general secretary.

David Pitt (1913–94) was the chairman of CARD and a Labour Party politician. He was born in Grenada and came to Edinburgh in 1933 to train as a doctor. After working in the Caribbean, Pitt returned to England in 1947 and set up a surgery in Euston, North London. In 1959, he became the first black person to stand as a candidate for parliament. Pitt suffered racial abuse during his campaign in Hampstead and lost the election. He was a local Labour councillor throughout the 1960s and 1970s. Pitt believed that the best way for CARD to fight discrimination was to lobby the government and become a partner in shaping national legislation (see Source 3). Glean took a very different view: she wanted CARD to work directly with the immigrants themselves and fight discrimination at the grassroots level (see Source 2).

> 1 How far do you think the disagreements between Marion Glean and David Pitt were connected to assimilation and autonomy?

5.2 How did immigration transform Britain in the twentieth century?

The 1965 Race Relations Act
As a result of the pressure faced by the Labour government, the first ever legislation against discrimination was passed. The Race Relations Act came into force in 1965. The Act banned racial discrimination in public places and made the promotion of hatred on the grounds of 'colour, race, or ethnic or national origins' an offence. Following the Act, a Race Relations Board was created to deal with cases of discrimination.

Reactions to the Act
CARD thought the Labour Government's Race Relations Act of 1965 was weak and ineffective:

- The new law only outlawed racial discrimination in 'places of public resort' like hotels and pubs; it did not apply to housing, employment, education or the police.
- The government had agreed with CARD's suggestion that conciliation should be the remedy for cases of racial discrimination, but they ignored CARD's demands that the Race Relations Board be given tough powers to summon offenders.

Pitt said:

> 'the Bill is merely intended as a sop and not as a serious measure … to cover up the reactionary measures which are being introduced for enforcing stricter immigration control.' (See page 86.)

> **Fenner Brockway (1888–1988)** was born in Calcutta, India, the son of English Christian missionaries, and went to school in England. He was a radical socialist politician all his life. As a Labour MP he tried nine times, between 1956 and 1964, to pass a bill in parliament that would make racial discrimination illegal. It was rejected every time. Finally, in 1964, the leader of the Opposition Labour Party, Harold Wilson, supported his idea.

◀ **Source 3** David Pitt with the government's minister responsible for immigrants in Britain, Maurice Foley, 3 March 1965

a) How far does this photo reflect the ambition and success of CARD in the 1960s?
b) Compare this image with the 1948 photograph on page 85. Do the images show progress between 1948 and 1965?

Extending the Race Relations Act
In 1966, CARD organised a Summer Project, led by **Dipak Nandy** (see page 102), exposing racism in three key centres: Leeds, Manchester and Southall (West London). They found that because of discrimination nearly all the South Asians in Southall who had immigrated as skilled workers under visa categories A and B (page 86) were working in unskilled jobs. Furthermore, over 70 per cent of the 327 complaints made to the new Race Relations Board could not be investigated under the terms of the 1965 Act.

In July 1967, the Labour Government agreed to bring in a new, extended Race Relations Act. Although CARD's campaigning had paid off, the organisation continued to suffer divisions and, in 1967, the moderates resigned, leaving Black Power activists (see page 134) in control. CARD lost its national influence.

▼ **Table 1** Race Relations Acts, 1965–2000. All of these were passed by Labour governments

Year	Race Relations Acts
1965	The first law against racist behaviour in Britain, outlawing discrimination in public places and making inciting racial hatred a criminal offence. Created the Race Relations Board.
1968	Racial discrimination made illegal in housing, employment and financial services.
1976	Indirect racial discrimination was recognised, so the law considered the *impact* of a situation on people of different racial groups, not just whether arrangements were the same for everyone. The Commission for Racial Equality replaced the Race Relations Board.
2000	Racial discrimination by the police was finally declared illegal, after the Macpherson Report that investigated the mishandling of the investigation into Stephen Lawrence's murder in 1993.

2 What did David Pitt think was the connection between new race relations laws and anti-immigration measures?

3 Explain what part each of these people played in the fight against racial discrimination in Britain in the 1960s: David Pitt, Marion Glean, Martin Luther King, Fenner Brockway.

4 How significant was the Campaign Against Racial Discrimination in Britain?

5 How far should the Race Relations Act of 1965 be considered a turning-point in the history of immigration in Britain? Consider whether the answer to this would be different for a) a lawyer, b) a Labour Party politician and c) a black person living in England.

PART 1: Migrants in Britain, c.800–present

Case study: Bristol in the mid-twentieth century

Bristol has had a long connection with the Caribbean since the growth of the transatlantic slave trade (see page 38). After the Second World War its port was still a major destination for Caribbean produce. Bristol was also a city with many different industries, such as aircraft production and tobacco processing, and lots of job opportunities. Its first Caribbean settlers were servicemen who stayed in Britain after the war. Then chain migration brought growing numbers of Caribbean people to Bristol, mainly from Jamaica. The Caribbean population in Bristol increased from approximately 1,300 in 1958 – (0.3 per cent of the city's population) to 7,000 by 1963 – (over 1.5 per cent of the total). One such migrant was **George Odlum** (see biography box) who arrived in Bristol in 1956 to study English.

> 1. How significant was George Odlum's migration to Bristol for a) himself and b) the city?
> 2. How did the Bristol Bus Boycott show the power of local activism by an immigrant community?
> 3. Study the lives of Roy Hackett and Guy Reid-Bailey. How did they continue their social and political activism after the boycott? Complete autonomy and assimilation circles (see page 9) for the two immigrants.

George Odlum (1934–2003) was born in Saint Lucia. The son of a barber, he first arrived in Bristol in 1956 to study English at Bristol University. In 1958, he was elected President of the Bristol Students' Union; he was the first black leader of a students' union anywhere in the UK. He then went on to study at Oxford University from 1959 to 1961.

Odlum said, 'Living here in England, you get the feeling you are in touch with the nerve centre of the world.'

After graduating, Odlum returned to Saint Lucia, where he became a politician. He went on to serve there as Deputy Prime Minister (1979–81) and Foreign Minister (1997–2001).

The Bristol Bus Boycott

Many Caribbean migrants hoped to work for the Bristol Omnibus Company (BOC buses), as their friends had with London Transport, but they found that a 'colour bar' existed on Bristol buses. They were accepted as maintenance workers in the bus garages, but not as drivers or conductors, even though there were plenty of vacancies. **Ena Hackett**, who had arrived in Bristol from Jamaica in 1958 to marry her childhood sweetheart Roy, was refused a job as a conductor in 1962. **Roy Hackett** decided to organise a campaign to tackle this racial discrimination, and formed the Commonwealth Coordinated Committee.

Paul Stephenson came to Bristol in 1962 and was the city's first black social worker. He was born in Essex in 1937 and was of dual West African–English heritage. One of Stephenson's night-school students, **Guy Reid-Bailey**, wanted to apply for a bus conductor's job, and Stephenson agreed to help him. He phoned the BOC, spoke to them in his Standard English accent, and arranged an interview. On a second phone-call, the company was told that Reid-Bailey was from the Caribbean and they withdrew the interview offer. Stephenson, Roy Hackett and the other Committee leaders decided to protest. Inspired by the successful Montgomery campaign in the USA in 1955, they organised a boycott of Bristol's buses.

The protest was supported by many of Bristol's white residents, particularly students, as well as the black communities. The Bristol Bus Boycott was a success, and on 28 August 1963 the BOC announced it was going to end any racial discrimination in its recruitment process. The campaign had been supported by local Labour MP Tony Benn, and his party leader Harold Wilson, as well as Sir Learie Constantine (see page 84). The boycott gained national media attention and its success showed that the 'colour bar' could be defeated.

Roy Hackett was born in 1928 in Jamaica and arrived in the UK in 1952, living first in Liverpool and then in London. In 1957, he moved to Bristol and settled in the St Paul's district. Hackett founded the Commonwealth Coordinated Committee in 1962 and helped to organise the Bristol Bus Boycott. He continued to advocate for the rights of migrants in the city through his work in various posts:
- Chairperson of the Management Committee of the Bamboo Club (see opposite page)
- One of the founders of St Paul's Festival in 1968, which later became the St Paul's Carnival
- A member of the Bristol Race Equality Council, 1965–2005

Guy Reid-Bailey was born in 1945 in Jamaica and arrived in Bristol in 1961 to finish his schooling in the 'mother country', but was disappointed by the school curriculum and the lack of black history. He:
- was at the centre of the Bristol Bus Boycott at the age of nineteen
- was a founding member of the Bristol West Indian Cricket Club in 1963, and later team captain
- studied for a degree in social science at Bristol Polytechnic in the early 1970s
- was an education welfare officer (supporting school attendance) until 1997
- founded Bristol's first black housing association in 1985.

5.2 How did immigration transform Britain in the twentieth century?

The Bamboo Club and cricket

There were very few parts of Bristol where Caribbean migrants could rent or buy property when they first arrived, so they ended up living in the poorer, war-damaged parts of the city, particularly the district of St Paul's. There were limited places where they could socialise and they would organise their own parties and activities. Cricket was a very popular sport amongst people from the Caribbean and, in 1964, Guy Reid-Bailey and others set up the Bristol West Indian Cricket Club.

In 1966, Paul Stephenson helped Tony Bullimore to open a music club and restaurant that would specifically cater for Bristol's Caribbean community, and would be open to white and black Bristolians. Bullimore was born in Southend-on-Sea, Essex, in 1939, the son of a market trader, and of Portuguese-Jewish heritage from his mother. He migrated to Bristol in the early 1960s and married Lalel, a Caribbean woman. Bullimore's Bamboo Club was a great success, hosting musical legends like Bob Marley, Tina Turner and Millie (see page 117). The Bamboo Club also became the headquarters for the West Indian Cricket Club.

St Paul's Festival

Carnival is an important part of Caribbean culture and the community in St Paul's decided to follow the example of London (see page 129) and host a festival in 1968. **Carmen Beckford** and Roy Hackett were two of the organisers; Beckford said:

> 'We wanted the people of St Paul's to develop a certain amount of national pride.'

The first events were multicultural festivals, with elements from Caribbean and British cultures, such as steel pans and Scottish dancers. **Francis Salandy**, from Trinidad, took over organising the festival in 1975, and promoted more elements of traditional Caribbean carnival, including the Mas parade and sound systems. The themes of the Festival featured issues of social justice that affected the black community: 'Survival' (1979), 'Resistance' (1980) and 'Not Guilty' (1981).

▲ **Source 4** A wall mural of Carmen Beckford on the Seven Saints of St Paul's trail in the centre of Bristol

Carmen Beckford (1928–2016) was born in St Thomas, Jamaica, and arrived in England in 1945 to study nursing in Kent. She then moved to Bristol in 1965 to become a midwife. Beckford served on the Commonwealth Coordinated Committee with Hackett and Stephenson, and went on to help organise the first St Paul's Festival. She was also involved in dance and established Bristol's West Indian Dance Team.

From 1978 until 1986 she served as Bristol Council's first race relations officer.

Source 5 Tony Bullimore, talking about the success of his Bamboo Club:

> … our members are proud … that friends of West Indians can come in here and enjoy themselves and it takes away this inferiority complex that we haven't got anywhere to take our English friends.

a) How does Tony Bullimore suggest that his Bamboo Club helped the integration of Bristol's communities?

Source 6 Guy Reid-Bailey speaking in 2020, about playing for the Bristol West Indian Cricket Club:

> I used cricket as a sword, a weapon to show I could be as good as anyone else. Cricket was the only thing we could hold on to. It helped us to be seen as a force to be reckoned with and it was something we could actually say was ours.

a) How does Reid-Bailey help to explain the significance of cricket in the lives of Caribbean immigrants in Bristol?

4 How did the development of the St Paul's Festival show elements of assimilation and autonomy, 1968–80?

5 Explain how Caribbean immigrants responded to the challenges of living and working in Bristol in 1955–80.

6 Who would you choose as the most inspirational community leader of the time?

PART 1: Migrants in Britain, c.800–present

Altab Ali
Racial violence hit the Bengali community in East London in 1978 when Altab Ali, a 25-year-old textile worker was murdered in a racial attack. Altab Ali had arrived in London in 1969, and had recently returned from Bangladesh with his new wife. He was murdered on his way home from work in Whitechapel. The three youths who chased and killed him had often been involved in violence against Asians. The local community reacted strongly and on 14 May, 7,000 of them marched behind his coffin to Hyde Park. They demanded better protection for the Bengali community against right-wing extremist thugs. The area where he died has now been renamed Altab Ali Park.

Anti-racist community activism

The late 1970s and 1980s were politically, economically and socially challenging times for Britain and its diverse communities. In order to oppose right-wing extremists, various groups of activists were formed, from the local All Lewisham Campaign Against Racism and Fascism (ALCARAF) of 1977, to the nationwide Rock Against Racism (RAR), which organised major concerts in London and Manchester in 1978. The second generation of immigrant communities were less prepared to tolerate racism than their parents. They were determined to claim the liberties and equality that they deserved, and many formed organisations in the 1970s to do just that.

▲ **Source 7** The march behind Altab Ali's coffin in May 1978, at Hyde Park

a) How does the photograph show the solidarity and strength of the Bengali community of East London?

OWAAD and Southall Black Sisters

Anti-racist struggles also connected with the fight for equality for women. The Imperial Typewriter Strike in Leicester (see page 94) and the Grunwick Strike, led by Jayaben Desai, in 1976–78, showed the potential of Asian women's organised resistance to racism. In 1978 a group of women, including **Olive Morris**, formed the Organisation of Women of Asian and African Descent (OWAAD), which prompted the establishment of local Black Sisters groups. Southall Black Sisters (SBS) was founded in 1979 in a predominantly Asian area of West London, led by women of Asian and African heritage. They regarded 'Black' as an inclusive organising principle that included any ethnic group suffering racism from a white-dominated society (see Source 9).

> **Source 8** Rahila Gupta of Southall Black Sisters wrote in 2020:
>
> My own personal journey to 'Black' began with me self-identifying as Indian when I first arrived in the UK in 1975. This slowly morphed into 'Asian' … and stayed that way until I joined the anti-racist struggle and adopted 'Black' gratefully almost overnight as a marker of my politicisation.

OWAAD and SBS protested in January 1979 about Asian women immigrants being given forced 'virginity tests' (see information box). The SBS also fought on behalf of many women, who suffered extreme domestic violence. The case of Kiranjit Ahluwalia was particularly significant. She was imprisoned for murdering her highly abusive husband in 1989, but the SBS succeeded in getting her conviction overturned on appeal.

Virginity tests
Immigration rules in the 1970s allowed women who were due to marry their fiancée within three months to enter the UK without a visa. British immigration officials used medical tests attempting to check if engaged Asian women were virgins, thinking this would prove whether or not the women were really unmarried. These tests are now understood to be unscientific and a violation of human rights. Between 1975 and 1979 around 80 women endured this indignity. It was stopped in 1979 after the *Guardian* newspaper exposed the practice.

1. What was the significance of Altab Ali's murder?
2. Why did Labour Prime Minister James Callaghan cancel the virginity testing of Asian women so swiftly in 1979?
3. Why was the inclusive approach to 'Black' identity of the Southall Black Sisters a) so powerful, and b) difficult to maintain?

5.2 How did immigration transform Britain in the twentieth century?

Public services: immigrants and the NHS

The establishment of a National Health Service (NHS) in 1948 by Clement Atlee's Labour government was a major turning-point in Britain's welfare provision for its people. From the outset, it was also an area of employment in Britain that attracted migrants from a range of nations.

Doctors from overseas

Hospitals had benefited greatly from the work of German Jewish doctors who had fled Nazi rule in the 1930s, and the expansion of hospitals after 1948 would not have been possible without immigrants. More than 10 per cent of NHS doctors working in 1953–55 had been trained overseas, mostly in Central Europe. They were pioneers in new aspects of medicine, particularly psychiatry. **Joshua Bierer** had fled to England from Nazi control in Austria in 1938, and in 1946 he founded the Marlborough Hospital, the first social psychotherapy day hospital in the world.

By the 1960s, the largest group of immigrant doctors was from South Asia. They were concentrated in certain regions and in junior ranks of the service: in 1964, 40 per cent of junior hospital posts were filled by overseas doctors. Indian and Pakistani doctors concentrated on fields that did not attract white British doctors, particularly geriatric medicine. In 2009, a South Asian doctor commented in a research study that, 'without racism there would be no discipline of geriatrics'.

Irish nurses

Thousands of Irish women came to train and serve as nurses in the NHS; by the 1960s, just over 10 per cent of all NHS nursing staff were born in Ireland, and in 1971 there were 31,000 Irish nurses. There was always some prejudice towards Irish migrants in England, and nurses sometimes faced hostility and abuse. In a research study, Sheila (who migrated in 1952) said, 'The sisters were really snappy with the Irish.' But others found Irish women were welcomed: Dympna (who migrated in 1951) said, 'They loved the Irish nurses … always kind of looked up to. Well, I suppose it is the charm, and the sensitivities.'

Black nurses

Women from the Caribbean and West Africa were encouraged to come and train as nurses. In 1951 the gold medal trainee at Chase Farm Hospital in Enfield was Mabel Dinah Coke from Kumasi in the Gold Coast colony (known as Ghana since 1957). By 1955, sixteen British colonies had set up selection and recruitment agencies to ensure a good supply of candidates to train as nurses in Britain.

However, black women faced prejudice as early as the recruitment stage. They were often advised to take the quick route to become a state *enrolled* nurse (SEN), rather than be state *registered* (SRN), and then found that the SENs could not progress any further. SRNs were able to train as midwives and seek promotion, which was always more difficult for the black nurses.

> **Dame Elizabeth Anionwu (1947–)** is the daughter of a Liverpool-Irish mother and Nigerian father. She was brought up in a care home near Birmingham and only met her father in 1972. It was at this point that she became aware of her Nigerian African heritage.
>
> With good qualifications, Anionwu applied to study nursing in London, but was rejected many times before being accepted at Paddington. She passed as an SRN in 1968. In 1971 she trained as a Health Visitor, but was failed by her supervisor when she questioned the misuse of public funds that were supposed to help black and Asian immigrants. She was passed and exonerated on appeal.
>
> Anionwu became a pioneer in the treatment of sickle cell disease, which particularly affects African and Caribbean people. With Dr Milica Brozovic, she set up the Brent Sickle Cell Centre in 1979, the first of its kind. In 1990, she moved into nurse education, eventually becoming Professor and Dean of Nursing at the University of West London.

4 How important were immigrants in the provision of an NHS in Britain?

5 How was Elizabeth Anionwu a pioneer for racial equality?

Source 9 Beatrice Norman, born in Uganda in 1956, migrated to Britain in 1962. She trained as a nurse aged seventeen at St George's, Tooting. At North Middlesex University Hospital she became the Head of Child Nursing. Norman said in 2016, when she retired:

> I think we [black nurses] need to have that belief that actually we're just as good as the person next to you. You have to shine, you have to really show that people don't have a choice but to give you that job.

a) Why was Beatrice Norman's advice necessary for migrant nurses?

▲ **Source 10** Dame Elizabeth Anionwu

Case study: Asian immigrants in Leicester

It is believed that the first modern South Asian settlers in Leicester were a family of Punjabi Muslims who opened a spectacles shop in the 1920s. Large-scale Asian migration came to Leicester from the 1960s. By 2011, 37 per cent of the city's residents described themselves as Asian or Asian British.

> **Dipak Nandy** was born in 1936 in Calcutta, India, and arrived in Britain in 1956 to study. He was a lecturer in English Literature at the University of Leicester, 1962–68. Nandy led the Leicester Campaign for Racial Equality, including a successful sit-in at the Admiral Nelson pub when it refused to seat black people in its saloon bar. He was a founder member of the national Campaign Against Racial Discrimination (see page 88), and the founding director of the Runnymede Trust (a leading race equality research organisation) in 1968.

The challenges for Leicester's Ugandan Asians

Early in 1968 about 3,000 Kenyan Asians (see page 79) arrived in Leicester. It was a prosperous city and had a lot of light industry, particularly hosiery (socks, stockings and tights) manufacturing and textiles, with most of the jobs considered suitable for women. This was important for East African Asians, as whole families, rather than just men, were fleeing Kenya and then Uganda, and the opportunity for two wages was attractive.

When the possible arrival of Asians from Uganda was announced in 1972, the Labour leaders of Leicester Council took the extraordinary step of putting an advertisement in Ugandan newspapers that urged the Asians not to come to Leicester (see Source 11). Leicester was labelled 'the most racist city in Britain' by some newspapers.

> **Source 11** Part of the advertisement placed by Leicester Council in Uganda in 1972
>
> The City Council of Leicester, England, believe that many families in Uganda are considering moving to Leicester. If YOU are thinking of doing so it is very important you should know that PRESENT CONDITIONS IN THE CITY ARE VERY DIFFERENT FROM THOSE MET BY EARLIER SETTLERS.
>
> IN YOUR OWN INTERESTS AND THOSE OF YOUR FAMILY YOU SHOULD ACCEPT THE ADVICE OF THE UGANDA RESETTLEMENT BOARD AND NOT COME TO LEICESTER.

However, the Council's tactic didn't work. In fact, it may have had the opposite effect. Ugandan Asians knew from the advertisement that there were already East African Asians in Leicester, so it became one of the obvious places to migrate to, where fellow Asians would welcome them. About 6,000 Ugandan Asians came to Leicester in 1972, and six years later there were around 10,500 living in the city.

> 1. Why did Leicester City Council's advertisement fail to deter Ugandan Asian immigrants?
> 2. How does Source 14 help to explain the growth in Leicester's Asian population after 1972?

> **Source 12** The writer Judith Vidal-Hall recalled the approach of many Ugandan Asians to the problems of racism in Leicester:
>
> Remember, this was our second migration. In Africa we already knew what it was to be an unloved but tolerated minority. We knew how to keep our heads down, blend in and get on with people. We'd learned all that before we came here.

Imperial Typewriters strike

On 1 May 1974, 39 Asian workers, including 27 women, walked out on their duties in the assembly section at Imperial Typewriters, and within two days up to 500 more had joined them. They were protesting against racial discrimination in the factory: Asians were given higher quotas of work to be done and were paid lower wages than white workers.

The local trade union negotiator said the Asian protest group had: 'not followed the proper disputes procedure' and 'have no legitimate grievances'. Union leader Bill Batstone said in an interview with Radio Leicester: 'The Asians cannot come here and make their own rules.'

After three months, the workers had to admit defeat and return to work. By the end of 1974, the factory had been closed down. For the workers, especially the Asian women, the dispute gave them a new confidence and sense of empowerment.

> **Source 13** Shardha Behn, a former worker at Imperial Typewriters:
>
> The first day I got back to work, my foreman asked me what I had gained … He was making fun of me I know … I told him I had learnt how to fight against him for a start … In the past when I used to get less money in my wage packet I used to start crying … Next time I won't cry, I'll make you cry.

5.2 How did immigration transform Britain in the twentieth century?

> **3** Using the sources and your knowledge, explain the significance of the Imperial Typewriters strike for the Ugandan Asian immigrants in Leicester.

◀ **Source 14** A march by the Asian workers at Imperial Typewriters during the strike in 1974

> **a)** How does this picture show East African Asians in a very different way from Source 8 on page 87?

Asian culture and activism in Leicester

The Labour City Council decided that it needed to work hard to make up for their dreadful message of 1972. Leicester's Labour Party became the first in Britain to print its election material in Indian languages in 1974. The council allocated considerable funding to community organisations that would support the Asian immigrants and build a proudly diverse Leicester.

Radio Leicester

In 1976, local radio station BBC Radio Leicester revolutionised broadcasting to Asian communities in England by launching a five-nights-a-week Asian programme in English. *Six-Fifteen* first aired on Monday 16 October and the *Radio Times* featured the new Asian presenters, Don Kotak and **Mira Trivedi**, in the studio with the caption, 'Six-Fifteen – a good time to get to know your neighbours.' Within three months, research showed that two-thirds of Asians in Leicester were listening.

Belgrave Road: the 'Golden Mile'

By the end of the 1970s, Belgrave Road, just north of the city centre, had become the premier destination for South Asians in the Midlands to shop for weddings and festival clothing, jewellery and foodstuffs. It was nicknamed the 'Golden Mile' probably because of the jewellery shops. Its annual Diwali celebrations for the Hindu, Sikh and Jain festival of light are considered to be the largest such celebrations outside of India. Belgrave Road is also the location of a pioneering community centre led by two South Asian women: Rita Patel, from India, and Karen Chouhan, from Pakistan. Their Belgrave Baheno Peepul Centre organises arts, culture and sports activities.

> **Source 15** Mira Trivedi, who arrived in England from Uganda in 1970, interviewed in 2017:
>
> There was such a big vacuum where entertainment was needed ... in India we used to listen to the radio the whole day, in Africa we used to listen to the radio the whole day and when we came here there was very little Indian music.

> **4** How did Asian women leaders help to transform the culture of Leicester in the late twentieth century?

PART 1: Migrants in Britain, c.800–present

Multicultural Britain

Liberty had been considered an important aspect of British society since the seventeenth century (page 40), but until the 1800s it was only white Protestant immigrants, such as Huguenots, who were free to fully assimilate. The acceptance of Catholics (1829, page 55) and Jewish people (1858, page 73) made it clear that Britain was not monocultural, but a century later the increased immigration of people of colour challenged Britain's ideas on identity and diversity.

From assimilation to multiculturalism

The idea of assimilating immigrants into white British society was complicated with the arrival of large numbers of mainly black and Asian peoples different in appearance, culture and faith. Government responses from the 1960s promoted integration so that British identity could develop and be enriched by interaction with different cultures. This interaction was meant to all happen under the umbrella identity of 'British', so integration still involved a denial of autonomy for the immigrants' cultures. In contrast to this, many black and Asian migrants in Britain, especially those of the second and third generations, started to think of themselves as black British and Asian British.

Multiracial British parliamentary politics

Britain's parliament in the 1980s started to really reflect the diversity of the British nation. Conservative politicians of Jewish heritage served in major positions in Margaret Thatcher's government of 1983: Nigel Lawson as Chancellor of the Exchequer, Leon Brittan as Home Secretary (both sons of East European Jewish immigrants), and Sir Keith Joseph as Education Secretary. Then, in 1987 the first four black and Asian MPs since 1945 took their seats in the House of Commons. Diane Abbott, **Paul Boateng**, Bernie Grant and Keith Vaz were all members of the Labour Party, the first three serving constituencies in North London, and Vaz in Leicester.

▲ Source 16 Paul Boateng, then Minister at the Home Office, speaking at the memorial service for murdered schoolboy Damilola Taylor in December 2000

> **Paul Boateng (1951–)** was born in Hackney, London to a Ghanaian father and Scottish mother, but then lived for eleven years in Ghana. In 1966, the family returned to the UK as refugees after a military coup in Ghana. They lived on a council estate and Boateng finished school in Hemel Hempstead. He studied law at Bristol University and became a solicitor. He specialised in civil rights law, representing many black community organisations opposing racism in the housing and justice systems. This included the Scrap Sus Campaign, which worked to repeal the Vagrancy Act that was often used unfairly to criminalise black young people merely on suspicion that they were about to commit an unspecified offence.
>
> Boateng entered politics and was elected to the Greater London Council in 1981, and as Chair of the Police Committee worked to make the police more accountable to Londoners. In 1987, he was elected MP for Brent South. Boateng became the first black government minister (in the Department of Health) in 1997, and in 2002 was appointed Chief Secretary to the Treasury, a Cabinet position, and another first. He returned to Africa in 2005 to become Britain's first black High Commissioner to South Africa. After serving four years, he was appointed to the House of Lords as Baron Boateng of Akyem in the Republic of Ghana and Wembley in the UK.

1. How had the British parliament become more representative of a multiracial Britain by 2020?
2. How does Paul Boateng show both assimilation and autonomy as a black Briton?

In the General Election of 2019, 10 per cent of members of the House of Commons were from minority ethnic backgrounds. The Conservative government of 2020 saw three prominent Cabinet ministers of Indian Hindu heritage: Rishi Sunak as Chancellor of the Exchequer, Priti Patel as Home Secretary (both families migrated from East Africa), and Alok Sharma as Business Secretary. Both Sunak and Sharma swore their parliamentary oaths on the Bhagavad Gita (Hindu scriptures).

Migrants and British culture: sport

The national sporting teams of the twenty-first century reflect the strength of involvement of immigrant communities in British sport:

- **2012 Olympics:** 24 of the 65 medals won by British people in the London Olympic Games were won by first- or second-generation immigrants, including Mo Farah, gold medal winner in the men's 5,000 and 10,000 km races, who was born in Somalia and migrated to England as a child; and Jessica Ennis, the heptathlon gold medal champion, who has a Jamaican father and English mother.
- **Men's cricket:** the World Cup winning team of 2019 had a high proportion of immigrant players: the captain from Ireland, players born in Barbados, New Zealand and South Africa, and two second-generation Pakistani players.

Football

Football is recognised as a national sport with very diverse representation in its men's national team and top professional clubs, particularly by players of African and Caribbean heritage. By 2008, 60 per cent of Premier League players (331 men) came from 66 different countries. For most of the twentieth century, Irish men were the biggest group of immigrants playing in English clubs: in 1888–2010 over 1,200 male footballers in England had birthplaces in Ireland. Arsenal football club had a tradition of recruiting Irish players from the nineteenth century, with the peak of their influence under an Irish manager, Terry Neil, from 1976 to 1983. The number of Irish Premier League players declined in the 1990s when the free movement of people in the EU (page 84) brought greater global mobility.

The breakthrough for black footballers in England came after 1970. West Bromwich Albion became the first English club to regularly field three black footballers at the end of the 1970s. Batson, Cunningham and Regis were all of Caribbean heritage, and manager Ron Atkinson nicknamed them 'The Three Degrees', after the black female singing trio. These early pioneers faced a lot of racist abuse from supporters, including hate mail, especially Cunningham who had a white fiancée. Batson remembered:

> 'We'd get off the coach at away matches and the National Front would be right there in your face. In those days, we didn't have security and we'd have to run the gauntlet. We'd get to the players' entrance and there'd be spit on my jacket or Cyrille's shirt.'

Jawahir Roble is a recent refugee succeeding in English football as a referee and coach of both men and women players. She was born in Somalia in 1995, and fled to the UK from the civil war (see page 83) aged ten. Her family settled in north-west London and she pursued football all the way through school. Jawahir started refereeing in 2012 and is now England's first female Muslim Football Association referee. She said:

> 'Once I am on the pitch and I blow the whistle to start the game, I am not a refugee, my hijab does not matter, my gender or colour of my skin does not matter, I am a referee and I know how to do my job.'

▲ **Source 17** Jawahir Roble refereeing a men's football match in South London

a) How does this picture show how football in England had become more multicultural by the twenty-first century?

'Three Degrees'

- **Brendon Batson** (1953–) was born in Grenada and arrived in England in 1962. The first black player at Arsenal in the early 1970s, he joined West Bromwich Albion in 1978.
- **Laurie Cunningham** (1956–89) was born in London. His father was a Jamaican racehorse jockey. He joined West Bromwich Albion in 1977 and earned six England caps.
- **Cyrille Regis** (1958–2018) was born in French Guiana and arrived in England in 1963. He became an electrician and then a footballer. He joined West Bromwich Albion in 1977 and earned five England caps.

▲ **Source 18** A statue of the Three Degrees at the West Bromwich Albion ground, celebrating their contribution to the football club, unveiled in 2019

3 What was the significance of 'The Three Degrees' at West Bromwich Albion at the end of the 1970s?

PART 1: Migrants in Britain, c.800–present

Migrants and British culture: food

As immigrant communities grew in the second half of the twentieth century so did the variety of cuisines available in Britain. Migrant communities observed that British people who had travelled to different parts of the world had developed a taste for exotic foods and the first popular Chinese and Indian restaurants established in Britain were designed to cater to this group. These restaurants also became an important pull factor for future migrants as they could easily find employment in this sector. Throughout the twentieth century the dishes at these restaurants were adapted to suit British tastes and became very different from what migrant communities would eat in their own homes.

Turkish and Cypriot cuisine

Cyprus was another part of Britain's empire that influenced British eating habits after 1945. The island had Greek and Turkish Cypriot communities, and migrants from both groups were particularly involved in restaurant businesses in London and elsewhere. Greek Cypriots owned quite a lot of fish and chip shops, and Turkish Cypriots and Turks pioneered the introduction of the kebab into British food habits.

Indian curry

Large-scale migration from South Asia after 1950 boosted interest in Indian cuisine. Food writer Pat Chapman, whose family had longstanding connections to the British Raj in India, founded the Curry Club in 1982 to popularise Indian food with British people. By 1995 there were around 8,000 Indian restaurants in the UK, nearly 90 per cent owned by Bangladeshis. Curry had become a staple feature in the British diet (see information box).

Chicken Tikka Masala

In 2001, the Foreign Secretary, Robin Cook, made a speech about the importance of multiculturalism in the development of British identity and pride. He chose a food as his example of 'the way Britain absorbs and adapts external influences' – chicken tikka masala. Cook called it 'Britain's true national dish'. He described how the British had adapted the Indians' chicken tikka by adding masala sauce 'to satisfy the desire of British people to have their meat served in gravy'.

Chinese cuisine

Chinese restaurants were initially located around areas of Chinese settlement in large cities but over the course of the twentieth century grew in popularity and number, so much so that by 2020 there were over 10,000 Chinese restaurants and takeaways in Britain.

> **Laxmi Pathak (1925–97)** and **Shanta Pathak (1927–2010)** were a young married couple with a food business in Kenya. They migrated to Britain in 1956 to escape the unrest that had broken out against British rule. They settled with their young family in Kentish Town in London and Laxmi had to take a job as a road-sweeper to survive. Shanta started making samosas in her kitchen and selling them. Laxmi and Shanta then set up a shop for Indian foods in Drummond Street, Euston. From there they expanded to large premises in Northamptonshire and in 1970 their seventeen-year-old son, Kirit, joined the business. Patak's (they dropped the 'h' to make it easier for their customers to pronounce) manufactured curry sauces, pastes and pickles as well as selling Indian foodstuffs, and supplied lots of restaurants.
>
> When Ugandan Asian people arrived in 1972 (page 83), the Pathaks won the contract to cater for them in their temporary refugee camps, and they supplied printed information for them about English life. When the migrants settled and many opened shops and restaurants, they became Patak customers. In 1976 Kirit's marriage to Meena, a graduate of Sofia College of Food Technology in Bombay, India, brought her excellent knowledge of Indian cuisine into the business.
>
> By the 1990s non-Asian consumers had become very important for the Indian food market in Britain. In 1996 around a quarter of British people ate an Indian meal at least once a month, and they were cooking them at home, as well as using Indian restaurants. Patak's products supplied many of these cooks' ingredients.

?

1. How did the Pathak family business grow and make its mark on English society in the late twentieth century?
2. Construct an 'assimilation and autonomy' diagram for the Pathaks.

◀ Source 19 Shanta Pathak with her firm's van in the 1960s

5.2 How did immigration transform Britain in the twentieth century?

Migrants and British culture: music

Black musicians have contributed to music in Britain through the centuries (see pages 66 and 107) and in the twentieth century they were pioneers in new musical forms, such as jazz, 'ska' and reggae.

Jazz musicians

Caribbean and African-American musicians led the development of jazz music in Britain in the 1920s and 1930s. Jamaican trumpeter **Leslie Thompson** (1901–87) began as a musician in the West India Regiment and trained in 1919–20 at Kneller Hall in England. He migrated to England in 1929 and, in the mid-1930s, formed a band with **Ken 'Snakehips' Johnson** (1914–41) called the Jazz Emperors. After splitting from the band, Thompson continued to play until 1954, and then studied at university and became a probation officer in 1963.

Ken 'Snakehips' Johnson was born in British Guiana and was sent to school in England in 1929. He was supposed to study medicine, but was more interested in dance and music. After travelling in America, he took up the leadership of the Jazz Emperors. Johnson wanted to promote talented black musicians and, in 1937, he formed his own West Indian Dance Orchestra. When war broke out in 1939, he boosted people's morale with popular jazz-swing music. Una Marson (page 84) interviewed 'Snakehips' on her BBC West Indian radio programme in 1940. His orchestra was playing during the **Blitz** on London in March 1941 at the Café de Paris, when two bombs fell through a shaft to the underground dance-floor. Johnson was one of the 34 people killed in the explosion.

Caribbean music: 'ska'

One of the passengers on the famous *Emperor Windrush* voyage in 1948 (page 85) was a Trinidadian musician known as Lord Kitchener (real name Aldwyn Roberts). He sang a **calypso** entitled 'London is the place for me' on landing, although the song didn't reflect the attitude of the British authorities or the experience of many of the Caribbean immigrants. A more influential Caribbean musical genre was **ska**, which combined calypso with American rhythm and blues. The first major ska hit in England was Jamaican Millie Small's 'My Boy Lollipop', produced by Island Records, an Anglo-Jamaican company set up by Chris Blackwell, who brought Millie to London in 1963.

Ska music developed into **reggae**, which was led by the drum and bass, used off-beat rhythms, and was a little slower-paced than ska. Reggae songs would often focus on political and social themes of justice and liberation. Jamaican artists brought the music to England and it was taken up by British-born black artists like Janet Kay and Musical Youth.

In the late 1970s there was a revival in ska music in England, led by a group from Coventry in the Midlands. Jerry Dammers, Horace Panter and Jamaican-born Lynval Golding, formed a band in 1977 that fused ska with punk and new wave influences, to create a sound known as two-tone. They became The Specials and always had a mix of black and white musicians. Their music reflected the hardships of the 1980s when economic distress and racial tensions produced major riots in urban areas, including St Paul's in Bristol, Brixton in London and Toxteth in Liverpool, notably in the 1981 hit, 'Ghost Town'. In 1984 they recorded 'Free Nelson Mandela' as part of the global **anti-apartheid** protests.

> **3** How did Caribbean musicians contribute to British life during the Second World War?

▲ Source 20 Ken 'Snakehips' Johnson leading his band

> **4** How did Caribbean musical genres influence popular music in England from 1960 onwards?

▲ Source 21 The Specials

Source 22 Lyrics from 'Ghost Town' by The Specials

This town (town) is coming like a ghost town.
Why must the youth fight against themselves?
Government leaving the youth on the shelf.

This place (town) is coming like a ghost town,
No job to be found in this country
Can't go on no more
The people getting angry.

> **a)** What were some of the social and political messages of The Specials and their music?

PART 1: Migrants in Britain, c.800–present

Migrants and British culture: religion

Religion continued to be an important aspect of immigrants' lives in Britain in the twentieth century. However, the major change was the arrival of large numbers of people with faiths that were not Christian, and the transformation made by these religions to the urban environment by the 1980s.

Muslim migrants

The earliest worshipping communities of Muslims in Britain were the lascars in port cities (page 62), but the earliest purpose-built mosque in Britain was in Woking, Surrey. It was attached to The Oriental Institute set up by Gottlieb Leitner, a Jewish Hungarian scholar, in 1889.

In 1910, a meeting at the Ritz Hotel in London launched a project to establish the East London Mosque, led by Syed Ameer Ali (1849–1928), an Indian lawyer who retired to England in 1904 and became the first Indian to serve on the **Privy Council** in 1909. The non-Muslim trustees included Baron Nathaniel Rothschild, prominent Jewish MP and banker. The project took decades: the purpose-built mosque in Whitechapel was not built until 1985. In 2001, Prince Charles launched the project to build the London Muslim Centre next to the mosque, which was opened in 2004.

By the year 2000 there were over 150 mosques in London, and around 1,500 in the UK. The 2011 Census suggested that almost 5 per cent of the population of England and Wales was Muslim.

▲ **Source 23** The Central London Mosque, Regents' Park. In 1940 Churchill's government funded the land for this project, in gratitude for Muslim contributions to Britain's war efforts

Hindu migrants

Hindu temples were first established in the UK in existing buildings, including homes, warehouses and disused churches. The migration of thousands of Ugandan Asians in the early 1970s (page 79) hugely increased the number of Hindus in Britain. By 2020 the Hindu population in the UK had reached 1 million. The project to construct Britain's first traditionally built place of Hindu worship was launched in 1990 and the building opened five years later. The funds of £12 million were raised by British Hindus and the workforce included hundreds of volunteers.

> 1 How have religions contributed to the development of a multicultural Britain?

Christian migrants

Black people migrating to Britain were often strongly committed to the Christian faith. British missionaries had been very successful in West Africa and the Caribbean in previous centuries and, in turn, migrants brought new perspectives to help transform the churches in England, including:

- Archbishop of York John Sentamu (from Uganda, born 1949), who was one of the trio who produced the Macpherson Report in 1999, finding the police to be 'institutionally racist' after the failed investigations into Stephen Lawrence's murder in 1993.
- Bishop of Croydon, **Wilfred Wood** (see biography box).
- Reverend Sybil Phoenix (from Guyana, born 1927), a leading Methodist minister and social activist, who supported black communities in south-east London struggling against racial attacks including the New Cross Fire of 1981.

▲ **Source 24** Rev. Wilfred Wood, in the 1980s

> **Rt Rev. Wilfred Wood (1936–)** was born in Barbados and trained there as an Anglican priest. In 1962 he arrived in England to be ordained in the Church of England at St Paul's Cathedral. He then worked in a parish church in Shepherd's Bush, West London. In 1974 he served in the Diocese of Southwark and, in 1985, he rose to become Bishop of Croydon – the first black bishop in the Church of England.
>
> Rev. Wood was active in racial justice inside and outside the Church:
>
> - He set up the Shepherds' Bush Housing Association with Rev. John Asbridge in the 1970s, to support the poor and homeless, including a lot of black immigrants.
> - He was on the management board of the Institute of Race Relations when it took up a more radical position. He encouraged the appointment of Darcus Howe (page 126) as editor of their journal *Race Today*.
> - He also helped lead the national Housing Corporation in 1986–95.

> 2 How did Wilfred Wood work for change in English society?

5.2 How did immigration transform Britain in the twentieth century?

Visible learning: Revise and remember

Technique 1: Recording and assessing the role of a migrant group

During your course you will need to record and assess the experiences and impact of different migrant groups – Vikings, migrants from Europe and the British Empire and other groups of migrants. It will be much easier to revise their stories and write about them in exams if you use the same kind of chart for each of them. This means the pattern of the chart will be clear in your mind when you need it. The questions included below will help you create charts for other migrant groups, but don't be afraid to think for yourself about what needs to be included.

'Role of the migrant group' chart

Asian migrants in Leicester When: 1920–present	
Reasons for migration and patterns of settlement: Why did the group migrate to Britain? Where did the migrant group settle, and why?	
Positive experiences of migrant group: Explain how they were welcomed in Britain/the community.	Negative experiences of migrant group: Explain how they were not welcomed in Britain/the community.
The impact of the migrant group in Britain: How did the migrant group change Britain/the community?	
Key individuals: Record the names and stories of key individuals from the migrant group.	

Technique 2: Set your own questions and test each other

Go back over the work in your exercise book if necessary. Write ten to fifteen knowledge-based quiz questions for a partner. Make sure that you also record the answers somewhere!

Your questions could be multiple choice, multiple select, true or false, or even require short sentences as answers. Use a mix of question types. Just by composing these questions, you are already revising key content. Swap your questions with a partner. Have a go at their quiz and then mark each other's answers.

Practice questions

1. Explain one way in which the impact of migration to Britain in the years c.1700–c.1900 was similar to the impact of migration to Britain in the years c.1900–present. (4 marks)
2. Explain one way in which the experience of migrants in the years c.1500–c.1700 was similar to the experience of migrants in the years c.1900–present. (4 marks)
3. 'The impact on politics was the most significant consequence of migration to Britain in the years c.1700–present.'

   How far do you agree? Explain your answer. (16 marks)
   You **may** use the following in your answer.
   - Culture
   - Public services

   You **must** also use information of your own.

1. Complete the 'Role of the migrant group' chart for Asian migrants in Leicester on an A4 sheet of paper in order to establish the pattern of the chart.
2. Complete a similar chart for the different migrant groups you have learned about during this course. Ask your teacher for a list if you need help remembering.

Technique 3: Repeat your memory map

At the end of Chapter 2 you drew a memory map to help you record the main features of migrants in Britain. Draw a similar memory map for all time periods in this book using Chapters 3, 4 and 5. Use two different colours to show changes and continuities from earlier periods.

Technique 4: Writing the Big Story

It is really important to continue to keep the Big Story of migrants in Britain clear in your mind as this is a great help in the exam.
Use the notes in your book and write a brief story of migrants in Britain for each of the following periods:
- c.800–c.1500
- c.1500–c.1700
- c.1700–c.1900
- c.1900–present

Conclusion: The Big Story of migrants in Britain: change and continuity in the period c.800–present day

We are now going to review the history of migrants in Britain across the whole course. You should review your notes and also look back at the Migration Highways. There will be many different ways of considering the changes and continuities in migration to Britain since the Viking invasions. Look back to the 'levels of openness' activity on page 77 and choose a few dates to cover the final section of the course.

Significant migrants

Here is a list of 36 migrants from across the whole course. They represent different homelands, motivations for migrating, and different experiences in Britain. Their impact on British society was also very varied.

- Altab Ali
- John Blanke
- Peter Bonyn
- Robert Cain
- Samuel Coleridge-Taylor
- Joseph Emidy
- Desiderius Erasmus
- Carlo Gigli
- George Frederick Handel
- Caroline Herschel
- Hans Holbein
- Menasseh Ben Israel
- Ken 'Snakehips' Johnson
- Lanfranc
- Sake Dean Mahomed
- Una Marson
- Abraham de Moivre
- Dadabhai Naoroji
- Beatrice Norman
- Emma of Normandy
- William of Orange
- Shanta Pathak
- David Pitt
- Eleanor of Provence
- Paul Reuter
- Ignatius Sancho
- Johann Schweppe
- Warsan Shire
- Cornelia Sorabji
- Anne Tanqueray
- Mira Trivedi
- Damian Wawrzyniak
- Licoricia of Winchester
- Gustav Wolff
- Wilfred Wood
- Wynkyn de Worde

You are going to link people across the centuries of this course who share common features, and compare their experiences and impact. Write the names of the migrants above into lists, using the following headings:

- Art and books
- Business and finance
- Food and drink
- Law and politics
- Music
- Religion
- Science and medicine
- Textiles

You may find that a few people could go on more than one list, and that is fine.

Once you have placed all the migrants listed above into a category, consider the changes across the centuries that are shown through their experiences. You should also look for elements of continuity over time.

Choose one of the lists that you think shows a great deal of change over time. Write an account of the changes and the continuities shown by the particular examples in the list.

Develop your writing further by considering:

- the aspects of change that have been discussed throughout the book: *extent, pace, direction.*
- the factors that might have caused the changes: *economic influences, government, religion, social attitudes.*
- how far you think the people in the list *represent* the widespread experiences of migrants in their period.
- other migrants that you could add to your account.

Conclusion: The Big Story of migrants in Britain: change and continuity in the period c.800–present day

The impact of migrants: change and continuity

The government and the media have been very important factors in the history of migrants in Britain across the centuries. Our Big Story now looks at change and continuity in these areas of British life.

Government

Sources 1 and 2 show a group of powerful political leaders in Britain roughly 400 years apart.

a) What major differences can you see in the political leaders pictured in the different years?

b) How could the change be seen as a sign of progress in the experiences and opportunities for immigrants in Britain?

▲ **Source 1** 1604: Senior political figures at a conference in Westminster to negotiate peace with Spain

▲ **Source 2** 2020: The British front bench in Westminster: Prime Minister Boris Johnson, Chancellor of the Exchequer Sajid Javid and the Home Secretary Priti Patel

Media

Immigration has been a focus for British media for centuries. Study Source 3 which is a media text from 400 years ago.

> **Source 3** In 1701 the famous English author/journalist Daniel Defoe wrote about the importance of immigration for the history of England in the introduction to his satirical poem 'The True-born Englishman':
>
> I could go on to prove 'Tis also Impolitick in us to discourage Foreigners; since 'tis easie to make it appear that the multitudes of Foreign Nations who have took Sanctuary here, have been the greatest Additions to the Wealth and Strength of the Nation; the greatest Essential whereof is the Number of its Inhabitants: Nor would this Nation have ever arriv'd to the Degree of Wealth and Glory, it now boasts of, if the addition of Foreign Nations, both as to Manufactures and Arms, had not been helpful to it. This is so plain, that he who is ignorant of it is too dull to be talk'd with.

a) Explain what you think Defoe's message is in Source 3.

b) How far do you find his attitudes surprising for the year 1701?

There are a number of media texts particularly from newspapers, throughout this book (see pages 2, 32, 46, 50, 60–66, 94, as well as Source 3). Some of the writing in the press has been based on prejudices rather than considered observations. In September 2021 a number of popular newspapers had front-page headlines championing the idea of turning back boats of refugees trying to cross the English Channel (see page 2). They also showed large pictures of **Emma Raducanu** with headlines praising this young immigrant for her victory in the US Open women's tennis championship (see biography box), often referring to her as a 'British teenager'.

> **Emma Raducanu** Born in 2002 in Toronto, Canada, to a Chinese mother and a Romanian father, Raducanu migrated to England when she was two. She became a professional tennis player at age fifteen.

1 What different attitudes towards immigration have appeared in the media since the seventeenth century? Look for common themes across time. What situations seem to provoke hostility towards migrants in the media?

2 Are there other responses, like the situation in September 2021, that appear contradictory?

PART 2: The historic environment: Notting Hill, c.1948–c.1970

Part 2: The historic environment: Notting Hill, c.1948–c.1970

There are three major differences from your work on the Thematic Study on Migrants in Britain:
1. This unit focuses on a single place, a historic site – Notting Hill, an area of West London.
2. It focuses on a short period, the years c.1948–c1970.
3. It looks much more closely at contemporary sources and how we use them in an enquiry.

The map on these pages shows how the streets were laid out in the period of your study. Most of the roads still remain, but there have been some changes. The biggest changes have been in the decoration and luxury of the buildings. Most of Notting Hill has been 'gentrified', meaning it has become an area where wealthy people live. The pictures on these pages are of places that you will learn about in the course as they look now. You will see these pictures repeated throughout the unit.

Caribbean immigrants settle in Notting Hill

Look back at the thematic study on page 85, on the background to large-scale migration from the Caribbean region to the UK after 1945. You will find out about a number of different Caribbean men and women in this unit: Clifford Fullerton (tailor), Duke Vin (DJ), Kelso Cochrane (carpenter), Carmen Bryan (factory worker), Pansy Jeffrey (nurse), Frank Crichlow (railway worker); make a note of their migration and the life they had in Notting Hill.

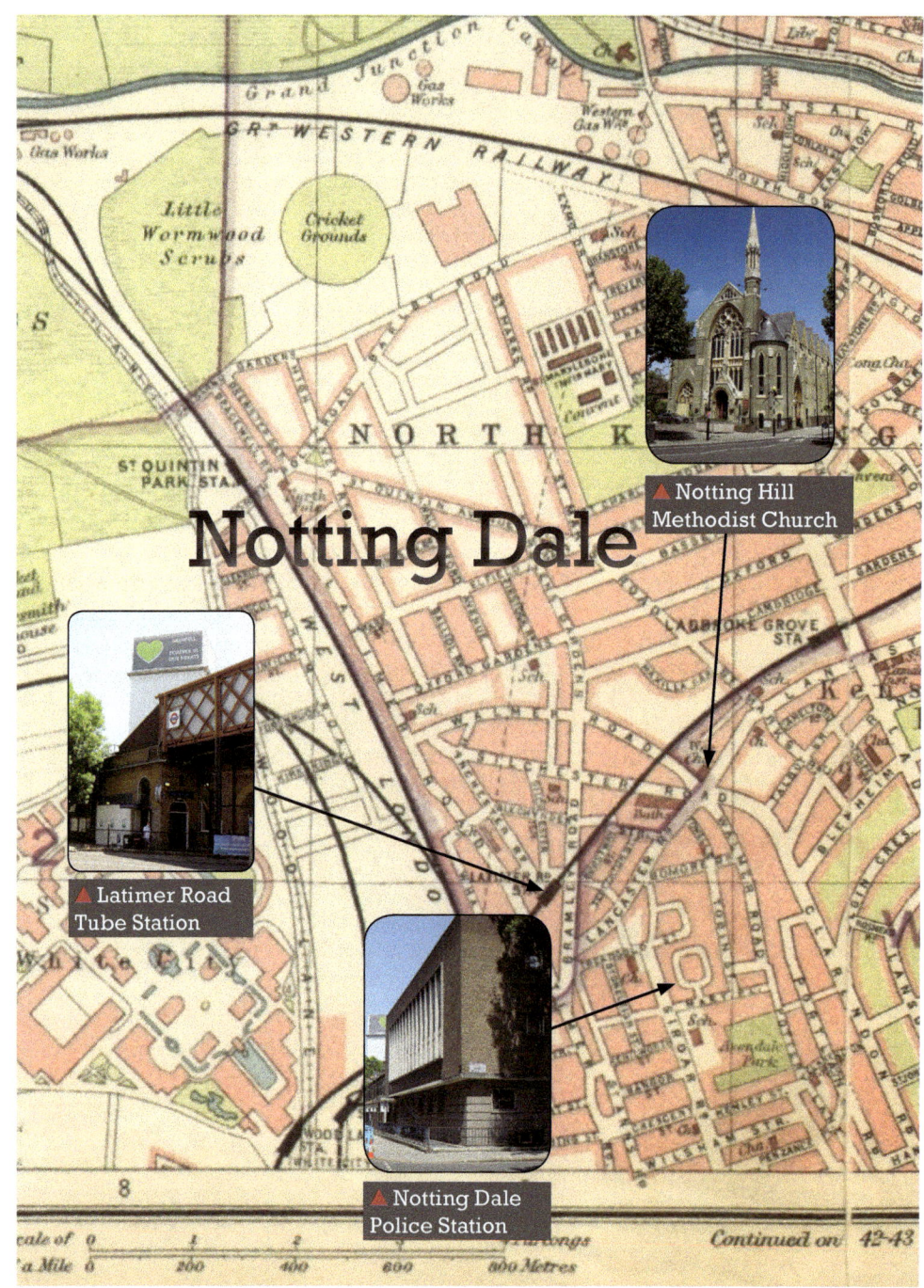

▲ Notting Hill Methodist Church

▲ Latimer Road Tube Station

▲ Notting Dale Police Station

Part 2: The historic environment: Notting Hill, c.1948–c.1970

This unit on the historic environment of Notting Hill complements your studies of Migrants in Britain. This was a very mixed area of London. In the nineteenth century, Notting Hill had large Victorian style houses owned by wealthy middle class families who had servants to do the cooking and housework. Notting Dale was always a rougher working area. By 1948 a lot of the wealthier houses had also become run-down. Houses were divided into small units and were not looked after very well. Our study focuses on the poorer parts where landlords were willing to rent property to immigrants from the Caribbean in the 1950s and after. The area we know as Notting Hill was actually divided into three separate districts:

- ☐ Notting Dale - where residents such as Irish families had migrated in the nineteenth century
- ☐ Colville - which was also known as 'Brown Town' by the 1960s because of the concentration of Caribbean people living there
- ☐ Notting Hill - the wealthy area at the top of the hill.

▲ Corner of Talbot Road and Portobello Road

▲ 34, Tavistock Crescent

▲ 105-107, Talbot Road

▲ 24, Colville Terrace

▲ Hedgegate Court

▲ 8, All Saints Road

Portobello Road

This key street ran through the Colville area and into the wealthier part of Notting Hill. There was a fresh food market on Portobello Road from the nineteenth century, but in the late 1940s traders selling antiques and other household items set up stalls there as well. By the 1960s, stallholders were selling Caribbean vegetables for the new migrant community.

This unit is made up of four enquiries. You will be investigating each enquiry question through the use of historical sources. Keep detailed notes on the different kinds of sources that you study within each enquiry. Think carefully about how useful each source could be in answering the enquiry question. Record your work in a table like this for each enquiry:

Source number and caption	Type of source (photo/text/ official/ personal)	Evidence it suggests	Usefulness for this enquiry

PART 2: The historic environment: Notting Hill, c.1948–c.1970

6.1 How did Caribbean people try to make themselves 'at home' in Notting Hill in the 1950s and 1960s?

Clifford Fullerton on Talbot Road

Clifford Fullerton was born in Kingston, Jamaica, in 1910. He became a tailor, but he was also a trumpet player in The Deluxe Syncopators, a top Jamaican band. In 1948, he was one of the Jamaican immigrants who arrived in England on the SS *Empire Windrush* (see page 85). In a recorded interview Fullerton explained what had motivated him to make that journey (see Source 1).

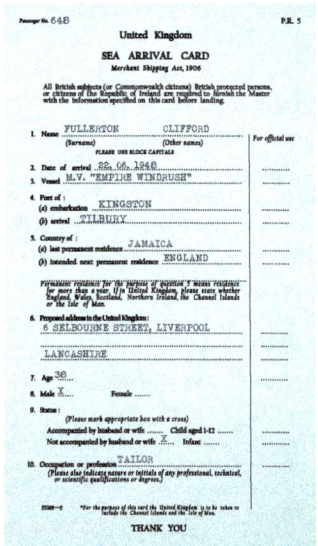

▲ **Source 2** A representation of Clifford's landing card from the *Windrush* voyage of 1948. This was part of an art installation that highlighted the destruction of the originals (see page 93). It gives his destination as Liverpool, but we know he didn't go there. He went to the shelter in Clapham (see page 85)

> **Source 1** Fullerton's testimony about the *Windrush* journey from an interview with him in 1988. You can listen to Clifford presenting this testimony on the Black Cultural Archives website at: https://blackculturalarchives.org/sounds-of-the-rush:
>
> Well, I came because I wanted to gain more knowledge towards making tailor-made clothes. As a matter of fact, I wanted to get down to the fundamentals of drafting … I used to be able to spot an Englishman after some experience … And they were always well dressed you know, quite big difference between they and the American … their suits were well styled and the drapery that was infused in those stylings, I admired very much. So, I would like to come to England to be able to learn that method of work.

a) What do we learn from Fullerton's testimony about his motivation for migrating to England?
b) How far do you think his motivation would help him make himself 'at home' in Notting Hill?
c) What can we learn from Clifford's reproduced landing card (Source 2) to help our enquiry?
d) Why might Clifford have given his address as Liverpool? (There were three tailors on board the *Windrush* who listed the same street in Liverpool as their address.)

Talbot Road tailor's shop

Clifford's first job was with the Salvation Army, making uniforms, and he enrolled to study and qualify on English terms. His wife and two-year-old son joined him in 1949. In 1952 he completed his studies and was admitted as a member of the City of London Master and Foreman Tailoring Society: its first black member. Clifford Fullerton's first premises was a basement on Talbot Road, opposite an electrical appliances shop at 105–107 Talbot Road, owned by Mr Cohen, a Jewish businessman. Fullerton eventually took over Cohen's place, but it was a struggle (see Source 4 on page 115, and page 118 has a picture of 105–107 Talbot Road in 2021).

a) How far does this photograph show that Clifford Fullerton has been successful in Notting Hill?

◀ **Source 3** Clifford Fullerton in his tailor's shop, photographed by George W. Hales in April 1969

6.1 How did Caribbean people try to make themselves 'at home' in Notting Hill in the 1950s and 1960s?

Source 4 Clifford's testimony about how he came to acquire his premises with the support of the Jewish owner of the shop, Mr Cohen:

I went to Beale and Capp (property agents on Ladbroke Grove) and told them I wanted to buy. 'No, no sir, not you'. The next day Mr Cohen rang me and asked me if I took the money to Mr Beale and Capp. I said 'Yes, but they wouldn't take it'. He drove up in his car and asked me to jump in. When we came to Beale and Capp's office… he said, 'This man came in to your office, and brought the money to buy that shop in Talbot Road, and you wouldn't take it from him… I know him, he's done me a lot of favours and I'm going to see that he gets the shop. It's mine. You take his money now.' And by two o'clock they had someone doing the lease!

a) What do we learn about inter-community relations in Notting Hill from Source 4?

b) How far do Sources 1–4 suggest that Clifford Fullerton assimilated into English society in Notting Hill?

Teddy Boys

Clifford Fullerton's testimony (see Source 5) tells us that Teddy Boys were some of his best customers, so we should investigate who they were. Their nickname came from the word 'Edwardians' which referred to the period of British history at the start of the twentieth century when some young men dressed in similar clothing.

Source 5 Clifford speaking about the fortunes of his business, from his testimony:

The best times for the shop were the '50s. All the fellows wanted a hand-made suit, mostly West Indians and we worked a lot with the Teddy boys. At that time Teddy boys used to be well-dressed. We had brought a lot of our styles, which I incorporated in what I had learnt. When you incorporate English and West Indian styles, you get a master suit.

◀ **Source 6** Teddy Boys attending the church service for youth held by American evangelist Renee Martz at Kensington Temple, Notting Hill, on 16 July 1956

a) How far does this photograph support what Clifford Fullerton said about the Teddy Boys?

b) What further questions could you ask about this service to find out more about why the Teddy Boys were there?

Do your own research to explore these questions.

Teddy Boys in the press

Most of the British newspapers of the mid-1950s would have given you a quite different impression of these youths. Although they were very smartly dressed, their behaviour was sometimes rough and aggressive.

Dance Halls, Cinemas, Police and Public join forces to wage WAR ON TEDDY BOYS

The menace of the Teddy Boys is being broken by the concerted action of police and public … to combat the thugs in Edwardian dress who, often armed with bicycle chains, knuckle-dusters, and razors, have terrorised peace-loving citizens for two years.

▲ **Source 7** A front page of the *Sunday Dispatch* paper in June 1955

a) How does this newspaper report clash with the view in the picture (Source 7)?

b) How far does the newspaper report contradict Clifford Fullerton's statement in Source 5?

1 Who were Clifford's customers in the 1950s? Why would the suits be important to them?

2 What further questions could you ask to investigate your answers more deeply?

3 How important was Fullerton in making Caribbean people 'at home' in Notting Hill in the 1950s?

PART 2: The historic environment: Notting Hill, c.1948–c.1970

▲ Source 8 Hedgegate Court in June 2021

Housing in Notting Hill

Bombing of Britain during the Second World War had caused a lot of destruction and so, throughout the 1950s Britain was experiencing a severe housing shortage and the government's solution to this crisis was to remove the controls that kept rents low. Their thinking was that if landlords could charge higher prices they would maintain properties better in order to attract renters and also to divide large homes into smaller apartments. When the Rent Act of 1957 removed controls on rent, there was a large increase in the number of houses of multiple occupation (HMOs) in Notting Hill.

Peter Rachman

Perec (Peter) Rachman (1919–62), a Polish immigrant, became especially skillful at finding loopholes in the 1957 Rent Act to make large profits from renting property in Notting Hill. Rachman grew wealthy in the early 1950s through criminal activities, particularly managing sex workers; he began buying properties in Notting Hill in the mid-1950s. Most of the properties he acquired were large, five-storey homes that had been designated as 'unfit for human habitation' in the 1930s, but were still being lived in. Hedgegate Court in the heart of Colville was a small street of such houses (see Source 8).

Most of the initial tenants in Rachman's properties were white, working-class people who had legal protection against high rent increases, even after the introduction of the 1957 Rent Act. Rachman could only make huge profits if he could force these tenants out and he did this by using extreme methods, such as: hiring local thugs to intimidate them with threats of violence; encouraging tenants in adjoining flats to play loud music; moving prostitutes into the building; and, on occasion, having family pets killed to send tenants the message that they needed to leave. If these tactics didn't work, Rachman would send thugs to the property to cut off the water and electricity, remove the locks and eventually empty tenants' belongings onto the street.

Once Rachman had cleared his properties of existing tenants and brought new ones in, he could legally increase the rent to whatever he liked. One group of people willing to pay over the odds for accommodation was the Caribbean migrants who had been arriving in London in growing numbers over the previous decade. Many white landlords refused to let property to Caribbean people due to widespread racism, and Rachman, despite being motivated by greed, was able to present himself as an immigrant who, out of goodwill, was helping fellow immigrants find accommodation.

> 1. How was Peter Rachman able to acquire so much property in Notting Hill?
> 2. How far was Rachman a 'friend' to Caribbean immigrants?
> 3. How did Peter Rachman contribute to the transformation of Notting Hill?

> a) If each window represents one room, roughly how many families would live in this row of four houses?
> b) How useful is this photograph as evidence of Rachman's exploitation of Caribbean renters?
> c) How could you follow up this source to find out more about Rachman's exploitation of Caribbean renters?

▲ Source 9 Rachman properties on Chepstow Road, Colville, in 1963. When these houses were built, they would each have housed one family. When these became HMOs, there would be one family in each room in the house

> In the exam you will be asked to consider what you should do to 'follow up' a particular source in an enquiry. You should pick out particular details of the source that you want to find out more about, and decide what further questions you want to ask. Then, think about the different kinds of sources that you could use to understand that aspect better.

6.1 How did Caribbean people try to make themselves 'at home' in Notting Hill in the 1950s and 1960s?

Rachmanism

Peter Rachman died of a heart attack in November 1962, at the age of 43. Early in 1963 the Profumo Scandal (see page 128) revealed the connections between Rachman and criminal activity, particularly organised prostitution. Politicians and national newspapers made Rachman a notorious national celebrity. Study these two sources:

> **Source 10** Leader of the Labour Party and future Prime Minister, Harold Wilson speaking about Peter Rachman in the House of Commons, July 1963, the year after Rachman died:
>
> The Rachman story is a lurid version of a story which goes on in more sombre, sepia tones in other slum empires and other cities as well as London. ... Rachman was only part of a much wider conspiracy ... the disease of Rachmanism, if one likes to call it that, can be described in this way. It is to buy controlled properties at low prices and to use every means, legal or illegal, blackmail, or physical violence, to bring about evictions ... because the Rachman property empire was a vice empire.

> **Source 11** An article in the *Guardian* newspaper by Jean Stead published on 6 August 1963, described the ongoing legacy of the methods that Rachman had started in Notting Hill:
>
> The new committee say the same men with their heavy-glove accomplices are still collecting the rents today, even though Rachman has gone, and the landlords' names have changed. The rent agents' methods remain the same. Families are still put forcibly onto the street, tenants are still terrorised out by a variety of legal and illegal methods ... The choice for the tenants is always overcrowding and high rents or the streets. In these circumstances, the human choice is to settle for the evil you know.

4. What do these sources suggest about how difficult it would be to wipe out Rachman's legacy in Notting Hill?
5. Discuss how people in Notting Hill could have acted to undo the legacy of Rachmanism.

a) What kind of language did Wilson use to describe Rachman and his activities? Look at the words 'lurid', 'slum', and 'vice', for instance, and check their meanings.

b) Why do you think Peter Rachman's name became a synonym for greed and criminality?

a) What does Stead suggest had happened in Rachman's Notting Hill properties after he died?

b) How does Stead present Peter Rachman's legacy?

a) Joe Gannon's 1970 documentary called *Getting It Straight In Notting Hill Gate* described the area as, 'the world's most integrated ghetto'. How far do you think Phillips' picture supports Gannon's description?

▲ **Source 12** Silchester Road in 1967, before it was demolished to make way for a new roadway, photographed by Charlie Phillips

Photographs of 1960s' Notting Hill

Two photographers have provided important sources for our enquiries: Charlie Phillips (pages 117 and 119 and George W. Hales (pages 114 and 135). Look for more of their Notting Hill photographs online. Compare their work. How are their approaches different?

PART 2: The historic environment: Notting Hill, c.1948–c.1970

▲ **Source 13** A photograph of 105–107 Talbot Road, Fullerton's shop, in June 2021

Leisure time on Talbot Road

The colour bar was a feature of life in Notting Hill for its Caribbean immigrants (see page 96). They did not have open access to the same facilities that white English people did which meant that they had no choice but to organise their own services and entertainment. In this way they brought their own culture to the area.

Barbers

We know that the Caribbean men liked to look smart, and they helped Clifford Fullerton to have a successful tailoring business. A vital part of looking smart was to have a good haircut ('trim'). White English barbers would not have been skilled at cutting black men's hair, so we can assume that there would have been a number of black barbers operating in the Colville district.

We found a photograph of Aston George Clifford working in his barbershop on the same day in 1969 that the photographer took the picture of Clifford Fullerton (Source 3 on page 114). See if you can find that photograph online.

Duke Vin and his sound system

'Duke' Vincent Forbes was born in Kingston, Jamaica, in 1928. When he grew up he became involved in a local **sound system** and was nicknamed 'Shine-Shoes Vinny' because of his smart appearance. In 1954 he and a friend stowed away on a boat headed to England and he carried his records with him.

Source 14 Duke Vin talking about his early months in England in a film made in 2008:

When I come here in '54, I look around and I see what's up. I said 'boy, the country is dead'. Nowhere a sound, nowhere to go; I said 'this is not me'. I couldn't find where to go for a dance. So, I start my own sound system, 1955. I made the first sound system in the country. People, used to use them grams*. Grams didn't have the power to keep the crowd going.

*'Gram' refers to a gramophone player that would be used in people's houses to play records.

Fullerton's basement blues

The Caribbean people in Colville held many of their 'blues' parties in their own accommodation, but these were usually small rooms (see page 116). Duke Vin looked for a larger venue for his sound system.

Source 15 Clifford Fullerton explains how he got involved with a blues club:

Black people had nowhere to go to amuse themselves, if they go to the West End they reject them, they don't want them. So I used to do a big business here with the tailoring and they used to complain to me that they had nowhere to go. They said to me 'You have a big place here, why don't you help us?' So I considered it ... but I was afraid of disturbance. My business was getting on alright and everybody respect me so I didn't want anything to disturb it. So, after a time with them pressing and pressing, I gave in. So I started a blues club, this was in 1957, but it wasn't really me who wanted it, two other fellas decide to manage it, to run it themselves, so I eventually gave in. It was going alright and then all of a sudden the bad elements started to creep in ... I came here to behave myself and learn what I can, I did not come here to break no law ... So we had to close it, it was sad but I had to do something.

The Tickler

The blues club moved from Talbot Road to premises on All Saints Road, which later became the Mangrove restaurant (see page 135). Duke Vin's sound system was called The Tickler and, in 1958, he was in London's first '**sound clash**', winning the crowd's approval against his friend and rival Count Suckle. Duke was one of the people who brought Jamaican music to England, including ska (see page 107).

a) How did Clifford Fullerton end up hosting a blues club for Duke Vin's sound system in his basement at Talbot Road?

b) What does Clifford's testimony tell us about the tensions between assimilation and autonomy in his immigrant story in Notting Hill?

The Tickler playlist

This is a list of top tunes that Duke Vin might have played each year between 1958 and 1964. (You can find these tunes on YouTube.)
1958 Laurel Aitken: 'Boogie in My Bones'
1959 The Blues Busters: 'Early One Morning'
1960 Owen Gray: 'Jenny Lee'
1961 Buster's Group: 'Little Honey'
1962 Ska-talites: 'Snow Boy'
1963 Prince Buster: 'Madness'
1964 Millie: 'My Boy Lollipop'

1 Compare the contribution of Duke Vin and Clifford Fullerton to making Caribbean people 'at home' in Notting Hill in the 1950s and 1960s.

6.1 How did Caribbean people try to make themselves 'at home' in Notting Hill in the 1950s and 1960s?

Shebeens

Caribbean migrants, like a lot of people, wanted to be able to enjoy alcoholic drinks at their parties and nights out. The English enjoyed going to their local pubs (public houses) to drink, but many of those pubs operated a colour bar. **Shebeens** were places where Caribbean migrants could purchase alcohol as well as dance to the sound system, smoke, and sometimes gamble as well. Venues in England have to have a licence to sell alcohol and operate gambling, and licences were not granted to the shebeens, which made them illegal.

▲ **Source 16** The corner of Talbot Road and Portobello Road, site of the Piss House, in June 2021

> **Source 17** Johnny Edgecombe was a petty criminal in Notting Hill in the 1960s and a key figure in the Profumo Scandal (page 128). He described his shebeen in his book *Black Scandal*, published in 2002:
>
> There was a front room where you could listen to the latest sounds … In this room was a bar, where we served any type of drink you wanted. Next door in the bedroom was the casino … where people sat and played poker … In the front room would be some nice jazz going down, with people drinking and smoking dope. I would roll joints myself, and sell them for five shillings a spliff. While the men were gambling, the chicks sat around getting stoned and drunk.

> **Source 18** The testimony of an unnamed Caribbean immigrant is recorded in Mike and Charlie Phillips' book *Notting Hill in the Sixties*:
>
> Sometimes we gambling in Bell Street and they playing 79 and one of the pots would be £150 (*about £3,500 in 2021*). In them days! £5 a stake … If you think of the Klondike [see box], that's how we used to live. The police didn't take kindly to it. A lot of things made them annoyed … the police used to regularly raid them, kick their speakers in … That aggravated the blacks no end and gave them the determination to persevere and the whole police hatred came out of that.

a) What activities were going on in Edgecombe's shebeen? Distinguish between the legal and illegal activities.

b) Why did the speaker in Source 18 describe Notting Hill as like the 'Klondike'?

Klondike was the location of a famous 'gold rush' in the 1890s. Thousands of people arrived to try to get rich quickly through gold digging. The place was a wild frontier town where drinking and gambling dominated social life.

The Colville pub: the 'Piss House'

On the corner of Talbot Road and Portobello Road was a pub called The Colville. Unlike a lot of bars, this pub happily served Caribbean immigrants. It also had a lot of Irish customers. The pub was affectionately nicknamed the 'Piss House'.

▲ **Source 19** Customers at the bar of the 'Piss House' on Talbot Road in 1969, taken by Charlie Phillips

a) How far does Charlie Phillips' picture of the 'Piss House' bar show that Caribbean people were welcome in pubs in Notting Hill in the 1960s?

2 Review the work you have done for this enquiry. Discuss the challenges and opportunities that Caribbean migrants faced in Notting Hill in the 1950s and 1960s. How far do you think they 'made themselves at home'?

3 What further evidence could you seek out to answer the enquiry question?

119

PART 2: The historic environment: Notting Hill, c.1948–c.1970

6.2 How did racial tensions spill over in Notting Hill in 1958–59? What were the consequences?

This is your second enquiry question in your study of Notting Hill. Use a table for sources like the one on page 113. The development of racist ideas and actions is central to this enquiry.

▲ **Source 1** Latimer Road tube station in June 2021

SIR OSWALD MOSLEY

A British politician who led the British Union of Fascists in the 1930s. This was an openly anti-Semitic organisation that engaged in street violence. Mosley was on friendly terms with Hitler and in the Second World War he was imprisoned by the British government as an enemy sympathiser.

After the War he re-entered politics with his Union Movement and campaigned against immigration using racist ideas about migrants from the Caribbean. Mosley hoped to re-enter Parliament in the late 1950s as the MP for North Kensington.

Growing tension in Notting Hill

The already difficult lives for the residents of North Kensington had been made worse in the 1950s by a national housing shortage that was exploited by landlords. Other social problems such as crime, increasing gang activity and unashamedly racist groups stoking division, added to these tensions.

Racial hatred

In the weeks before August 1958, when the tensions came to a head, **fascist** organisations like the Union Movement and the League of Empire Loyalists distributed leaflets urging the white residents of North Kensington to 'protect your jobs – stop coloured invasion'. Racist attitudes towards Caribbean migrants had led to a few isolated attacks in the build-up to the Notting Hill riots, but the catalyst was the outbreak of violence against black migrants over a hundred miles north on 23 August 1958, in Nottingham. The Nottingham riots had the same root causes as the those about to begin in Notting Hill and the catalyst was the same: the strong hatred a section of white working-class men had for inter-racial relationships.

The riots begin

On 29 August 1958, outside Latimer Road tube station, a white Swedish woman, Majbritt Morrison and her Jamaican husband, Raymond, began arguing with one another. The argument grew increasingly loud and attracted the attention of passers-by. At some point during their quarrel someone from the crowd shouted a racial slur at Raymond. Majbritt and Raymond stopped arguing and she confronted the person who had abused her husband. The abuse was then aimed at her as some of the white people in the crowd called her 'a black man's trollop' and other similarly offensive terms. In time, some of Raymond's Caribbean friends came to his aid and a small fight broke out. Although there were no serious injuries from this incident, it was the start of one of the most infamous riots in modern British history. By 1 September the area had been rocked by three days of increasingly violent unrest.

Early on 1 September, the local MP, George Rogers, had toured the area in a van with a loud speaker calling for 'common-sense, decency and tolerance'. Later that afternoon, a young student from the Caribbean, Seymour Manning, came to Notting Dale to visit a friend. Manning must have been unaware of the riots that had gripped the area as reports described him exiting Latimer Road tube station with a 'confident stride'. As he turned into Bramley Road, Manning was confronted by a large group of white men blocking the road. Manning, realising the danger he was in, ran back towards the train station and, although the mob briefly caught him, he was able to escape to a nearby greengrocers. It was owned by an older white woman who was angry with the rioters for a number of reasons, not least the damage they had caused to shops during their rampage. She took Manning inside and bolted the doors. The mob of nearly 200 were heard shouting 'lynch him' as Manning hid inside the grocers. It took police in cars and on horseback, and over twenty constables, half an hour to disperse them.

In the course of the riots that followed, police arrested 140 people during the two weeks of violence, with 108 of them being charged. Roughly two-thirds of those charged were white people and the rest were from the Caribbean, most of whom were charged for possession of weapons.

?

1. What role did racist political groups play in causing the riots?
2. Imagine you were the local MP during the height of the riots. What could you say to the crowd to encourage the two sides to refrain from rioting and violence?

6.2 How did racial tensions spill over in Notting Hill in 1958–59? What were the consequences?

Experiences of the Notting Hill riots

The three sources on this page can help you to investigate the experiences of the riots on Caribbean migrants and local white citizens.

Source 2 From the novel *Absolute Beginners* by the white English author Colin MacInnes; he wrote extensively about life in West London in the 1950s and was also an anti-racist campaigner:

Because what I'd just seen in there made me feel weak and hopeless: most of all because, except for that old vegetable woman (who I bet will go straight up to heaven like a supersonic rocket when she dies – nothing can stop that one), no one, absolutely no one, had reacted against this thing. You looked round to find the members of the other team – even just a few of them – and there weren't any. I mean, any of us …

a) What do we learn from Source 2 about the depth of racist attitudes in Notting Hill in the 1950s?

b) To what extent would the novel this quote was taken from be considered a useful source about the Notting Hill riots?

◀ **Source 3** A Caribbean woman speaking to detectives shortly after a racist mob attacked her home

Source 4 From an interview given by Baron Baker in 1994 about the Notting Hill riots. Baker, born in Jamaica, had served in the RAF between 1940 and 1944:

When they told us that they were coming to attack that night I went around and told all the people that was living in the area to withdraw that night … We made preparations at the headquarters for the attack. We had men on the housetop waiting for them, I was standing on the second floor with the lights out as look-out when I saw a massive lot of people out there. I was observing the behaviour of the crowd outside from behind the curtains upstairs and they say, 'Let's burn the n_____s, let's lynch the n_____s.' That's the time I gave the order for the gates to open and throw them back to where they were coming from.

I was an ex-serviceman, I knew **guerrilla warfare**. I says, 'Start bombing them.' When they saw the Molotov cocktails coming and they start to panic and run. It was a very serious bit of fighting that night, we were determined to use any means, any weapon, anything at our disposal for our freedom. We were not prepared to go down like dying dogs. But it did work, we gave Sir Oswald Mosley and his Teddy boys such a whipping they never come back in Notting Hill. I knew one thing, the following morning we walked the streets free because they knew we were not going to stand for that type of behaviour.

a) What can you learn about the Caribbean responses to the Notting Hill riots from Sources 3 and 4?

b) What do Sources 3 and 4 suggest about the ferocity of the attack against the Caribbean community of Notting Hill?

c) Study Source 4. How could you follow up this source to find out more about Caribbean responses to the riots in Notting Hill in late August and September 1958? In your answer, you must give the questions you would ask and the types of sources you could use.

PART 2: The historic environment: Notting Hill, c.1948–c.1970

▲ **Source 5** Site of the White Defence League bookshop at 74 Princedale Road, Notting Dale, in 2021

The aftermath of the riots

The days of rioting provoked a good deal of serious reflection in different parts of society. Britain was aware that its global reputation would be affected by such outbursts of racial violence.

Teddy Boys and the courts

Around a hundred people were arrested during the nights of rioting on the streets of Notting Hill, and about two-thirds were white youths. The magistrates' courts dealt with these cases and gave out fines and prison sentences ranging from a few weeks to several months. Nine youths – who were part of the group known as Teddy Boys – had been arrested on 24 August, before the riots, and were charged with wounding and actual bodily harm on a number of black men during a night of vicious attacks. These young men were tried at the Old Bailey on 15 September and they pleaded guilty. The judge, Justice Cyril Salmon, himself a descendent of Jewish immigrants in the East End, issued heavy sentences of four years' imprisonment.

> a) How does Justice Salmon explain his use of severe punishment for the young men's offences?
> b) How far does Justice Salmon's decision 'scapegoat' the nine youths for the country's racial problems?

Source 6 This is an extract from Justice Salmon's statement in the trial of the nine white youths:

It was you then who started the whole of this violence in Notting Hill. You are a minute and insignificant section of the population who have brought shame upon the district in which you lived, and have filled the whole nation with horror, indignation and disgust … Everyone, irrespective of the colour of their skin, is entitled to walk through the streets in peace, with their heads erect, and free from fear … I am determined that you and anyone anywhere who may be tempted to follow your example shall clearly understand that crimes such as this will not be tolerated in this country, but will inevitably meet in these courts with the stern punishment which they so justly deserve.

Source 8 This is part of the transcript of a filmed interview with Colin Jordan, founder of the White Defence League, recorded after the riots:

The facts are the people not having previously a political outlet for their indignation at the evils of the coloured invasion, resorted to blind violence. We now offer them a political outlet, and we therefore think that our presence in this area militates against violence rather than for it …

There are many immediate evils of the coloured invasion … the most important is the long-term one of mass interbreeding … We believe in preventing the evils … by stopping all further coloured immigration into our country and by **repatriating**, with every humane consideration, the coloured immigrants who were already here.

"Go on, boy! I may have lost that war, but my ideas seem to be winning…"

◀ **Source 7** This cartoon by Victor Weisz (also known as 'Vicky') appeared in the *Daily Mirror* in September 1958

> a) How does Vicky make a connection between the Notting Hill riots and Nazi Germany?
> b) How far does this cartoon confirm the scapegoating of the Teddy Boys?

Racist political activity

There were a number of extreme right-wing political groups that wanted to put an end to non-white immigration in Britain. Many people felt that these ideas had fuelled the racial tensions that led to the riots. One of the newest groups was the White Defence League; its headquarters was in a house in Notting Dale, at 74 Princedale Road. (See Sources 5 and 8.)

> a) How did Colin Jordan try to make use of the riots to justify his group's appearance in Notting Hill?

6.2 How did racial tensions spill over in Notting Hill in 1958–59? What were the consequences?

Claudia Jones and the 1959 carnival

Claudia Jones was a leading figure among London's Caribbean immigrants, and she had just launched her *West Indian Gazette* (*WIG*) newspaper (see page 126) before the riots happened. She was deeply upset by the riots and wanted to take action to unite Caribbean people and give them hope in the midst of these hostilities. Claudia launched a Caribbean Carnival Committee in November 1958 to organise a cultural event that would show the positive contribution Caribbean people could make to British society. This carnival was held indoors, in St Pancras Town Hall, because it was to take place around January or February, the same time as carnivals in the Caribbean.

The first Caribbean Carnival, 30 January 1959

The evening's entertainment included a cabaret of Caribbean and black British artists singing and dancing, including the jazz singer Cleo Laine, and the Trinidad All Stars and HiFi steel bands. There was also a carnival queen beauty contest for Caribbean women, to show that black women should not be seen as less beautiful than white women.

However, Claudia Jones saw the carnival as much more than an enjoyable evening's entertainment. Proceeds from sales of the carnival souvenir brochure were 'to assist the payment of fines of coloured and white youths involved in the Notting Hill events'. The title of the brochure was 'A people's art is the genesis of their freedom'.

> **Source 10** These are extracts from the message that Claudia Jones published in the souvenir brochure for the first Notting Hill Caribbean Carnival:
>
> Rarely have the energies of a people indigenous to another homeland been so quickly and spontaneously generated to such purpose as witness the work of the Caribbean Carnival Committee 1959, … A pride in being West Indian is undoubtedly at the root of this unity: a pride that has its origin in the drama of nascent [emerging] nationhood, and that pride encompasses not only the creativeness, uniqueness and originality of West Indian mime, song and dance – but is the genesis of the nation itself … We have a determination to make the *WIG* Caribbean Carnival an annual event.

a) How does Jones connect the 1959 Caribbean Carnival to national pride of Caribbean people?

▲ **Source 9** The blue plaque commemorating Claudia Jones in Notting Hill

Claudia Jones (1915–64)
Claudia Jones was born on the British Caribbean island of Trinidad in 1915. From 1924, Jones' family lived in New York, where Claudia became politically active during the Great Depression of the 1930s. She became a journalist and joined the Young Communist League of America. In 1955, Jones was imprisoned for her activism, and when released she was deported to Britain after the British authorities in her native Trinidad refused to let her return to the colony.

a) How far does the photograph show that the 1959 Caribbean Carnival gave Caribbean people in London a new confidence and sense of pride?

b) How could you follow up Source 11 to find out more about the success of the first Caribbean Carnival of January 1959?

1 How far do the sources on these pages show that the Notting Hill riots had important consequences, both positive and negative?

▲ **Source 11** Some of the people attending the Caribbean Carnival at St Pancras Town Hall, 30 January 1959

123

PART 2: The historic environment: Notting Hill, c.1948–c.1970

▲ Source 12 A photograph of Kelso Cochrane taken in May 1959

Kelso Cochrane Kelso Cochrane was born on 26 September 1926 in Antigua and when he grew up he followed his father's trade as a carpenter. In September 1954 he travelled to England; his plan was to stay for a few years and study law. However, when he met Olivia Ellington, a student nurse from Jamaica, he decided to marry and settle in England.

a) How did Castle claim that Cochrane's death was part of a much bigger racial problem for Britain?

The Hola Massacre

The British authorities in the colony of Kenya in east Africa reacted to the Mau Mau campaign for independence by holding thousands of the black African people in detention camps and forcing them to work. When a group at the Hola camp refused to work, eleven of them were beaten to death on 3 March 1959.

a) What seems to be the priority for this Home Office advisor?

The death of Kelso Cochrane, 1959

The brutal murder of Kelso Cochrane in May 1959, following the riots of the previous year, caused considerable anxiety about the state of race relations in Notting Hill, and in the country as a whole. Right-wing extremists, led by Mosley, hoped that this would help his campaign in the General Election later that year.

The murder

Kelso Cochrane injured his thumb at work, and when it kept hurting, he decided to go to Paddington General Hospital on the night of Saturday 16 May. On his way home, after midnight the next day, Kelso was attacked by a group of young white men at the corner of Southam Street and Golborne Road. He was killed by a stab wound to his chest. There were witnesses to the attack, and the police did detain two suspects, but they did not gather enough evidence to charge them with the murder. The police do not appear to have searched the suspects' homes for weapons, and they held them in adjoining cells in the police station. Nobody was ever charged with Kelso Cochrane's murder.

Official responses to Cochrane's murder

The three sources here show the responses of public officials to the tensions surrounding Cochrane's murder. Compare the different approach they each take to the situation.

Source 13 Detective Superintendent Ian Forbes-Leith, the youngest officer ever to reach that rank in the Metropolitan Police, issued a statement to the press on 19 May:

We are satisfied that it was the work of a group of about six anti-law white teenagers who had only one motive in view: robbery or attempted robbery. The fact that he happened to be coloured doesn't come into the question.

He also told one journalist:

You will be doing the community a service by refraining from any suggestion that this is a racial murder.

a) Why might Forbes-Leith have been so adamant that Cochrane's death was not a racial murder?

Source 14 Labour MP Barbara Castle spoke about the responsibility for the violence and murder in Notting Hill on 18 May 1959:

You read today of the horrible race murder in Notting Hill. It is not for us to sit back and blame the Teddy boys. We have on our own shoulders the responsibility of failure to our coloured brethren not only in this country but in our colonies, where some of them are still languishing in detention centres under colonial rule. If the British people are going to allow those responsible for the beating to death of eleven detainees in the Hola detention camp in Kenya to go untraced and unpunished, then we shall have given the green light to every n_____r-baiting Teddy boy in Notting Hill.

Source 15 A month after the murder, the Home Secretary was asked to make a statement against racist behaviour. A Home Office advisor was against the idea:

The most impressive point was, in my view, the need of the coloured people in Notting Hill to be reassured. If a broadcast of the kind proposed had been made very soon after the murder of Kelso Cochrane it might have been very helpful and reassuring.

The position now is very different. My impression is that immediate interest in the subject has subsided in the country generally … It seems to me that it would appear odd for the Secretary of State, out of the blue, to make a broadcast specially to condemn racial intolerance at this time …

1 How do Sources 13, 14 and 15 help you to find out about the impact of Kelso Cochrane's death?

6.2 How did racial tensions spill over in Notting Hill in 1958–59? What were the consequences?

Community responses to Kelso Cochrane's murder

Black community groups were very clear that Kelso Cochrane's death was a racial murder. Alao Bashorn of the Committee of African Organisations led a group of African and Caribbean activists who presented an open letter of protest to the Prime Minister, Harold Macmillan, stating:

> Kelso Cochrane was murdered because he was coloured … Are we to be mauled down just because we are black?

These activists included Claudia Jones and David Pitt (see page 96), and they organised a burial committee to raise funds for Cochrane's funeral. On 1 June there was a twelve-hour demonstration on Whitehall near 10 Downing Street, and a small group of demonstrators carried placards displaying slogans such as 'Speak Out against the Colour Bar' and a drawing of Cochrane's photograph. However, his funeral five days later would be a much more powerful public ceremony.

▲ **Source 16** The blue plaque commemorating Kelso Cochrane's murder at the corner of Southam Street

Cochrane's funeral

Over a thousand people turned out on the streets of Notting Hill near St Michael and All Angels Church on Ladbroke Grove on 6 June 1959, for the funeral procession of Kelso Cochrane. The Bishop of Kensington led the service, and a number of African and Caribbean politicians attended.

MOSLEY IN THE 1959 ELECTION

Many people blamed Mosley for stirring up the hatred that lay behind racial violence and Cochrane's murder. In the October General Election, the voters of Kensington North soundly rejected him: Mosley got less than 10 percent of the vote.

▲ **Source 17** A crowd of onlookers at Ladbroke Grove watches the arrival of the hearse for the funeral of Kelso Cochrane

a) What impression does the photograph give of the impact of Kelso Cochrane's death on the communities of Notting Hill?

b) How could you follow up Source 17 to find out more about the significance of Kelso Cochrane's funeral for the communities of Notting Hill?

> **Source 18** Journalist John Gale visited the area where Kelso was killed and interviewed some of the youths in the area. He published some of what they said on 24 May in his 'Notting Hill Notebook' in the *Guardian*:
>
> 'I live 200 yards from where that coloured bloke was done. Couldn't care two hoots. One less. What happens if they find the bloke and they top him? There'll be riots then. And they'll keep on.'

a) How far does this source overturn the ideas that are conveyed by Source 17?

2 Which of Sources 12 to 18 would prove most useful to you in studying the impact of Kelso Cochrane's death?

PART 2: The historic environment: Notting Hill, c.1948–c.1970

The *West Indian Gazette*

One of Claudia Jones' first projects in London in March 1958 was to establish the *West Indian Gazette* (WIG), a monthly newspaper that aimed to publish national and global news that Caribbean people in Britain would be interested in reading. The newspaper published news from the Caribbean and also publicised black cultural developments like the work of Cy Grant and Corinne Skinner-Carter in entertainment.

> **Source 19** In the first edition of the *West Indian Gazette*, Claudia Jones wrote:
>
> There are at least 80,000 good reasons why we believe a West Indian newspaper is necessary and will be welcomed. They are the 80,000-odd West Indians now resident here. Together we form a community with its own wants and problems, which our own paper alone would allow us to meet.

a) What does this source tell us about Claudia Jones' vision for the *West Indian Gazette*?

> **Source 20** In September 1959, the WIG reported a speech made by the world-famous African-American actor-singer and activist Paul Robeson at an event hosted by Claudia Jones:
>
> This has become one of my favourite newspapers as I am sure it is of yours – a paper courageous, deeply human, concerned with a decent life for us all; a paper calling upon us all to realise that a new day has come; a time when we all can and must be free ... How proud we must always be of our mothers and sisters, newly-born Harriet Tubmans and Sojourner Truths, struggling without stint without sparing any sacrifice ... I am proud to be on this platform by the side of a dear, dear friend Claudia Jones ...

a) How does Paul Robeson emphasise the significance of Claudia Jones in his speech? (Research the other two African-American women he mentions, if you have not heard of them.)

a) What do you learn from this source about Claudia Jones' political views and priorities?

b) How far do you think Jones' vision for the work of the newspaper has developed since 1958?

> **Source 21** In November 1961, Claudia Jones wrote this front-page opinion piece on the forthcoming Commonwealth Immigrants Act (see page 86):
>
> BUTLER'S COLOUR-BAR BILL MOCKS COMMONWEALTH
>
> It is now nakedly revealed to be an official colour-bar against the coloured and the poor ... For if one is rich enough the same formality – to have a job to come to; a house to go to, and enough money to sustain you – its provisions need not apply. But if you are an immigrant from Kingston or Port-of-Spain, from Karachi or New Delhi, acceptance would first have to be vetted not only by Mr Butler but would have to be accompanied by a voucher from the Ministry of Labour.
>
> There is no excuse for this Bill. In London alone, official figures show that of 50,000 needing jobs there are 87,000 vacancies today! Regards housing, it is not the immigrant who causes the shortage, but the failure of a Tory Government to build them, the infamous Rent Act, and the diverting of funds for people's social needs to the programme to build H-bombs ...

a) What impression do you get of a) Claudia Jones and b) the fortunes of the WIG from this picture?

1. Explain what you have learned about the impact of Claudia Jones on the Caribbean community in Notting Hill and other parts of the country in this enquiry. Which sources have you found most useful?

▶ **Source 22** Claudia Jones working in the office of the *West Indian Gazette*

6.2 How did racial tensions spill over in Notting Hill in 1958–59? What were the consequences?

Carmen Bryan's story

Carmen Bryan was caught up in a crisis about the government's immigration policies in 1962. She arrived in Britain from Jamaica in 1960 and worked in a factory. Carmen was engaged to be married and was living in the Notting Hill area. In 1962 she was made redundant from her job. She was struggling to survive and was caught shoplifting £2 worth of goods from a shop: nylon stockings, tomatoes, milk and a clothesline. The Commonwealth Immigrants Act had just come into force (see page 86). Carmen pleaded guilty in court. It was her first offence.

The magistrate took account of her situation and gave her a conditional discharge, which meant she would not be punished unless she committed a new offence. However, he also decided that she 'seemed not to have settled down successfully' in Britain and ordered her deportation under the Commonwealth Immigrants Act! Carmen spent around six weeks in Holloway Prison waiting to hear if the Home Secretary, Henry Brooke, would agree to deport her. Brooke did sign the deportation, but Labour MPs mounted a huge commotion in parliament. A week after saying he thought shoplifting was a serious offence, Brooke changed his mind and cancelled the order. Carmen was free to marry her fiancé, Leslie Walker, but they soon decided to go back to Jamaica.

> **Source 23** An extract from the Hansard records of the debate in the House of Commons on 23 July 1962; the speaker is George Brown, Labour MP. Brown is describing what happened to Carmen Bryan after the magistrate recommended her deportation back to Jamaica:
>
> Miss Bryan was then taken straight off to prison… It was four weeks before anybody was told anything about it… During that four weeks during which the (Jamaica) High Commission knew nothing about her… Miss Bryan was never told what her rights were… she appears to have been told of a number of things that might happen to her if – you know – she did not fit in. Miss Bryan was very frightened, very worried. She thought that she was not only up against the law here, but that her friends, her own people, had deserted her, since no one came to her.

a) Study Sources 23 and 24. How useful are these sources for an enquiry into how well Caribbean immigrants settled in Notting Hill in the 1960s?

b) Study Source 23. How could you follow up Source 23 to find out more about political debate regarding Caribbean immigrants in 1962?

▲ **Source 24** A photograph taken of Carmen Bryan on her wedding day, 30 July 1962

PART 2: The historic environment: Notting Hill, c.1948–c.1970

> This is our third enquiry question in our study of Notting Hill. The development of community activism is central to this enquiry.

6.3 How far did Notting Hill communities change during the 1960s?

The 'swinging sixties' in Notting Hill

The period of the 1960s was a time when some young people were strongly opposed to the expectations of their parents' generation, and some chose to live a 'counterculture' that often shocked older generations. Notting Hill became a centre of this 'underground counterculture' in what was often referred to as the 'swinging sixties'.

Counterculture

Young adults of the 1960s became more politically motivated and active than previous generations. Following the Profumo Scandal (see box), many rejected the idea that the country's serving politicians were trustworthy. The Profumo Scandal of 1963 showed the problems with politics very clearly. The rebellion of young people against the establishment was expressed in their dress, music, sexual behaviour and use of recreational drugs. A small minority actually dropped out of society altogether, and became known as 'the underground'.

> **The Profumo Scandal, 1963**
>
> Government Defence Minister John Profumo was revealed to have had an affair with a young model, Christine Keeler, who had another lover who was a Russian spy. Profumo resigned in disgrace.

> **Source 1** Barry Miles, an underground author and bookseller, born in Cheltenham in 1943, spoke about Notting Hill in the 1960s in a book of interviews published in 1988:
>
> The hip society in Notting Hill in those days was basically very involved with the West Indians. They were the only people around who had good music, they knew all about jazz and ska and bluebeat. They also smoked rather good dope ... We knew a lot of black guys like Michael de Freitas and Asiento Fox, known as Priest, who was the head of the Rastafarians.

> a) Why did Barry Miles connect Caribbean immigrants so strongly with the growing counterculture of the 1960s?

> **Rastafarians**
>
> A religious movement that developed in Jamaica in the 1930s. It emphasises a strong spiritual connection with Africa, and Ethiopia in particular. Rastafarians refer to Western society as 'Babylon' and regard it as oppressive to black people. This feeling of oppression was made worse by the strict enforcement of the laws against cannabis, a drug which Rastafarians used in their worship.

> **Source 2** Courtney Tulloch spoke about the significance of Rastafarians in Notting Hill in 1988:
>
> The Rastafarians were the first group in the Western World to actually drop out of white society, saying, 'This is Babylon, we don't want anything to do with it'.

> a) How does Courtney Tulloch confirm the importance of Caribbean people for the 'underground'?

The London Free School and Rhaune Laslett

Rhaune Laslett was born in 1919 in the East End of London. Her mother was a Native American and her father was of Russian Jewish heritage. She worked in social care and arrived in Notting Hill in the early 1960s, living at 34 Tavistock Crescent, where she set up a children's playgroup. In March 1966, Laslett joined John 'Hoppy' Hopkins, a photographer and political activist, and others, to establish the London Free School (LFS). The project was part of the counterculture, and the idea was for older people with skills in fields like photography, film and music, to tutor young people. The project produced a radical newsletter that became the *International Times* in October 1966.

> **Courtney Tulloch** was born in Jamaica in 1942, and came to join his parents in England at the age of sixteen. He was a community activist in Notting Hill, and went on to become a social worker and lecturer at Goldsmiths, University of London.

> **Source 3** Courtney Tulloch wrote about the London Free School in the activist newspaper *International Times* at the end of August 1967:
>
> There are many ways of being secure in places like Notting Hill. One of them is to show actively and bravely that one loves people. Unashamedly love people ... Anyone and everyone belongs to the Free School Community – artists, writers, painters, trippers, labourers, dolers, singers, meters, hangers-on ... policemen ... and blacks ... All Saints Church Hall has the hippiest vicar in London and soon we hope the hippest cops.

> a) How does Tulloch see the vision of the London Free School?
> b) How far does the London Free School appear to belong to the 1960s underground?

6.3 How far did Notting Hill communities change during the 1960s?

Rhaune Laslett's Notting Hill Street Festival

In 1965, Rhaune Laslett appears to have organised a small street event for the children in her playgroup, with a truck for them to stand on and Caribbean music playing. Laslett then teamed up with Michael X (see page 130) to develop a festival and raise the profile of the Free School. In 1966, the event became a week of festivities called The Notting Hill Fayre and Pageant. Russell Henderson's steel pan group was a leading attraction (see Source 8), and joining them were Ginger Johnson and his Afro-Cubans, and Agnes O'Connell and her Irish Girl Pipers. The children dressed as Charles Dickens characters for the big parade through the streets. This became an annual celebration and by the mid-1970s it had grown into the Notting Hill Carnival.

▲ **Source 4** 34 Tavistock Crescent, site of Rhaune Laslett's playgroup, in June 2021

> **Source 6** Larry Ford, a Trinidadian who ran a restaurant called Fiesta One on Ledbury Road, talked about the LFS festival:
>
> Mrs. Laslett, a charming Polish [*sic*] woman, who used to have a playgroup in Tavistock Crescent, looked after all sorts of kids – black, white, pink, blue – the lot. Well, she had a little parade, trucks for the kids – that was the first time … we saw all these trucks going by and all the kids and thought, that's nice.

> **Source 7** Rhaune Laslett commented on their motivation in launching the street festival:
>
> We felt that although West Indians, Irish, Africans and many other nationalities all live in a very congested area, there is very little communication between us. If we can infect them with a desire to participate, then this can only have good results.

> **Source 8** Russell Henderson, the steel pan band leader spoke about Rhaune Laslett:
>
> Rhaune Laslett was a good woman … I'd hate to think people have left her out (of the Carnival story) because of her colour. I never went on the streets playing for anyone before I did it for her … Carnival started with Mrs. Laslett.

▲ **Source 5** The plaque remembering Rhaune Laslett-O'Brien at the corner of Portobello Road and Tavistock Road

> a) How useful are Sources 6–8 in establishing the significance of Rhaune Laslett's festival for the development of the Notting Hill Carnival?
>
> b) What further historical questions would you want to ask about Laslett's festival in an enquiry into the Notting Hill Carnival?

Notting Hill Neighbourhood Service

This was a development of the Free School. Laslett set up the service to give legal, financial and other advice to local people. The *Kensington News* said this was:

> an organisation run on entirely selfless and voluntary lines by dedicated men and women who have turned a part-time aid programme into a full-time social mission.

Courtney Tulloch said:

> Rhaune Laslett's Notting Hill Neighbourhood Service, was a Free School throw-up. It shows how a comparative **square** [Rhaune Laslett] can in the end swing with a community.

> 1. How far do you think Rhaune Laslett would have been pleased with the judgements of both the *Kensington News* and Courtney Tulloch (see 'Notting Hill Neighborhood Service' box)?
>
> 2. The blue plaques for Rhaune Laslett-O'Brien (she married in 1968) and Claudia Jones (page 123) have been placed opposite each other on the corner of Portobello Road and Tavistock Road in the heart of Notting Hill. Why do you think this was done?

PART 2: The historic environment: Notting Hill, c.1948–c.1970

Michael de Freitas

Notting Hill had always been a place where some of London's criminals operated illegal activities, including drug-dealing, prostitution and gambling, or all three. If job opportunities were in short supply, because of the colour bar, it was tempting for some Caribbean people to seek income from crime; Michael de Freitas was one of those who 'hustled' for a living.

Michael the migrant

Michael de Freitas was born in Trinidad in 1934 to a black mother and a white Portuguese father, who lived on the island of St Kitts. His grandmother in Trinidad did not allow Michael to play with black children because he was of mixed heritage, but he was also shunned by the white children. In 1948, he went to live with his father, but after an argument, went back to Trinidad and became a seaman, travelling the world on Norwegian trading freighters. In 1957, he left the sea and came to Britain, first to Cardiff, and then London, where he found a place to live in Notting Hill. He met a young Guyanese mother called Desree, and they set up home with her daughter in Southam Street (near to where Kelso Cochrane was killed). De Freitas tried to get a regular job but without success.

▲ Source 9 24 Colville Terrace, photographed in June 2021

> **Source 10** Michael de Freitas wrote an autobiography in 1968. In it he describes the search for a room in Notting Hill:
>
> It was impossible to believe you were in twentieth-century England: terraced houses with shabby, crumbling stonework ... garbage and dirt strewn all over the road, derelict cars ... a legion of filthy white children swarming everywhere and people lying drunk across the pavement.

> a) What does de Freitas tell us about his reaction to seeing the conditions in Notting Hill in 1957?
>
> b) How far is his account supported by what you have already learned about housing in Notting Hill?

Hustling in Notting Hill

De Freitas quickly became involved in organising small-scale prostitution and robbery just before the Notting Hill riots broke out in 1958. He was arrested during the riots, but afterwards he seized opportunities offered by the attention that the authorities were giving to the area. In his autobiography, de Freitas describes a visit by a group of MPs, whom he took to a shebeen, where they drank and mixed with sex workers and learned 'how to roll a marijuana cigarette'. Through these activities he came to the attention of Rachman (page 116) who hired him as an 'enforcer' for collecting rents. De Freitas also moved into a Rachman property at 24 Colville Terrace. He lived with Desree at the top of the house, and his mother, who arrived from Trinidad, managed a brothel in the basement. This brought him more trouble with the police.

▲ Source 11 Michael X photographed in 1967

De Freitas and the Racial Adjustment Action Society

In January 1965, de Freitas met the African-American activist Malcolm X in London and took him on a tour of Notting Hill. He started to refer to himself as Michael X, and then, after announcing his conversion to Islam, used the name Michael Abdul Malik. He took a greater interest in political activities, and soon afterwards joined two Guyanese activists, Roy Sawh and Jan Carew, to set up a new black political organisation in London called the Racial Adjustment Action Society (RAAS). The new group was a direct challenge to the more moderate CARD (see page 96), because RAAS demanded swift action against racism in Britain, and self-defence against racist aggression.

> 1 Compare Michael X's story of life in Notting Hill with Clifford Fullerton's (pages 114–115 and 118). What further questions would you want to ask about the two men? What sources could you use to answer them?

Michael Abdul Malik and 1960s counterculture

Malik became involved in a number of the activities in the countercultural life of Notting Hill in the mid-1960s. He was part of the London Free School and may have helped them set up in a former Rachman property in Powis Square, as well as helping Mrs Laslett with the street festival. Malik also helped Courtney Tulloch with Defence, which was a black legal advice project. Through his American connections, Malik met with Muhammad Ali when he came to London to fight British boxer Henry Cooper in May 1966. He persuaded Ali to visit the London Free School playgroup.

▲ **Source 12** Tavistock Crescent, photographed in June 2021

> **Source 13** A Caribbean resident of Notting Hill in the 1960s gave his testimony to Mike Phillips about Malik:
>
> He was a visionary right, all this Carnival down in the Grove [Ladbroke Grove] is down to Michael you know. Down to Michael because what happened was those guys decided to come on the road one day and they come up out and they following he, and the next thing he's talking to this woman who's running a neighbourhood thing down on Tavistock Road, Ronnie Laslett and they twos up. And that kick off from there ... I ain't say make an epitaph to him ... but.

▲ **Source 14** Muhammad Ali on the doorstep of 34 Tavistock Crescent. Mrs Laslett's head can be seen on the right of the picture, under Ali's chin

> The following questions are in the style of your examination:
>
> **a)** How useful are Sources 13 and 14 for an enquiry into Notting Hill community action in the 1960s?
> Explain your answer, using Sources 13 and 14 and your knowledge of the historical context.
>
> **b)** Study Source 14. How could you follow up Source 14 to find out more about community activism in Notting Hill in the 1960s?
> In your answer, you must give the question you would ask and the type of source you could use.

PART 2: The historic environment: Notting Hill, c.1948–c.1970

▲ **Source 15** Notting Hill Methodist Church, in June 2021

Improving housing in Notting Hill

Following the Notting Hill riots of 1958 and the murder of Kelso Cochrane in 1959, Notting Hill became the focus of many people and organisations around Britain committed to economic and racial justice.

Notting Hill Methodists and Kenrick

The Notting Hill Methodist Church was transformed in 1960 by a new approach to teamwork and social activism, led by three ministers who were inspired by a project in East Harlem, New York, USA. They began to organise local community groups with the aim of encouraging Kensington Borough Council to buy properties in order to rent them to the local poor who were either homeless or living in sub-standard accommodation. The council was unco-operative until the mission to improve housing in Notting Hill was energised by the arrival of the Reverend Bruce Kenrick, who moved into a small, decaying house on Blenheim Crescent in Notting Hill in 1962. This part of Notting Hill was particularly run down and landlords, such as Peter Rachman, made the situation worse by demanding high rents for accommodation.

Source 18 The conclusion of a letter written by Kenrick to the Labour Government, in 1967, asking for national funds to pay for renovating properties:

At well under £500 per person the conversion of existing properties is much cheaper than new building – and they will last at least 30 years. The capital will be repaid twice as fast as repayments for new building over 60 years. And damn it (if I may use a biblical expression) homeless people will be housed much faster.

Source 16 Kenrick saw the actions of landlords like Rachman up close:

I came home from work one summer evening and saw all the belongings of our next-door neighbour piled out on the street. While she was out with her child, the landlord had come and removed all her things from the one room, locked the door and dumped them all on the pavement.

Source 17 An extract from an article by Kenrick called 'Homeless near a Thousand Homes' published in the *New Christian* magazine, November 1965:

What struck me painfully was the extent to which people's problems stemmed from damnable housing conditions. Marriages broke up because one or other partner could no longer stand the strain of living in one room with a stove and sink squeezed into one corner.

a) What do Sources 16, 17 and 18 reveal about Kenrick's ambitions for his work in Notting Hill?

b) How far are his experiences supported by what you have already learned about housing in Notting Hill?

The Notting Hill Housing Trust

Kenrick, along with other activists, formed the Notting Hill Housing Trust (NHHT), which had its headquarters in a four-storey, terraced house at 107 Blenheim Crescent. Their aim was to buy up property, renovate it to an acceptable standard and then rent it at a fair price to the needy poor. Their first fundraising activity was running a stall in Portobello Road market in December 1963, which raised the modest sum of £24. Soon after that, Kenrick was given an interest-free loan of £7,000 by an initially anonymous donor. He was allowed to take the bold step of using this money to pay for a national advertising campaign, rather than immediately spending it on a property (see Source 18).

The impact of the Notting Hill Housing Trust

Kenrick, through the NHHT, raised thousands of pounds in its first year and used these funds to buy 5 houses and to house 57 people. The NHHT continued to raise large sums of money and within five years had become a major presence in West London, housing nearly 1,000 people. As the NHHT acquired more property it became increasingly prominent both in Notting Hill and throughout the country. The Trust received more donations for its work, some of which were spent on advertising campaigns that further increased its prominence, which in turn led to even more donations. The Trust quickly outgrew its offices and, in 1969 moved to All Saints Road, down the road from the popular Caribbean-owned Mangrove restaurant (see page 125), putting it right at the heart of the community it wanted to serve.

1. How useful are Sources 16, 17, 18 and 19 for studying the work of the Notting Hill Housing Trust?
2. What further sources could you seek out to explore the story of Kenrick's work?

6.3 How far did Notting Hill communities change during the 1960s?

a) What impact do you think the NHHT wanted the advert to have on the *Observer* readers? Pick out three words or phrases from the text that support your answer.

b) How accurate are the details used in the NHHT's appeal? Use information from the rest of this book to support your points.

c) Why do you think that the NHHT chose not to use a Caribbean immigrant family for the image in their advert?

d) What arguments would people have used in letters of support or complaint to the editor of the *Observer* newspaper responding to the NHHT advert.

Source 19 The full-page advertisement that the NHHT placed in the *Observer* newspaper on 28 June 1964

Housing and self-help: Pansy Jeffrey

The need to support the growing community of Caribbean migrants in Notting Hill had become clear and urgent after the riots of 1958. The Kensington Citizens' Advice Bureau appointed Pansy Jeffrey, a nurse, social worker and recent migrant to Britain from Guyana, to work in the community and help improve race relations in the area. She was an active member of the Notting Hill Social Council, which was established to give residents a greater say in how their area was being run, as well as the Notting Hill Housing Trust. Jeffrey would go on to found the West Indian Mothers Club in 1960 to bring together Caribbean women who, as recent migrants, felt isolated in Notting Hill. In 1980, she also established the Pepper Pot Club in Ladbroke Grove as a community centre for elderly Caribbean people.

Housing and self-help: Pardner schemes

The Caribbean migrants brought an important self-help practice with them. It was a form of financial credit based on group savings. A group would be formed and each person would contribute a fixed amount each week to the 'hand'. That large sum would be given to a different person each week, in order. The allocation of the hand could be arranged according to particular individual needs. The pardner scheme could help people find a deposit for accommodation.

PART 2: The historic environment: Notting Hill, c.1948–c.1970

6.4 How far was the trial of the Mangrove Nine in 1971 'the high water mark of Black Power in Britain'?

> This quote, which forms our fourth enquiry question in our study of Notting Hill, is from Rob Waters' book *Thinking Black – Britain 1964–1985*. The development of local power and protest is central to this enquiry.

'Black Power' in Notting Hill

The African-American civil rights movement had already inspired black British activism in the Bristol Bus Boycott (page 98) and the establishment of CARD (page 96). Both of these followed the non-violent resistance of the African-American protest movement. But in the mid-1960s new thinking emerged in the USA under the banner of Black Power. Malcolm X pioneered this idea, but since his death in 1965 its most prominent leaders were Stokely Carmichael, Angela Davis, and the Black Panthers under Huey Newton and Bobby Seale. Black Power encouraged new energy in black British politics, and struck fear in the minds of British authorities.

Stokely Carmichael and Michael X, 1967

In July 1967, Stokely Carmichael and Angela Davis visited London to attend a counterculture conference called the Dialectics of Liberation, held at the Roundhouse, Camden, and Michael X took them on a tour of Notting Hill. The visit revived Michael's RAAS group and provoked a campaign against Black Power in the British press, which called Carmichael 'the most effective preacher of racial hatred at large today'.

British authorities were scared that American-style race riots would happen in England. The Special Branch of the police pressed Carmichael to leave England before he was due to speak at an RAAS meeting in Reading. Michael X took his place, and made references to violence against white people. He was arrested under the terms of the Race Relations Act (page 97) and sentenced to a year in prison for racial hate speech.

▲ **Source 1** Stokely Carmichael speaking at the Dialectics of Liberation conference in London, July 1967. Michael X is sitting on his right

> **Source 2** The extract from Michael X's Reading speech that led to his imprisonment:
> In 1958 I saw white savages kicking black women in the streets and black brothers running away. If you ever see a white laying hands on a black woman, kill him immediately.

> **Source 3** Darcus Howe commenting on Michael X:
> Michael X was quite simply a hustler, who was hustling off of Malcolm's name. He was a crook! He didn't set up anything you could commit to – he didn't organise anything political.

a) What events of 1958 was Michael X referring to?
b) How does this quote help explain the authorities' fear of Black Power?

Darcus Howe and the Black Eagles

Darcus Howe arrived in London from Trinidad in 1961 to study law, but after two years had become a postman. In the evenings he was a regular at the Rio café in Notting Hill (see page 135). Howe had been involved in the struggle for independence in Trinidad and was drawn to local political activism on behalf of Caribbean people in London. He had been a childhood friend of Stokely Carmichael and was inspired by the Roundhouse conference to promote Black Power in London. Howe recognised that the police would be a serious barrier to activism in Notting Hill.

In 1968, Howe set up a protest group called the Black Eagles, whose major activity was a programme of street patrols observing the police in the 'execution of their duty' to try to protect black people from harassment. This was modelled on the practice of the Black Panther Party in the USA, which used armed patrols. The Black Eagles were not armed, but they were aggressively targeted by police, and the organisation petered out by 1969. Michael X was involved with the Eagles, but Howe's older cousin CLR James, a Trinidadian intellectual and Marxist activist, advised Howe to have nothing to do with Michael X.

a) Why might Darcus Howe have come to this judgement of Michael X?
b) How useful is Howe's comment in assessing the significance of Michael X in Notting Hill?

6.4 How far was the trial of the Mangrove Nine in 1971 'the high water mark of Black Power in Britain'?

Frank Crichlow

Frank Crichlow was another of the famous Trinidadian immigrants of Notting Hill. He arrived in London in 1953, and after working for British Rail for a while and then playing in a successful band, he opened the Rio café at 127 Westbourne Park Road in 1959. His vision was to provide a place for people from the various Caribbean islands to integrate. It became a focal point for the counterculture and community activism.

> **Source 6** Frank Crichlow commenting on the Rio in an interview in 1979:
> It got a lot of hustlers … [and] attracted people who were rebellious and a bit smart, those with street intelligence, those for whom the factory was not their speed.

> a) What did Crichlow mean by 'those for whom the factory was not their speed'?
> b) Why would Darcus Howe spend most evenings and weekends at the Rio in the early 1960s?

▲ **Source 4** 127 Westbourne Park Road, in June 2021, site of the Rio café

The Mangrove

Some of the people at the centre of the infamous Profumo scandal of 1963 (see page 128) had been customers of the Rio, so from then on the police and media paid unwelcome attention to the café. Crichlow was prosecuted several times by the police for minor offences, such as 'allowing music and dancing without a licence' and 'bad language'. Police harassment prompted Crichlow to close the Rio in 1968 and open a new restaurant at 8 All Saints Road, called the Mangrove. Celebrities, such as Nina Simone, Jimi Hendrix and Vanessa Redgrave, were customers, as well as black intellectuals like CLR James.

▲ **Source 5** The site of the Mangrove at 8, All Saints Road, in June 2021

▲ **Source 7** Frank Crichlow in his Mangrove restaurant in Notting Hill, photographed by George W. Hales in 1969

> **Source 8** Barbara Beese, a local activist and Darcus Howe's partner, said in a later interview:
> The Mangrove was the 'go to' place for black people in the area. Frank used to make the most wicked pineapple punch … There was good food, but there was way more to it. All Saints Road and the Mangrove were popularly known as 'the frontline'. People associate that term with drug dealing, but what I mean is that the Mangrove was the frontline of support for the black community. They'd get advice on things like housing. Frank's restaurant became the crucible for all of that.

> a) What impression of the Mangrove restaurant do you get from Sources 7 and 8?
> b) What sources do you think might present a less positive view of the Mangrove? Why would it be important to study those sources as well?

British Black Panther Party

Obi Egbuna, a Nigerian writer, established a British Black Panther Party in April 1968. Like Howe, Egbuna was concerned about the police, and he published an article in which he argued that black people should fight back 'like one big black steamroller to catch up with the cops'. He was sent to prison for 'conspiring to murder police officers'. The Panthers carried on, setting up community support and work in schools.

PART 2: The historic environment: Notting Hill, c.1948–c.1970

▲ **Source 9** A photograph of All Saints Road in June 2021

a) What do the police authorities say about Black Power in England? Why do you think they make this claim?

b) How does this document deal with the issue of police harassment of the Mangrove?

Source 12 An extract from a police report on the march, written on 11 August 1970, commenting on the pig's head:

This action alone in my submission shows this to be a procession called by people who are over aggressive and determined to exploit any situation to their advantage and not by people who are troubled about the social problems of some members of their community.

1 How far do Sources 10, 12, and 13 show the breakdown of relations between the police and Caribbean people in Notting Hill by 1970?

2 What further sources could you seek out to explore the story of the Mangrove protest in Notting Hill?

Police and the Mangrove

The Metropolitan Police in the Notting Hill area took a very different view of the Mangrove, seeing it as a 'den of iniquity and evil which was frequented by pimps, prostitutes and criminals' according to Constable Frank Pulley. The Notting Hill police put the Mangrove under even more scrutiny than the Rio, and there were several raids on the restaurant for misuse of drugs, despite the local knowledge that Crichlow had a firm policy against the use of illegal drugs on the premises. No drugs were found in any of the raids. The key police officer to push the raids was Constable Pulley (see page 137).

Source 10 From Metropolitan Police's Special Branch document on the Mangrove situation written on 11 August 1970:

Although, as has been pointed out, the concept of 'Black Power' is alien to this country, its advocates are politically dangerous for, in an effort to make their philosophy more meaningful to the coloured community, they have set out deliberately to manufacture complaints of white oppression. This process has been characterised by an **intemperate** anti-police campaign.

The Mangrove protest

In August 1970, community leaders decided that they had had enough of the police treatment of the Mangrove. The Action Group in Defence of the Mangrove was formed and they staged a protest march on Sunday 9 August, led by Howe, Jones-LeCointe (see page 137), Beese and Crichlow.

The demonstrators carried a lot of banners and Beese carried a pig's head. The pig was a derogatory symbol of the police, taken from its use in American struggles. The route of the protest march was to pass the three police stations in the area: Notting Dale, Notting Hill and Harrow Road. 'Kill the Pigs!' and 'Hands off Black People!' were two of the chants used by the protesters.

◀ **Source 11** Mangrove protest march, Notting Hill, London, 1970

Source 13 Darcus Howe made a speech to the protesters on All Saints Road before the march set off:

It has been for some time now that black people have been caught up in complaining to police about police; complaining to magistrates about magistrates; complaining to judges about judges; and complaining to politicians about politicians. We have become the own [sic] shapers of our destiny as from today … What our objective is today, and what it's going to continue to be is a concerted, determined attempt to prevent any infringement of our rights.

6.4 How far was the trial of the Mangrove Nine in 1971 'the high water mark of Black Power in Britain'?

The Mangrove Nine

The demonstration on 9 August 1970 remained non-violent for two hours as the protesters marched to Notting Dale and then Notting Hill police stations. However, on the final leg of the route to Harrow Road, violence broke out and nineteen people were arrested, mostly for possessing offensive weapons, assault and threatening behaviour. Of the nineteen, nine were to end up at the Central Criminal Court (Old Bailey) accused of the serious offence of inciting a riot.

The magistrates' court

The police decided to introduce the serious charge of riot against the leaders of the Mangrove demonstration, and that case was heard at Marylebone Magistrates' Court in January 1971. The police staked their case on the slogans that were chanted, arguing that 'Kill the Pigs!' should be taken literally. The magistrate, David Wacher, disagreed.

> **Source 15** From the record of the Marylebone Magistrates' hearing:
> Prosecution: One man said, 'We are going to smash up the Pig House'.
> Magistrate: But they passed at least one Pig House and nothing happened.

Wacher refused to accept the exaggerated ideas presented by the police, and dismissed the charges of rioting. However, the British government was not happy with this decision. The Home Secretary, Reginald Maudling, and police leaders wanted the Mangrove leaders to be severely punished as an example, so that the ideas of Black Power could be crushed for good. Nine of the demonstration's leaders were chosen and sent to the Old Bailey for a new trial on the same charge of inciting a riot.

> 3 Why did the British government overturn local justice in the case of the Mangrove Nine?

The Trial of the Mangrove Nine

The trial of Darcus Howe, Altheia Jones-LeCointe, Barbara Beese, Frank Crichlow and five others lasted twelve weeks in the autumn of 1971. The first two decided to represent themselves in court, which gave them the opportunity to confront police witnesses, including Pulley, directly. The trial began with a demand for an all-black jury, so that the ancient right to be tried 'by a jury of your peers' could be met. The judge dismissed the idea, but Howe and the others then used their right to reject over 60 of the potential jurors.

> **Source 16** Darcus Howe talked in an interview in 1980 about working-class support, in the absence of an all-black jury:
> We chose ... from the white working class ... sure in the belief ... that if there was any section of the population who could deliver us out of the mess in which we found ourselves, it would be white workers. And they did ... when I was making my closing speech ... one of the white women wept as I spoke.

The jury were faced with a choice between believing the evidence of the police or the evidence of the Nine. A number of witnesses spoke for the good character of Frank Crichlow and the positive atmosphere of the Mangrove restaurant, including the local Labour MP, Bruce Douglas-Mann. Such evidence contradicted the story that the police told, and in the end the jury decided in favour of the defendants. The Mangrove Nine were found not guilty of inciting a riot.

> 4 How did the Mangrove Nine case bring Notting Hill onto a national stage? Why had that happened?
> 5 Compare the way that Notting Hill had come to national attention in 1958 with the situation in 1970–71.

▲ **Source 14** Notting Dale Police Station (no longer in use), in 2021

PC Frank Pulley
Posted to Notting Hill police station in 1959, Pulley was awarded a medal for bravery in 1968 for tackling two armed criminals on Westbourne Park Road. Pulley was the focus of community anger against the police because of his fixation on the Mangrove.

Altheia Jones-LeCointe
Born in Trinidad, Jones-LeCointe's mother was a political activist for independence, women's rights and social justice. Altheia was an excellent chemistry student, and, in 1965, she came to University College London to undertake a doctoral study. She faced racism from lecturers and landlords. She led the Black Panthers when Egbuna went to prison, and increased their membership and community work.

PART 2: The historic environment: Notting Hill, c.1948–c.1970

▲ Source 17 The plaque at 8 All Saints Road, remembering Frank Crichlow

The Legacy of the Mangrove

The judge in the Mangrove Nine case, Justice Edward Clarke, had seemed unsympathetic to the defendants during the trial, but after the verdict he stated that the events had 'regrettably shown evidence of racial hatred on both sides'. This was the first time that anyone in authority in Britain had stated that there was a problem of racism in the police force; the Metropolitan Police made an unsuccessful attempt to get the statement withdrawn.

The significance of the Mangrove

Frank Crichlow went back to running the Mangrove restaurant, Darcus Howe joined Altheia Jones-LeCointe in the Black Panther Party, and PC Pulley left Notting Hill to work at New Scotland Yard. The police continued to raid the Mangrove. In 1988, Crichlow was found not guilty of drug offences, and the Metropolitan Police were ordered to pay him £50,000 in damages for false imprisonment, battery and malicious prosecution. The Mangrove closed down in 1992.

1 Use these sources and your own knowledge to explain the judgement of historian Rob Waters that the trial of the Mangrove Nine in 1971 was 'the high water mark of Black Power in Britain'.

Source 18 Ian Macdonald, one of the defence lawyers in the Mangrove case, said in a television documentary of the 1970s:

It seems clearly to have been an attempt by the state to prevent the growth of organised resistance within the black community, which had an independent leadership and that seems to me to have been the real point of the case … to smash that organisation before it got really solid firm roots within the community.

Source 19 Lord Boateng, Britain's first black cabinet minister (see page 96), speaking at Frank Crichlow's funeral service in 2012:

They were our places, and we welcomed a whole heap of people, black, white, African, Caribbean, Asian; film stars, musicians, community folk, lawyers, plenty of lawyers … all there in spaces that Frank made free, and there were people who couldn't stand that … and they did everything to destroy it; they did everything to take those places away from us … They were the people for whom the word 'Babylon' was invented.

a) What does Macdonald (Source 18) think lay at the heart of the authorities' issue with the Mangrove?
b) How far does Lord Boateng confirm Macdonald's much earlier view?
c) How far do you think these two people are in a strong position to make these judgements?

The story of the Mangrove Nine was presented in a feature film directed by Sir Steve McQueen, son of a Grenadian mother and Trinidadian father, as part of his Small Axe sequence about London's Caribbean communities through the 1970s and early 1980s.

Source 20 Letitia Wright, the actor who played Altheia Jones-LeCointe in the film, said:

[Steve McQueen] emphasised that the generation before us, of the elders that came from the Caribbean, were passing away and they hadn't seen themselves represented. It felt like it was a very important time to bring these stories to light.

a) What does Wright suggest about the significance of the Small Axe film, and the Mangrove case?

◀ Source 21 A still from the Steve McQueen Small Axe film *Mangrove*, showing the defendants in the Mangrove trial at the Old Bailey. The front row depicts Howe, Jones-LeCointe, Crichlow and Beese

6.4 How far was the trial of the Mangrove Nine in 1971 'the high water mark of Black Power in Britain'?

Communicating Your Answer: Notting Hill

These examination-style questions focus on the Mangrove restaurant and the events of 1970–71.

1. Study Sources A and B. How useful are Sources A and B for an enquiry into the Mangrove Nine (1970–71)? Explain your answer, using Sources A and B and your knowledge of the historical context.
2. Study Source B.
   How could you follow up Source B to find out more about the Mangrove Nine (1970–71)?
   In your answer, you must give the question you would ask and the type of source you could use.
   Complete the table below.

Detail in Source B that I would follow up:	
Question I would ask:	
What type of source could I use:	
How this might help answer my question:	

Source B Extracts from an interview with Frank Crichlow for a book by Mike and Trevor Phillips called *Windrush – the Irresistible Rise of Multiracial Britain*, published in 1998

Demonstrations was important at that time. Very important... When we called the demonstration Black Power was around and a lot of people gathered...

We were charged with very serious charges. Inciting members of the pubic to riot, affray, threatening behaviour, offensive weapons. Heavy stuff. And we had a big campaign. Darcus went up and down the country talking to different groups. We had support from the West Indies; we had support from America. And the trial started. Big trial. At the Old Bailey... we found out later that the trial got internationally known and the police made a mess of it, really.

◀ **Source A** A young woman standing outside the Mangrove restaurant on All Saints Road, Notting Hill, 10 August 1970

Part 3: Writing better history

Introducing the exam

Simply knowing a lot of content is not enough to achieve a good grade in your GCSE History exam. You need to know how to write effective answers to the questions. Pages 144–51 give you an insight into the exam and provide guidance on how to approach the different question types. This page and the next introduce the structure of Paper 1 of your exam. The guidance on page 142 will help you approach your exam with confidence.

Paper 1 is divided into two sections. Section A covers the **study of a historic environment** on Notting Hill, c.1948–c.1970. Section B covers the **thematic study** of Migrants in Britain, c.800–present.

Paper 1: Thematic study and historic environment

Option 13: Migrants in Britain, c.800–present

Time: 1 hour 15 minutes

You must have:

① Source Booklet (enclosed) with exam question paper.

Instructions

② • Answer Questions 1 and 2 from Section A.

③ • From Section B, answer Questions 3 and 4 and then **EITHER** Question 5 **OR** Question 6.

Information

④ The total mark for this paper is 52.

The marks for **each** question are shown in brackets.

SECTION A: Notting Hill, c.1948–c.1970

Answer Questions 1 and 2

⑤ 1 Describe **two** features of the 1959 Caribbean Carnival.   (Total for Question 1 = 4 marks)
   Feature 1: _____
   Feature 2: _____

⑥ 2 a) Study Sources A and B in the Source Booklet.
       How useful are Sources A and B for an enquiry into the reaction of the local community to the murder of Kelso Cochrane? Explain your answer, using Sources A and B and your own knowledge of the historical context.   (8 marks)

⑦   b) Study Source B.
       How would you follow up Source B to find out more about the reaction of the local community to the murder of Kelso Cochrane? In your answer, you must give the question you would ask and the type of source you could use. Complete the table below.   (4 marks)

   | Detail in Source B that I would follow up: _____ |
   | Question I would ask: _____ |
   | What type of source I could use: _____ |
   | How this might help answer my question: _____ |

   (Total for Question 2 = 12 marks)

   TOTAL FOR SECTION A = 16 MARKS

140

SECTION B: Migrants in Britain, c.800–present

Answer Questions 3 and 4. Then answer EITHER Question 5 OR Question 6.

3 Explain **one** way in which the experience of migrants in the years c.1100–c.1500 was similar to the experience of migrants in the years c.1500–c.1700. (4 marks)

4 Explain why the experience of migrants in Britain changed in the years c.1900–present. (12 marks)

> You may use the following in your answer:
> - the First World War
> - the Race Relations Act (1965).
>
> You **must** also use information of your own.

Answer EITHER Question 5 OR Question 6.

Spelling, punctuation, grammar and use of specialist terminology will be assessed in this question.

EITHER

5 'The impact on trade was the most significant consequence of migration to Britain in the years c.800–c.1500.' How far do you agree? Explain your answer. (16 marks)

> You may use the following in your answer:
> - York under the Vikings
> - Danelaw.
>
> You **must** also use information of your own.

OR

6 'There was little change in the reasons for migration to and within Britain in the years c.1500–c.1900.' How far do you agree? Explain your answer. (16 marks)

> You may use the following in your answer:
> - Trade
> - the British Empire.
>
> You **must** also use information of your own.

(Total for spelling, punctuation, grammar and the use of specialist terminology = 4 marks)

(Total for Question 5 or 6 = 20 marks)

Timing tip

It is important to time yourself carefully. One hour and fifteen minutes sounds a long time but it goes very quickly! Some students run out of time because they spend too long on Section A, thinking that it is worth spending half their time on this section. However, Section A is worth 16 marks whereas Section B is worth 36 marks. The final two questions you answer are worth over 60% of the total marks on Paper 1 (Question 4 is worth 12 marks and Question 5 or 6 is worth 20 marks) so you must allow yourself enough time to answer them fully. This shows the importance of having a time plan and sticking to it.

Look at the plan on the sticky note to the right. You could use this plan or develop your own and check it with your teacher.

> *Questions 1 and 2 approx. 25 minutes*
>
> *Questions 3 and 4 approx. 25 minutes*
>
> *Either Question 5 or 6 approx. 25 minutes*

PART 3: Writing better history

Planning for success

1. The Source Booklet
The exam paper on pages 140–41 gives you an idea of what your exam will look like. We have not included the Source Booklet. For practice, use the sources and activities in Part 2 of this book (pages 112–39). Make sure you spend time reading and annotating the sources in the Booklet before you attempt Question 2 in the exam.

2. Follow instructions carefully
Read the instructions very carefully. Some students miss questions they need to answer, while others waste time answering more questions than they need to. Remember to answer **both** parts of Question 2 and to choose between **either** Question 5 **or** Question 6. You will also see that for Question 1 you need to describe **two** key features, whereas with Question 3 you only need to explain **one** way in which people's reactions were similar.

3. Think carefully about which question to answer
You need to decide whether to answer Question 5 or Question 6. Do not rush your decision. Think carefully about which question you will perform best on. Plan your answer – it is worth 16 marks, nearly a third of the total marks for the paper.

4. Spend time de-coding the questions
The marks for each question are shown in brackets. This gives you an idea of how much you need to write, as does the space for your answer on the exam paper. However, do not panic if you do not fill all the space. There will probably be more space than you need and the quality of your answer is more important than how much you write. The most important thing is to keep focused on the question. If you include information that is not relevant to the question you will not gain any marks, no matter how much you write!

Read each question carefully before you start to answer it. Use the advice on de-coding questions on page 143 to make sure you focus on the question.

5. Describing key features
This question asks you to describe two features of an aspect of the historic environment you have studied. Headings on the exam paper help you write about each feature separately. Advice on how to gain high marks is on page 144.

6. Evaluating the usefulness of a source
This question asks you to evaluate how useful two sources are for a specific enquiry. Use the Source Booklet to annotate the sources. Make sure you use your own knowledge to place each source in its historical context.

This is a challenging task. Page 145 explains how to approach this question.

7. Following up a source
This question has four parts. You need to fill in the table on the exam paper. Page 146 provides advice on this question.

8. Exploring similarity and difference between two historical periods
This is the first question that tests you on your knowledge and understanding of migrants in Britain from c.800 to the present. It could ask you to explain a similarity or difference between the key features of two historical periods. Page 147 explains how to answer this question.

9. Explaining why migration to and within Britain changed (or stayed the same)
Questions such as this test your ability to write effective explanations. You may be asked to explain why the reasons for migration changed or why there was little change in the experiences of migrants during a period. Pages 148–49 will help you to write a good answer to this question.

10. Using the stimulus material
When you attempt Question 4 and either Question 5 or 6 you will be given bullet points as stimulus material to help you plan your answer. You do not have to include them but try to use them to get you thinking and to support your arguments. You must bring in your own knowledge too. If you only use the stimulus material you will not gain high marks for your answer.

11. Making judgements
This question carries the most marks and requires a longer answer that needs careful planning. You will be provided with a statement. It may be about the significance of a factor (for example Question 5) or the extent of change in a period (for example Question 6). Pages 150–51 provide advice on answering this question.

12. Checking the quality of your writing
Make sure you leave five minutes at the end of the exam to check your answers. If you are short of time check your answer to the final question first as spelling, punctuation, grammar and use of specialist terminology are assessed in this question. You can gain 4 additional marks on this question – page 151 provides advice on what to focus on. However, remember that the accuracy of your spelling, punctuation and grammar is important in all questions as it affects the clarity of your answer.

De-coding exam questions

The examiners are not trying to catch you out: they are giving you a chance to show what you know – and what you can do with what you know. However, you must answer the questions on the exam paper. Staying focused on the question you are answering is crucial. Including information that is not relevant or misreading a question and writing about the wrong topic wastes time and gains you no marks.

To stay focused on the question and give the answer that is needed, you will need to practise how to 'de-code' questions. This is particularly important for Section B of the exam paper. Follow these **five steps to success:**

Step 1 Read the question a couple of times. Then look at **how many marks** the question is worth. This tells you how much you are expected to write. Do not spend too long on questions worth only a few marks. Remember it is worth planning the 12- and 16-mark questions.

Step 2 Identify the conceptual focus of the question. What is the key concept that the question focuses on? Is it asking you to look at:
- the **significance** of a reason for migration or an aspect of British society
- **causation** – the reasons why the experiences or impact of migrants changed
- **similarities/differences** – between the key features of different periods
- **change** – the extent of change or continuity, progress or regress during a period?

Look at the exam question below. At first glance it appears this question is just about the reasons for migration to and within Britain between c.1700 and c.1900. This shows the danger of not de-coding a question carefully. If you simply describe the reasons for migration you will not get many marks as you are still not focusing on the actual question.

Step 3 Spot the question type. Are you being asked to:
- **describe** the key features of a period
- **explain** similarities/differences between periods or why something happened
- **evaluate** how useful a source or collection of sources is for an enquiry
- reach a **judgement** as to how far you agree with a particular statement?

Each question type requires a different approach. Look for key words or phrases that help you work out which approach is needed. The phrase 'How far do you agree?' means you need to weigh the evidence for and against a statement before reaching a balanced judgement. 'Explain why …' means that you need to explore a range of reasons why an event happened or why the pace of change during a period was fast or slow.

Step 4 Identify the content focus. What is the area of content or topic the examiner wants you to focus on?

Step 5 Look carefully at the date boundaries of the question. What time period should you cover in your answer? Stick to this carefully or you will waste time writing about events that are not relevant to the question.

The conceptual focus is change – you need to reach a judgement on whether there was 'little change' in the reasons for migration to and within Britain.

The date boundaries for the question are c.1500 and c.1900. If you include references to reasons for migration in the twentieth century you will waste time and not pick up any additional marks.

> 6 'There was little change in the reasons for migration to and within Britain in the years c.1500–c.1900.'
> How far do you agree? Explain your answer.
> (16 marks)

16 marks are available – this means the question requires an extended answer. It is definitely worth planning this answer!

The content focus is on the reasons for migration to and within Britain.

The phrase 'How far do you agree?' means that this question requires you to reach a judgement about the statement in quotation marks. This means analysing the reasons for migration to and within Britain, looking for change and continuity before deciding if there was little change.

Practice questions

Look at the other questions in Section B of the exam paper on page 141.
Break each question down using the five steps and check you have de-coded it effectively.

PART 3: Writing better history

Describing key features of a period

'Describe' questions only carry 4 marks so it is important to get to the point quickly so you do not waste precious time that is needed for questions that carry 12 or 16 marks.

Look at the question below:

Practice questions

1 Describe **two** features of the 1959 Caribbean Carnival. (4 marks)
   Feature 1: _____
   Feature 2: _____

Tip 1: Stay relevant to the question

One major problem with 'describe' questions is that students write too much! They include details that are not relevant to the question or needed. Make sure you stick to the question – describe two key features of the 1959 Caribbean Carnival.

You do **not** need to:

- include more than two features (extra features will gain you no more marks)
- evaluate and reach a judgement about the impact of the 1959 Caribbean Carnival.

If you write too much you could run out of time later in the exam when you are answering questions that are worth a lot more marks and need longer answers.

Tip 2: Keep it short and simple

You can get 2 marks by simply identifying two features of the 1959 Caribbean Carnival. For each feature you identify, add a sentence that adds further detail and develops your answer.

Look at the examples below. Then practise your technique by tackling the examples in the practice questions box.

Key feature 1 identified
The 1959 Caribbean Carnival was a celebration with singing and dancing.

 1 mark

Answer developed
There was a cabaret of Caribbean and Black British artists including the Trinidad All Stars.

 1 mark

Key feature 2 identified
The 1959 Caribbean Carnival supported the community of Notting Hill.

 1 mark

Answer developed
A brochure was sold to make money for those residents who needed help to pay fines.

 1 mark

REMEMBER
Stay focused and keep it short and simple. Four sentences are enough for 4 marks.

Practice questions

1. Describe two features of the Notting Hill Housing Trust.
2. Describe two features of Caribbean culture in Notting Hill.
3. Describe two features of shebeens.
4. Describe two features of the Notting Hill Riots (1958).
5. Describe two features of Black activism in Notting Hill.
6. Describe two features of the *West Indian Gazette*.
7. Describe two features of the British Black Panther Party.
8. Describe two features of the Mangrove protest.

Evaluating the usefulness of sources

In Section A of the exam you will be asked to evaluate the usefulness of a source for a specific enquiry. Look at the example below:

> **2 a)** Study Sources A and B. How useful are Sources A and B for an enquiry into the reaction of the local community to the murder of Kelso Cochrane? Explain your answer, using Sources A and B and your own knowledge of the historical context. (8 marks)

You should annotate the sources in the booklet before you start to write your answer. Also, to evaluate effectively you need to use criteria. Use the criteria opposite to help you.

Source A Journalist John Gale visited the area where Kelso was killed and interviewed some of the youths in the area. He published some of what they said on 24 May in his 'Notting Hill Notebook' in the *Guardian*:

I live 200 yards from where that coloured bloke was done. Couldn't care two hoots. One less. What happens if they find the bloke and they top him? There'll be riots then. And they'll keep on.

▲ **Source B** A crowd of onlookers on Ladbroke Grove watches the arrival of the hearse for the funeral of Kelso Cochrane

REMEMBER

The question is asking you how useful the sources are, not how useless they are. The sources will be useful. Do not tell the examiner what information is missing. Look at the strengths of each source as well as considering any limitations from the provenance. Try to begin and end your answer positively. Start your answer by writing how each source helps with this enquiry.

To evaluate the source use the criteria below:

☐ Criteria 1: Consider the content of the source

Highlight or underline useful information for the enquiry in both sources. Make sure you judge how useful it is for the enquiry specified in the question. For this question, the sources need to help you understand the reaction of the local community to the murder of Kelso Cochrane. Start your answer by highlighting how each source helps you with this enquiry.

☐ Criteria 2: Consider the provenance of each source

Look at the captions alongside the sources. Think carefully about the following key questions and the impact that this might have on how useful the source is. Remember, you only need to write about one: nature, origin OR purpose.

- **What is the nature of the source?**

What type of source is it? How does this affect its utility? For example, a private letter or diary can be useful because the person usually gives his or her honest view.

- **What are the origins of the source?**

Who produced it? Are they likely to have a good knowledge of the events they talk about? Are they likely to give a one-sided view?

- **What is the purpose of the source?**

Why was it produced? How might this affect the utility of the source? For example, a politician's speech or a newspaper report might be produced for propaganda purposes – to encourage people to react in a particular way.

☐ Criteria 3: Use your own knowledge of the historical context to evaluate the source

Compare the information and key messages contained in the source with your own knowledge of the enquiry topic.

- What knowledge do you have that confirms the content of the source?
- What knowledge do you have that explains the content or provenance of the source?

PART 3: Writing better history

Following up sources

One of the key aims of this book is to help you understand how we use the enquiry process to research history. Asking the right historical questions is a crucial part of enquiry and historical research. Exam questions like the one below provide you with the opportunity to show the enquiry skills you have been developing throughout your course.

> **REMEMBER**
>
> This question is only worth 4 marks. Do not go into detailed explanations of why you chose to follow up with a particular source – you do not have time. One or two sentences will be fine.

2 b) How would you follow up Source B (page 145) to find out more about the reaction of the local community to the murder of Kelso Cochrane? In your answer, you must give the question you would ask and the type of source you could use. Fill in the details below: (4 marks)

- Detail in Source B that I would follow up: _____
- Question I would ask: _____
- What type of source I could use: _____
- How this might help answer my question: _____

The key to answering this question is to make sure that the four different parts of your answer link together.

Step 1: Link the detail to the enquiry

Start by identifying the focus for the enquiry – in this case, the reaction of the local community to the murder of Kelso Cochrane. Make sure that the detail in the source that you say you would follow up is linked to this enquiry. For a written source, use a quotation. For a picture source, describe a detail that can be seen in the image. For example, if the crowd at Cochrane's funeral shows black and white residents, you could identify this as a detail that you would follow up as it is linked to the main enquiry.

Step 2: Link the question to the detail

The question you choose must be linked to the detail you are following up from the source. Do not simply choose an interesting question unrelated to the enquiry! If you were following up the detail about who attended Cochrane's funeral you could use 'Why did white residents of Notting Hill attend the funeral of Kelso Cochrane?' as your question.

Step 3: Link the type of source to the question

You now need to choose a type of source that would be useful for answering your question. Look at the list in the box opposite. Make sure you choose a source that would help answer the question, and make it specific to the enquiry. For example, in this case, written memoirs of local residents who attended the funeral would provide information about their reason for doing so.

Step 4: Link this with your own knowledge

Do not forget to explain the advantages of using this type of source and link it to the enquiry. The source type mentioned above would be useful as local residents would explain their reasons for attending the funeral honestly without trying to influence anyone's view. The written memoirs of local residents were unlikely to be produced for propaganda purposes (in contrast, newspaper accounts might try to influence the view of the reader).

Different types of sources

National sources:
- National newspapers
- Photographs
- Government records
- Census data
- Opinion polls
- Television reports
- Memoirs

Local sources:
- Local newspapers
- Publications written for the Caribbean community
- Local council and police records
- Housing and employment records
- Oral and written memoirs of local residents
- Photographs

Exploring the similarity/difference between the key features of two historical periods

Question 3 is the first question that tests your knowledge and understanding of the thematic study on Migrants in Britain, c.800–present. Remember this is where skills in de-coding questions come in useful. Look at the question below.

The date boundaries are important. You must focus on the right case studies, from the specified years – c.1100–c.1500 (medieval England) and c.1500–c.1700 (early modern England).

This is an 'explain' question. However, as it is only worth 4 marks, you only have to explain one similarity.

The conceptual focus of this question is 'similarity' – the ability to be able to compare different periods of history and spot a similarity.

> 3 Explain **one** way in which the experience of migrants in the years c.1100–c.1500 were similar to the experience of migrants in the years c.1500–c.1700.
>
> (4 marks)

This question has a very specific content focus. To save time, make sure you stay relevant – only write about the experience of migrants. There is no need to go into the background of different groups of migrants.

The first thing to notice is that the question is only worth 4 marks. It is important that you are clear on the focus of the question so that you can keep your answer short and to the point.

Explaining the similarity/difference between time periods

As this is an 'explain' question you must do more than simply identify a similarity or difference. You will need to support your answer with specific details from both time periods – a good motto is 'prove, don't say'. Would your explanation convince the reader that there was a similarity between the experience of migrants in the two different time periods?

For example, you might 'say' that one similarity between the experience of migrants was that they faced hostility. However, this would not get you high marks. Instead, you need to prove your big point (similarity) about hostility by providing supporting information from both time periods.

- BIG POINT – With a question only worth 4 marks do not spend time on an introduction. Start your answer with your 'big point', in this case that migrants in both periods experienced hostility.

- SUPPORTING INFORMATION – You need to develop your 'big point' and prove that this was the case by providing specific examples from both time periods. For the years c.1100–c.1500 you could refer to the experience of Jewish people during the reign of Henry III, while for the years c.1500–c.1700 you could explain the experience of Flemings in Sandwich.

Practice questions

1. Explain **one** way in which the reasons for migration to Britain in the years c.800–c.1500 were similar to the reasons for migration to Britain in the years c.1500–c.1700.
2. Explain **one** way in which the reasons for migration to Britain in the years c.1500–c.1700 were different from the reasons for migration to Britain in the years c.1700–c.1900.
3. Explain **one** way in which the experience of Jewish migrants in the East End of London in the nineteenth century was similar to the experience of Asian migrants in Leicester in the twentieth century.

REMEMBER

You should only be spending 5 minutes on this question. Keep your answer focused on supporting one similarity. Do not list lots of similarities.

TIP

Think about the connective you use to compare the two time periods. For a:

- similarity you can use words or phrases such as 'Also', 'Similarly' and 'This continued'.
- difference you can use words or phrases such as 'However', 'Whereas' and 'This was not the case'.

PART 3: Writing better history

Tackling 12-mark 'explain' questions

Look at the question below.

> 4 Explain why the experiences of migrants in Britain changed in the years c.1900–present.
> You may use the following in your answer:
> - the First World War
> - the Race Relations Act (1965).
>
> You must also use information of your own.   (12 marks)

This question is different in two ways from Question 3 on page 148. Firstly, the conceptual focus is different – in this case the key concept is causation (explaining why people migrated to Britain or explaining the pace of change). Secondly, this question is worth 12 marks. The examiner will expect you to give a range of reasons. The question also supplies stimulus material (see page 142, Point 10).

It is important to spend time planning this question during your exam. Follow the steps below to help you plan effectively and write a good answer.

Step 1: Get focused on the question

Make sure you de-code the question carefully. Note that the content focus is on 'the experiences of migrants in Britain' so do not go into reasons for migration or the impact of migration.

Step 2: Identify a range of factors

Try to cover more than one cause. If your mind goes blank, always go back to the key factors that influence change for migrants in Britain.

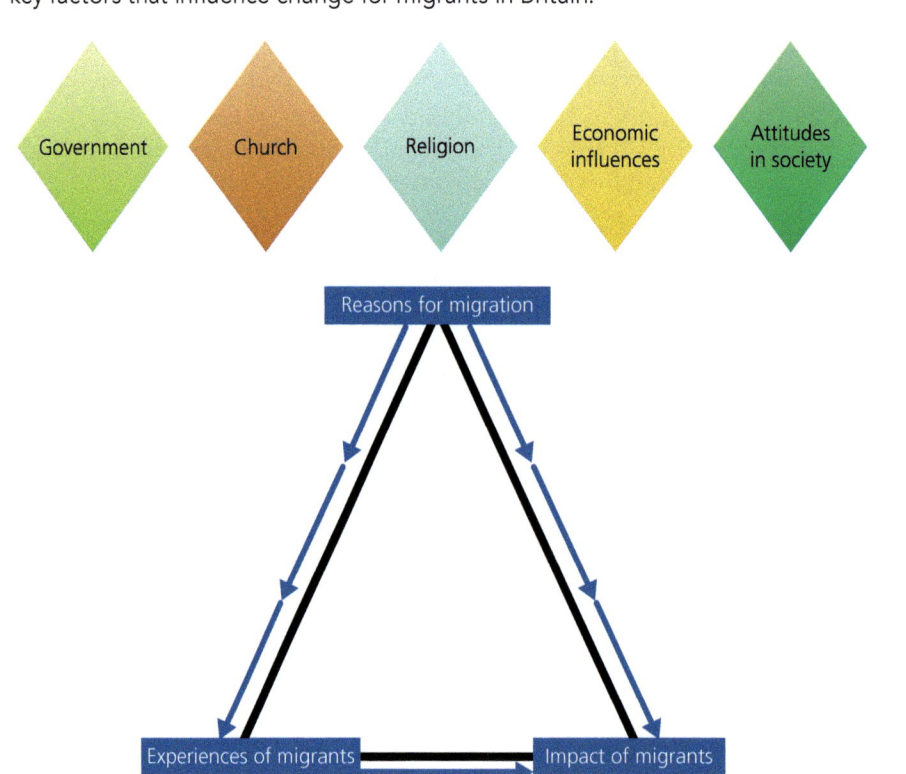

148

Tackling 12-mark 'explain' questions

Step 3: Organise your answer using paragraphs

Do not worry about writing an introduction. This is not needed. It will waste time and carries no marks.

Start a new paragraph each time you move onto a new reason (influenced by a factor) that caused change. Signpost your argument at the start of the paragraph. For example, you could start your first paragraph like this:

> The actions of government played an important role in changing the experiences of migrants in Britain in the years c.1900 to the present day.

Aim to write three paragraphs in your answer to this question.

Step 4: Do not 'say' that a cause was important – 'prove' it was

Remember that a list of reasons why the experiences of migrants in Britain changed will not get you a high-level mark. You need to **prove** your case for each cause. This means developing your explanation by adding supporting information and specific examples.

This is where your work on connectives will come in useful. Look at the advice on page 153 and remember to tie in what you know to the question by using connectives such as 'this meant that', 'this led to' and 'this resulted in'. For example, you may want to build on the opening to your first paragraph by using the example of the 1965 Race Relations Act as a way that the government helped to protect migrants in Britain from racial discrimination. Look at how the student below starts to prove a point.

> In 1965 the government introduced the Race Relations Act to protect people from racial discrimination. This resulted in it becoming illegal for pubs and hotels to discriminate against black, mixed and Asian people in Britain and improved the experiences of migrants in Britain as they could use the same facilities as white British citizens.

Aim to include three different features of knowledge (one in each paragraph) in your answer to this question.

Practice questions

1. Explain why migrants were attracted to Britain in the years c.1500–c.1700.
   You may use the following in your answer:
   - the cloth industry
   - Huguenots.

   You **must** also use information of your own. (12 marks)

2. Explain why the reasons people migrated to Britain changed in the years c.1700–present.
   You may use the following in your answer:
   - the Industrial Revolution
   - refugees.

   You **must** also use information of your own. (12 marks)

REMEMBER

Do not try to cover too many causes that led to change. Select no more than three that you can make a strong argument for. Remember, in the exam you will have approximately 15 minutes to answer this question.

PART 3: Writing better history

Making judgements – tackling the 16-mark question

The last question on the exam paper carries the most marks and requires a carefully planned, detailed answer. You will be provided with a statement in quotation marks and be asked to reach a judgement about **how far you agree** with it. The phrase 'how far' is important as it is unlikely that you will totally agree or disagree with the statement. The examiner will be looking for you to show that you can weigh the evidence for and against the statement.

> 5 'The impact on trade was the most significant consequence of migration to Britain in the years c.800–c.1500.' How far do you agree? Explain your answer. (16 marks)
>
> You may use the following in your answer:
> - York under the Vikings
> - Danelaw.
>
> You **must** also use information of your own.
> (Total for spelling, punctuation, grammar and the use of specialist terminology = 4 marks)
> (Total for Question 5 = 20 marks)

Look at the example in the green box.

Step 1: Focus

The content focus is important – you have to reach a judgement on the impact of migration to Britain in the years c.800 to c.1500. This includes culture, trade and language. The conceptual focus is on significance and consequence. You have to evaluate the significance of migration on trade, and other aspects of Britain, and may do so using the stimulus points (see page 142, Point 10). Focus on the phrase in the question – do you think the impact on trade was the most significant consequence of migration to Britain?

Step 2: Identify

In 16-mark questions you are required to reach a judgement on a statement. In order to do this effectively you need to identify **clear criteria** for reaching that judgement. Just as you need to cover a range of reasons in 'explain' questions, you need to **cover a range of criteria** in 'judgement' questions.

Possible criteria for reaching a judgement:

- If you are judging the importance of a cause or consequence of migration, you could analyse and evaluate the significance for different groups of migrants or impact on a location in Britain.
- If you are judging the extent of change you could analyse and evaluate how many people were affected (Did everyone experience change or was it just one group of people?) or how quickly a location in Britain changed (Were there immediate changes? Were they long last and permanent?).

In this example, you are being asked to reach a judgement on the 'consequences of migration' in Britain in the years c.800 to c.1500, so you could explore the main features of British society:

- trade
- culture
- authority
- the environment.

Step 3: Organise

The most straight-forward way of organising your answer is to plan 'for' and 'against' paragraphs:

- Paragraph 1: Evidence to **support** the statement (make sure that you use the criteria – the consequences of migration on trade in Britain)
- Paragraph 2: Evidence to **counter** the statement (once again, use the criteria – the consequences of migration on other features of British society)
- Paragraph 3: Your final conclusion – weigh the evidence. How far do you agree with the statement?

Step 4: Prove

Remember to tie what you know to the question. Do not include information and think it will speak for itself. Some students think that simply dropping in examples to the right paragraphs is enough. One of the stimulus points refers to York under the Vikings. The following statement from a student could be further developed and gain more marks.

> During the Viking settlement of York, which the Vikings renamed Jorvik, a lot of trade took place within Britain and into Europe. For example, tin, gold, silver and amber were traded.

This does not prove that trade was a significant consequence of migration to Britain. To gain more marks, the student would need to go on to explain that new items such as amber enabled the people living in York to make jewellery using a semi-precious stone that had not been available to them before. Also, it is important to show that goods, such as tin from Cornwall, were traded within Britain, allowing communities to benefit from goods that were closer but had not been made available to them before. 'Killer evidence' could be introduced to strengthen the argument – remember that combs, rings and pins made from Arctic reindeer antlers were also found during archaeological digs in York.

Making judgements – tackling the 16-mark question

Step 5: Conclude

Your conclusion is an important part of your answer. You have been asked to reach a judgement on a statement. You need to clearly state how far you agree with it and your reason why. It would be easy to sit on the fence and avoid reaching a final conclusion. But sitting on the fence is a dangerous position. Your answer collapses and you lose marks.

Instead of sitting on the fence, you need to be confident and reach an overall judgement. Imagine that you have placed the evidence on a set of scales. How far do they tip in favour of the statement or against it?

You can then move on in your conclusion to explain your judgement. Do not repeat everything you have already written. Think of the scales – what are the heaviest pieces of evidence on each side? Build these into your conclusion in the following way:

JUDGEMENT – Start with your judgement – try to use words from the question in this sentence.

I completely agree that the impact on trade was the most significant consequence of migration to Britain in the years c.800 to c.1500.

COUNTER – Show that you are aware that there is some evidence to counter this and give the best example.

The development of language was also a consequence of migration to Britain, and this can be seen when French became the main language at court and within the government after the Normans settled.

SUPPORT – Explain why, overall, you have reached the judgement you have. Give your key reason for reasons why.

However, the impact of trade was the most significant consequence of migration to Britain because it affected the lives of people living throughout the British Isles. People of all classes and in every region benefitted from the wider range of goods available to them from other parts of the country, Europe and beyond.

Practice questions

1. 'The wool industry was the main reason for migration to Britain during the Middle Ages.' How far do you agree? Explain your answer. (16 marks)
   You may use the following in your answer:
   - Flemish weavers
   - religious persecution.

   You **must** also use information of your own.

2. 'The Race Relations Act (1965) was a turning point in the experiences of migrants in Britain in the years c.1700–present.' How far do you agree? Explain your answer. (16 marks)
   You may use the following in your answer:
   - equal rights movements
   - the media.

   You **must** also use information of your own.

REMEMBER

Leave enough time to check your answer carefully for spelling, punctuation, grammar and use of specialist terminology.

Four important marks are available (this is as much as your answer to Question 1, 2b or 3).

- You will be marked for the accuracy of your spelling and punctuation.
- You will also be marked for your grammar – does your work make sense? Are your arguments clear?
- Finally, the examiner will consider your use of 'specialist terms' – have you used a wide range of historical terms?

151

PART 3: Writing better history

What are the key ingredients of effective writing in GCSE History?

The language you use to express your ideas is very important. One of the ways to get better at history is to be more precise with your use of language. For example, rather than simply saying that you *agree* or *disagree* with a statement you can use language that shows whether you agree to *a large extent* or only *to some extent*. Look at the different shades of argument below and experiment with using some of the phrases. Use them when you are debating or discussing in class.

Think carefully about the language you use

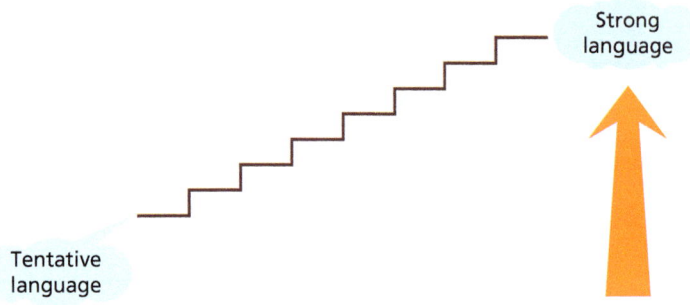

Varying your language to show how far you agree with a statement:	Varying your language to show how important a factor/cause is:
I totally/entirely/completely/absolutely agree with …	… was by far the most important reason why …
I substantially/fundamentally/strongly agree with …	The key/crucial/essential factor was …
I agree to a large extent with …	… was the main cause of …
I mainly/mostly agree with …	The most influential cause was …
I agree to some extent with …	… played a significant/important/major role in …
I partially/partly agree with …	… was of some importance in …
I only agree with … to a limited extent	
Varying your language to show the significance or importance of a group, event, feature or development:	**Varying your language to show the extent of change:**
… made the most important/significant contribution to …	… was revolutionised in ….
… had a crucial/major/highly significant impact on …	…. totally changed during …
… had an important/influential impact on …	… was transformed during …
… was of some importance/significance	… there was fundamental change in …
… only made a limited/partial/slight/minimal contribution to …	The period saw significant/important change in …
	… saw some changes in …
	… saw limited/slight/minimal change in …

What are the key ingredients of effective writing in GCSE History?

This table shows helpful phrases and sentence starters

When you want to explore the other side of an argument:	When you want to highlight similarity/difference:	When you want to make an additional point to support an argument:	When you want to show that a group, event, feature or development was important:
On the other hand …	In the same way …	Also …	… was a crucial turning point in …
However, …	Similarly …	Additionally …	… acted as an important catalyst for …
Alternatively, it could be argued that …	This is similar in the way that …	In addition …	Without this group/event/feature/development … would not have happened.
	However, …	Moreover …	This had an immediate impact on …
	This is different from the way that ….	Furthermore …	In the short term this transformed/revolutionised …
When you want to link points or show that one thing led to another:	**When you want to refer to evidence in a source:**	**When you want to give examples to support a point:**	In the long term this had a lasting impact on …
Therefore …	Source A suggests/implies/indicates that …	For example …	
Due to …	According to Source B …	For instance …	
Consequently …	Source A shows/illustrates/demonstrates that …	This can be seen when …	
One consequence of this was …		This is clearly shown by …	
This caused …		This is supported by …	
This led to …		This is proven by …	
This resulted in …			
This meant that …			

The History progression grid

You can use the **progression grid** below to get an idea of what getting better at history looks like. This is designed to give you a general idea of what you need to do to produce good answers in the exam. It focuses on the four key things in the coloured squares on the bingo card (page 154).

	Question focus	Organisation	Line of argument	Supporting information
High level ↑	The answer is consistently focused on the question.	The answer is structured very carefully and explanations are coherent throughout the answer.	The line of argument is very clear and convincing. It flows throughout the answer.	Supporting information has been precisely selected, and shows wide-ranging knowledge and understanding.
	The answer is mainly focused on the question.	The answer is well organised but some parts lack coherence.	The line of argument is clear, convincing and generally maintained through the answer.	Supporting information is accurate and relevant, and shows good knowledge and understanding.
	The answer has weak or limited links to the question.	Some statements are developed. There is some attempt to organise the material.	The line of argument is partly convincing but not maintained through the answer.	Supporting information is mainly accurate and relevant, and shows some knowledge and understanding.
	The answer has no real links to the question.	The answer lacks organisation.	The line of argument is unclear or missing.	Supporting information is limited or not relevant.

PART 3: Writing better history

Self-assessing and peer-assessing your work

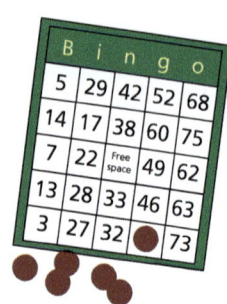

It is important that you check your own work before you give it to your teacher to be marked. Sometimes you may be asked to assess the work of someone else in your class. In both cases, you need to know what you are looking for. What are the key ingredients of great writing in history?

You can use the **bingo card** as a checklist – get competitive and try to show that you have covered all the squares and got a full house of ingredients!

The answer starts with a **clear focus on the question** (there is no long introduction). Key words from the question are used throughout the answer. For longer answers, each paragraph is linked to the question.	Statements and arguments are fully developed and explained – showing good knowledge and understanding. Arguments are **well supported** by accurate, relevant and well-selected evidence.	Connectives are used to help prove arguments and show significance/impact. Look for phrases like: • this led to … • this resulted in … • this meant that …
There is a **clear line of argument** at the start of each paragraph – think of it as a signpost for what follows. The rest of the paragraph supports this argument. The line of argument flows throughout the answer, building up to a clear conclusion.	Paragraphs have been used to provide a **clear structure**. Each paragraph starts with: • a difference cause/reason (12-mark 'explain' questions) or • different theme/criteria (16-mark judgement questions).	The answer shows wide-ranging knowledge and understanding. It considers a range of reasons/causes ('explain' questions) or explores the evidence for *and* against a statement (judgement questions).
The language used helps to construct very precise arguments – showing how important the writer thinks a reason/cause, event or development is. A good range of specialist **historical vocabulary** has been used.	There is a **clear conclusion**. For judgement questions, there is a focus on 'how far' the writer agrees with the statement.	The answer has been **carefully checked** for spelling, punctuation and grammar. The meaning is always clear throughout the answer.

Glossary

Abbot A man who is the head of an abbey of monks

Abolition The movement that campaigned for the end to the enslavement and trade of African people

Activism Campaigning to bring about change

Aliens (as used by the British government) People who are not British citizens and were born in another country

Allegiance A person's continued support of a political party, religion, leader, etc

Anglicised The process of people becoming English in their culture and way of life

Anti-apartheid Opposition to the oppressive system of racial segregation that operated in South Africa from 1948 until the 1990s

Anti-Semitic Displaying prejudice against Jewish people

Assimilation The process of changing people's culture and way of life to fit in with society as a whole

Asylum seekers People who have applied to be accepted as a refugee

Autonomy Maintaining aspects of people's culture and way of life within society as a whole

Ayahs Indian women employed by a British family to look after their children

Basilicas Large churches or halls with curved ends and two rows of columns inside

Bills of exchange A written commitment to pay someone a certain sum of money at a point in the future, usually as part of a trading deal

Blitz The period of aerial bombing by the Nazis that places in Britain suffered from during the Second World War

Boycott When people refuse to use a service or product as a form of protest

British Raj The system of supreme British authority that operated in India from the nineteenth to the twentieth centuries

Calypso A popular style of music in the Caribbean (previously known as the West Indies)

Chain migration When people migrating from one region are joined by others from the same region who follow them

Chancery The legal office in England that deals with issues of property law

Codes of laws The framework of laws for a society, usually written down

Coin-clipping Taking off the edge of metal coins to sell that precious metal for monetary gain

Colony A territory set up or ruled by another nation

Conciliation A process that aims to end an argument between people or groups

Cosmopolitan A place containing different types of people, or people from different countries, and that is influenced by their culture

Creditors A person, company, etc. that somebody owes money to

Death duties Tax that you must pay on the money or property that you receive from somebody when they die

Decolonisation The process of giving independence to places that had been colonies

Demobbed To release somebody from military service, especially at the end of a war

Denization The right, granted by a monarch, to live in England as a citizen

Denizens Immigrants who have been made citizens of England by law

Displaced To take the place of somebody/something

Divinity The quality of being a god or like God or a god

Duchy An area of land that is owned and controlled by a duke or duchess

Economic migrants People who have migrated to a country to earn income and then return to their native land

Entrepreneur Someone who starts and runs their own business

Exiles People who are forced to live away from their homeland against their will

EU15 Countries in the European Union in 1995: Austria, Belgium, Denmark, France, Finland, Germany, Greece, Ireland, Italy, Luxembourg, Netherlands, Portugal, Spain, Sweden, the UK

EU8 Countries that joined the European Union in 2004: Czech Republic, Estonia, Hungary, Lithuania, Latvia, Poland, Slovenia, Slovakia

EU2 Countries that joined the European Union in 2007: Bulgaria and Romania

Fascism A political system marked by authoritarian rule, nationalism, state and military power

Fascist Someone who follows a racist political ideology and believes there should be one strong leader

Fenians A group of extreme Irish nationalists who organised violent campaigns to get rid of British control over Ireland.

Feudal system A medieval system in which people served a lord by working and fighting for him and were given land to farm

Flemish Coming from the area of Flanders in north-west Europe

Grassroots The regular local people in a society who organise to bring change

Guerrilla warfare Fighting by a small group of soldiers who do not belong to a regular army. They usually fight as independent units and wage small-scale attacks on their enemies

Guilds Associations of crafts people and merchants who controlled their crafts and trade in each town

Heretics A person who believes in or practises religious ideas that clash with the accepted belief system

Home Office The British government department that deals with internal domestic matters, including immigration

Home Rule Giving internal control of a colony to its own people within the overall control of the British Empire

Houses of multiple occupation (HMOs) Properties that were divided up into small units, either rooms or flats, so many more people could be charged rent to live there

Humanism A belief that human beings have the capacity to develop the values and ideas that shape a worthwhile life

Hymns Religious songs of praise to God, sung by Christians

Immigrants People who come from a foreign country to settle permanently

Impresario A person who organises and often finances plays, concerts, etc

Indentured sailors Sailors who paid for their passage to a new country by signing a contract stating that they would work for a certain number of years for their master

Infrastructure The basic systems and services that are necessary for a country or an organisation to run smoothly, for example buildings, transport, water and power supplies

Integration The process by which groups of people with different cultures and ways of life mix together to develop a new social culture

Integrated A society where different groups have joined together

Intellectualise To deal with or explain things by thinking about them in a logical way, rather than responding emotionally

Intemperate Showing a lack of control over yourself

Investor   A person or an organisation that invests money in something

Joint-stock company   A business owned by shareholders

Kindertransport   A rescue effort that brought 10000 Jewish children to safety from Nazi Germany and Nazi – occupied Austria and Czechoslovakia

Liberal   People who have political ideas that emphasise the importance of liberty and equality, and are concerned with people's rights

Liberal constitutions   Frameworks for the government of a country that secure the rights of its citizens

Looms   A frame or machine used to weave cloth

Lutheran   A Protestant church that began in Germany during the Reformation and followed the approach of Martin Luther to how the church should function

Mariner   A person who works on the sea

Mercenary   A soldier who fights for people as a way of earning a living

Merchant navy   A country's commercial ships and the people who work on them

Migrant   A person who moves from one place to another, usually to find work and/or better living conditions, or to study

Missionaries   People who are sent to a foreign country to teach people about religion, especially Christianity

Monastery   A building in which monks (members of a male religious community) live together

Monocultural   Where people follow a single pattern of culture in their way of life

Monopoly   A royal licence which gave individuals the sole right to manufacture or sell a product

Multiculturalism   The idea that people of different cultural groups and ethnic backgrounds can create a diverse, successful society by keeping their cultures and also sharing in those of others

Nationalist   The belief that a nation of people should have their own independent country

Nationalist struggle   The actions taken arising from a belief in nationalism – that a nation of people should have their own independent country

Naturalise   Parliament granting someone the right to live in England

Net migration   The balance between the numbers of people arriving and leaving a country

Nobility   People who possess noble titles

Obituary   An article about somebody's life and achievements that is printed in a newspaper soon after they have died

Oratorio   A long piece of music for singers and an orchestra, usually based on a story from the Bible

Pageantry   Impressive and exciting events and ceremonies involving a lot of people wearing special clothes

Patrial   A citizen in Britain who had at least one British grandparent

Philanthropy   The practice of helping the poor and those in need, especially by giving money

Pilgrimage   A journey to a holy place for religious reasons

Political stability   A situation where the people in power in a country have peaceful control in the society and changes in power happen without violence and dramatic upheaval

Popery   An offensive way of referring to Roman Catholicism

Priory   A building where a community of monks or nuns lives, which is smaller and less important than an abbey

Priors   The men who were in charge of a monastery

Privateering   The use of privately owned ships and their crew to attack and rob enemy shipping

Privy Council   A group of high-ranking people who advise the English monarch

Puritans   Members of a fundamental protestant movement within the Church of England

Queen consorts   The title for the wives of kings reigning in England

Racism   The idea that there are different human 'races' and some are superior to others

Recanted   To say, often publicly, that you no longer have the same belief or opinion that you had before

Referendum   A vote in which all eligible people are asked to give their opinion of or decide on an important political or social issue

Refugee   People who are allowed to remain legally in a country, the government having accepted that they are escaping danger in their home country

Reggae   A type of popular music with strong rhythms, developed in Jamaica in the 1960s

Repatriation   Sending migrant people back to their country of origin

Samosas   A type of hot and spicy South Asian food consisting of a triangle of thin pastry filled with meat or vegetables and fried until it is hard and dry

Satirical   Using humour and ridicule to criticize somebody or something

Scapegoat   To blame somebody or something for a failure or for something bad that another person has done

Seamstress   A woman who can sew and make clothes or whose job is sewing and making clothes

Shebeens   Places where immigrants from the Caribbean islands drank, danced and socialised with each other without official permission

Sheriff (in the US)   An elected officer responsible for keeping law and order in a county or town

Sit-in   A demonstration by people who refuse to leave a certain location in order to persuade the authorities there to change something

Ska   A form of music that originated in Jamaica before reggae, and was popular among some groups in Britain in the 1960s

Socialist   A believer in a system where the government rules in the interests of the workers

Sop   A thing of no great value that is given or done as a concession to appease someone whose main concerns or demands are not being met

Squat   A place where people are living but they do not have the legal right to be there

Steel pans   Musical percussion instruments developed out of oil drums in Trinidad in the Caribbean

Sugar-bakers   Businesses that turned crystallised sugar into solid loaves of sugar for people to buy

Tabula   A frame on which important writings are inscribed

Temperance   The practice of not drinking alcohol because of your moral or religious beliefs

Tolerance   The quality of being willing to accept or tolerate somebody or something, especially opinions or behaviour that you may not agree with, or people who are not like you

Treasury   The office that looks after a government's finances

Unfree   People who cannot make all their own decisions about work and life

Unilaterally   Something carried out by one person, group or country involved in a situation, without the agreement of others

Ward   A local district in a town or city that has a representative on the local council

West Indian   The term 'West Indies' was used by Europeans to describe the islands in the Caribbean Sea after they were mistaken for a part of Asia around 1500. It is still the name of the islands' cricket team. The term 'West Indian' was used in the past to refer to people from those islands. Now the term is not considered suitable and 'Caribbean' is used instead

Xenophobia   Hostility and prejudice towards people from other countries

Index

Aaron of Lincoln 10, 26
Aethelred II, king 13, 15
Afghan refugees 91
African migrants 6, 7, 8, 44–5, 66–7
    East African Asians 87, 102
    musicians 66
    servants 45, 54, 66–7
    slaves 6, 38, 45
Africanus, George John Scipio 53, 63
agriculture 40
Al Annuri 45
Ali, Syed Ameer 108
Altab Ali 80, 100
American colonies 39
Angel, Moses 52, 72
Anglo-Saxons 12, 14, 17
Anionwu, Dame Elizabeth 79, 101
Archer, John 52, 58
Asian migrants 7, 87
    in Leicester 102–3
asylum seekers 3, 90
bankers 6, 28, 46
Bardi, Francesco de 42
Barrow, Jocelyn 96
Beckett, Thomas 22
Beckford, Carmen 79, 99
Ben Israel, Manasseh 32, 48
Bhownaggree, Sir Mancherjee 53, 70, 74
Bierer, Dr Joshua 79, 101
Black Death 11, 21, 29
Black Panthers 135, 138
Black Power 97, 134, 136
Blackman, Reasonable 44
Blanke, John 32, 44
Boateng, Paul 80, 104, 138
Bonyn, Peter 11, 25
Brexit 92
Bristol 98–100
British Empire 38–9, 60, 60–1
    decolonisation 7, 88, 89
British Isles 7, 10, 19
Brockway, Fenner 97
Bryan, Carmen 127
Bucer, Martin 33, 34
Bullimore, Tony 99
Cain, Robert 52, 59
Canterbury 33, 36, 37
Cantile, Dr James 60
Cardiff 8, 60, 83
Caribbean migrants 6, 7, 82, 84, 101
    see also Notting Hill
Carmichael, Stokeley 134
castles 16
Catholic Church 22–3, 28, 34, 40
    monasteries 10, 12, 22–3
Catholic emancipation 52, 55
Catholic migrants 49
    Irish 55, 59, 68, 69

chain migration 98
Chapman, Pat 106
Charles II, King 39, 48
Chinese migrants 7, 60
Christendom 10
Christian migrants 108
churches 17, 132
Cini, Filippo 29
Cistercian monks 10, 21, 23, 31
Cluniac monks 10, 22
Cnut the Dane 15, 19
Cochrane, Kelso 124–5, 130, 132
Coke, Mabel Dinah 101
Colchester 21, 29
Cold War 81, 89
Cole, Christian Frederick 67
Coleridge-Taylor, Samuel 53, 67
Commonwealth of Nations 89
Constantine, Learie 79, 84, 98
Corbet, Gabriel 11, 29
Crichlow, Frank 135, 136, 137, 138
Cromwell, Oliver 48
Crowther, Samuel Ajayi 67
Crusades 10, 19, 26, 28
Danelaw 12, 13
Dargan, William 57
Dee, John 38, 39
Defoe, Daniel 40
denization 11, 25, 42, 47, 49
Desaguliers, John Theophilus 32, 47
Dickens, Charles 74
Dutch migrants 40, 42
East India Company 39, 45, 60
Eastern Europeans 7, 72, 92
economic migrants 3, 5
Edward the Confessor 15, 16
Edward I, King 10, 19, 25, 27, 28, 48
Edward III, King 19, 21, 25, 29
Eleanor of Provence 11, 19, 25, 31
Elizabeth I, Queen 35, 38, 39, 45
Emidy, Joseph 52, 66, 67
emigration from Britain 7
Emma of Normandy 10, 15, 16
England 10
Engländer, Samuel 65
English Reformation 34, 35
Ennis, Jessica 105
Equiano, Olaudah 66
Erasmus, Desiderius 32, 34, 35
European Union/EEC 2, 7, 80, 89, 92
Evil May Day Riot 32, 42–3, 88
Farah, Mo 105
festivals 99, 103
Fetplace, Walter 29
feudal system 16
Fillis, Mary 33, 45
First World War 82–3
Flemish migrants 5, 6, 10, 17, 23, 36, 37, 46
    weavers 6, 11, 29, 31, 33, 42, 44

food 106
football 105
Forbes, 'Duke' Vincent 118
Franciscan friars 29
French migrants 5, 6, 19, 23
    Huguenots 38, 45–6, 46–7, 49, 104
    monks 22–3
    Walloons 33, 36, 37
French Revolution 53, 54–5
Fullerton, Clifford 114, 115, 118
Gerardot, Reverend 54
German migrants 5, 33, 42, 63, 64–5
    Palatines 49
Gestetner, David 53, 63
Gigli, Carlo 11, 28
Gigli, Giovanni 11, 28
Glean, Marion 96
Glorious Revolution 32, 33, 40, 46
Green, Bea 79, 90
guilds 21
Gupta, Rahila 81
Hackett, Roy 78, 98
Hall, Stuart 7
Handel, Georg Frideric 5, 52, 64
Hanseatic League 25
Harrying of the North 22, 23
Hawkins, John 38
Henry III, King 19, 25, 27, 28, 31
Henry VIII, King 34, 35, 42, 43, 44
Herschel, Caroline 53, 64
Hindu migrants 108
Holbein, Hans 5, 32, 35
Hong Kong refugees 7
Howe, Darcus 134, 135, 136, 137, 138
Huguenots 38, 46–7, 49, 104
humanism 34
Hundred Years War 11, 19, 25
immigration controls 86, 87, 88, 90, 92–3
Imperial Typewriter strike 100, 102, 103
Indian migrants 5, 7, 70–1, 84
    soldiers 82
Industrial Revolution 56–9
invaders 12–18
Ireland 7, 10, 19, 49, 55
Irish migrants 5, 6, 55, 59, 68–9
    medieval 19
    navvies 52, 57, 68
    women 72, 101
Italian migrants 6, 11, 28, 29, 65
Jaeger, August 67
Jamaican migrants 85, 93, 107, 114
James, II, King 33, 39
Jeffrey, Pansy 132
Jews 6, 7, 10, 17, 19, 48
    Clifford's Tower massacre of 26–7
    East End of London 72–3
    expulsion from England 27, 31
    hostility to 74
    and Nazi Germany 90, 101

Johnson, Ken 'Snakehips' 79, 107
joint-stock companies 39
Jones, Claudia 96, 123, 125, 126
Jones-LeCointe, Althea 137, 138
Kenyan Asians 87, 102
King, Sam 79
Kochertal, Joshua 32, 49
Kratzer, Nicholas 35
Lanfranc, Archbishop 10, 22
languages
    Norman French 16, 17
    Viking names 12, 13, 14
lascars 52, 58, 61, 70, 82, 84
Laslett, Rhaune 128–9, 131
League of Coloured People 83, 84
Leicester 102–3
Levant Company 39
Licoricia of Winchester 10, 27
Lincoln, John 42, 43
Liverpool 56, 58–9, 60, 69, 83
London 56
    Bevis Marks Synagogue 48
    St Katharine's Dock 57
Luther, Martin 33, 34
Mahomed, Sake Dean 53, 63, 70
Malebisse, Richard 26, 27
Manchester 56
Marson, Una 79, 84, 107
Marx, Karl 65
Meauty, John 42
medieval migrants 3, 12–30
    denization 11, 25, 28
    European traders 5, 19, 20–1
    invaders 12–18
    Italian bankers 6, 28
merchants 5, 6, 11, 17, 25, 29
Medina, Sir Solomon de 32
merchants 5, 6, 11, 17, 25, 29, 42
Michael X 129, 130–1, 134
missionaries 5
Moivre, Abraham de 32, 47
monarchy 19, 65
monasteries 10, 12, 21, 22–3, 31
Moody, Dr Harold 78, 83
More, Thomas 34, 35
Moroccans 45
Morris, Olive 78, 100
Mosley, Sir Oswald 120, 125, 126
multiculturalism 7, 8, 88, 96, 104
Murphy Riots 68–9
music 64, 66, 67, 99, 107
    Notting Hill Carnival 123, 129
Muslims 45, 61, 108
Nandy, Dipak 78
Naoroji, Dadabhai 52, 70
National Front 88, 105
Nazi Germany 90, 101
NHS (National Health Service) 101
Noble, Jawahir 81
Normans 6, 16–17, 31
Northern Ireland 7, 16–17

Notting Hill 86, 112–39
    Carnival 123, 129
    Colville Pub 119
    counterculture 128, 131, 135
    housing 116–17, 132–3
    Mangrove Restaurant 133, 134–8
    Methodist Church 132
    Neighbourhood Service 129
    Rastafarians 128
    riots 120–2, 130, 132
    shebeens 119
    Teddy Boys 115, 122
    West Indian Gazette 123, 126
Nugent, Father James 69
nurses 101
Odlum, George 78, 98
offensive terms for migrants 3
Palatine migrants 49
Paris, Matthew 20
Parliament 33, 40, 46
    Indian MPs 70
    legislation 49, 85, 86, 87, 88, 90, 97
    Aliens Acts 55, 74, 90
    medieval 19
    multiracial politics 104
Pathak, Laxmi and Shanta 106
Payne, John 29
Peto, Samuel Morton 68
Pathak, Shanta 78
Pitt, David 79, 96, 97, 125
Pocahontas 39
Polish migrants 85
Powell, Enoch 88
Preston 56
privateers 38
Protestant refugees 35, 36, 36–7
    German Lutherans 65
    Huguenots 2, 38, 46–7, 49
Protestantism 2, 5, 6, 33, 34, 35, 40
Pulley, PC Frank 136, 138
queen consorts 19
RAAS (Racial Adjustment Action Society) 130
Rachman, Peter 116–17, 130, 132
racism 3, 82, 88
Raducanu, Emma 80, 111
railways 56, 57
Reformation 6, 33, 34, 35, 38
refugees 2, 3, 5, 90, 91
    see also Protestant refugees
regional migration 56
Regis, Cyrille 78
Reid-Bailey, Guy 78, 98, 99
Renaissance 34
Reuter, Paul 52, 65
Revolutions of 1848 65
Riccardi company 28
Richard I, King 19, 26, 27
Rievaulx Abbey 23
Roble, Jawahir 105
Roman Empire 6, 12, 14

Romani Gypsies 3, 43
Rossetti family 65
Royal African Company 39
Royal Society 47
Russian Vapour Baths 73
sailors 7, 8, 58, 59, 60, 83
    lascars 52, 58, 61, 70, 82, 84
Salandy, Francis 99
Saloman, Johann Peter 66
Sancho, Ignatius 52, 66, 67
Sandwich 33, 36, 37
Schewzik, Benjamin 73
Schweppe, Johan 53, 63
Scientific Revolution 47
Scotland 7, 10, 19, 56
Second World War 7, 84–5, 89
sheep farming 21
Shiel, Richard 52, 59
Shire, Warsan 81
Sierra Leone 58, 67
slave trade 6, 38, 45, 52, 54, 58, 66
Somali migrants 7, 8, 61, 83, 91
Somerset, James 54, 66
Soper, William 29
Sorabji, Cornelia 5, 53, 71
Southall Black Sisters 100
sport 84, 99, 105
Stephenson, Paul 79, 98, 99
Stranger communities 36–7
Sun Yat-sen 53, 60
Syrian refugees 91
Tanqueray, Anne 32, 46
Thompson, Leslie 79, 107
Trivedi, Mira 80
Tulloch, Courtney 128, 131
Turnbull, George 57
Ugandan Asians 87, 102
universities 5, 34, 35, 47
Vermigli, Peter 34
Vikings 6, 12–15
Wales 8, 10, 11, 19, 56
Walloons 33, 36, 37, 44, 46
Wawrzynaiak, Damian 80, 92
weavers 6, 11, 21, 29, 31, 33, 42
    silk weavers 37, 44, 46
Willaume, David 46
William I (William of Normandy) 5, 16, 17, 22, 23
William of Orange (William III) 32, 33, 40, 46, 48, 68
Wilson, Paulette 80, 93
Windrush migrants 85, 93, 107, 114
Wolff, Gustav 52, 63
Wood, Rt Rev. Wilfred 108
wool trade 21, 23, 29, 36, 38
Wooton, Charles 79, 83
Worde, Wynkyn de 32, 34
xenophobia 2, 3
Yale, Elihu 45
Yemeni migrants 61
York (Jorvick) 12, 14